The Book of Revelation
Simplified

Sermon Notes from Dr. Sunny Ezhumattoor

(Sermons delivered from 2005 - 2012 at Colonial Hills Bible Chapel, Houston TX)

Thekkel Publications, a division of Narrow Path Ministries, Inc.

Dr. John Mathew (Sunny Ezhumattoor)

(c) Copyright reserved
April 2016

Published by
Thekkel Publications
A Division of Narrow Path Ministries

Web address: www.thekkel.com
narrowpathministries.net
thekkel45@gmail.com

Printed through:
CreateSpace
An Amazon Company

Copies can be bought from Amazon.com
If additional copies are needed in bulk,
contact Dr. John Mathew at his
email address listed above.

Price $ 24.50

CONTENTS

INTRODUCTION 1

Revelation chapter 1 5

Revelation Chapter 2 17

Revelation Chapter 3 43

Revelation Chapter 4 65

Revelation Chapter 5 89

Revelation Chapter 6 107

Revelation Chapter 7 123

Revelation Chapter 8 133

Revelation Chapter 9 141

Revelation Chapter 10 149

Revelation Chapter 11 155

Revelation Chapter 12 169

Revelation Chapter 13 201

Revelation Chapter14 215

Revelation Chapter 15 225

Revelation Chapter 16 233

Revelation Chapter 17 249

Revelation Chapter 18 265

Revelation Chapter 19 275

Revelation Chapter 20 291

Revelation Chapter 21 349

Revelation Chapter 22 367

INTRODUCTION

Almost everyone has some interest in prophecy. Millions read the daily horoscope in the newspaper. Astrology and fortunetelling are a big business today. The unstable political climate throughout the world and anxiety about economic Armageddon, generates an interest in prophecy. Government leaders have said that they do not have the answers. Many today seem to realize more than ever that the Bible has something reliable to say about tomorrow's headlines. In fact, it is the only accurate source of information about the future.

As the sun sank low over the Aegean Sea, the old man (Apostle John) stepped wearily into his residence. He longed for a night of renewing sleep, but as usual, it would not be his to enjoy. Sharing his cave was a band of criminals. All the men had been exiled to Patmos, that infamous desert island of the Aegean, for crimes that they had committed on the mainland. But the old man's only crime had been sharing his new life in Jesus with everyone he met. For this offense, Domitian, the emperor of Rome, had banished him to Patmos to die an old man or of starvation.

However, God had other plans. Here in the seclusion of exile, John was to receive the most sweeping survey of future events ever to be granted to the mortal mind.

John was commanded not to seal the book (Revelation 22:10), and those who read it are promised a special blessing (1:3). Apparently, therefore, the book was expected to be intelligible and helpful to those who read it. It is an apocalypse, designed not to mystify, but to clarify.

C I. Scofield wrote, "The book is so written that as the actual time of these events approach, the current events will unlock the meaning of the book." He pointed out that the book of Revelation did not have much meaning to people a few centuries ago. Revelation is written in such a way that its meaning becomes clearer with the unfolding of current world events.

Daniel wrote in the 12th chapter of his book that he was very disturbed about some visions he had seen because he could not understand them. Daniel was told that his visions were prophetic in nature, and that he or anyone else would not understand their fulfillment until the end of the age. The angel also informed him that as the end of this era approached, knowledge about prophecy would become widespread. (Read Daniel 12:8-10.) Daniel observed that at the end of time, the "wise" would understand. In Biblical terminology, the wise are the people who study what God has to say, and become enlightened to its meaning by the Holy Spirit.

The Time Machine

Suppose we were suddenly catapulted nineteen centuries into the future and confronted the marvels of that time, then were instructed to return to our own century and write what we had seen. You would be forced to try to communicate in terms of things we presently know. If someone were to read your account nineteen centuries after it was written, they would be forced to search for clues to unlock the meaning of your symbols.

This is how John used his symbols. Sometimes John employed terminology which can be understood only when the prophecy's fulfillment is near. For example, he describes a horrible way in which fire and brimstone are rained down on people. In John's day, the only thing capable of producing fire and brimstone was a volcano. It was one of the most dreaded forms of destruction. The volcano is really a classic description of the horrors of an atomic explosion, which is essentially fire and brimstone. Before the development of the atomic bomb, no destructive force known to man could equal the power of a volcanic eruption, or even come close to fulfilling the description of fire and brimstone.

Various Interpretations

Preterist is from the Latin word which means "past". Thus the Preterist interpreters are those who see Revelation as having already been fulfilled in the early history of the church. Chapters 5-11 are said to record the church's victory over Judaism, Chapters 12-19, her victory over pagan Rome, and 20-22, her glory because of these victories. The persecutions described are those of Nero and Domitian, and the entire book was fulfilled by the time of Constantine in 312 A. D.

The historical continuous interpretation states that in Revelation, there is a panorama of the history of the church from the days of John to the end of the age. It holds that the book has been in the process of being fulfilled throughout the whole Christian era. Those who hold this view see in the symbols the rise of the Papacy, the corruption of the church, and the various wars throughout church history.

Futurist or Plain Interpretation

The label "futurist" is derived from the fact that this interpretation sees the book from chapter 4 on as yet to be fulfilled. If one follows the plain, literal or normal principle of interpretation, he concludes that most of the book is yet in the future.

The concept of a literal interpretation always raises questions, since it seems to preclude anything symbolic, and the book obviously contains symbols. Perhaps saying normal or plain interpretation would be better than literal since futurists do recognize the presence of symbols in the book. The difference between the literalist and the spiritualizer is simply that the former sees the symbols as conveying a plain meaning. All recognize the presence of symbols in the Bible. For instance, Psalm 22 verse 18 prophesied the casting of lots for Christ's garments. This was a literal statement. Verses 12 and 13 depict the fierce enemies of the Lord as strong bulls and ravening lions. These are symbols with a very plain meaning. Apparently, the stars are literally the astronomical bodies in the heavens. In Revelation 9:1, 2, John records seeing a star fall from heaven. This is a plain symbol and one that is interpreted in the text itself as indicating a created being (probably an angel). The English word "star" is used today in both a literal and symbolic manner, just as it is in Revelation 8 and 9. We speak literally of the stars in the heavens. We also refer to stars on the athletic field and in so doing; we are using a symbol with a very plain meaning. Indeed, symbols often make the meaning plainer. The futurist does not deny the presence of symbols in the book, nor does he claim to be able to explain every detail with certainty. But he does insist that the principle of plain interpretation be followed consistently throughout the book.

REVELATION CHAPTER 1

There are three main divisions which mark Revelation. Most commentators see in 1:19 a divinely given outline. In this verse, the book is divided into three parts. (1) The things which John had seen, Chapter 1 through verse 19. (2) The present state of the Church, chapters 2 and 3. (3) The things which shall be after the Church is completed, chapters 4 through 22. The words translated "hereafter" (meta tauta) mean literally "after these things." The same words are found in 4:1, indicating that chapter 4 begins this last section of the book. However, it is possible to combine the first two sections because verse 19 may well be translated, "Write the things which thou hast seen, both the things which are and which are to come." In other words, John saw two things: present things and future things. The present things include the vision of Christ in 1:9-20 and the letters to the churches in chapters 2 and 3. It does make sense to see 1:9-3:22 as one unified section, simply because in the vision in 1:9-20 is that which John had seen, and thus as a separate division of the book. The important thing is to notice that according to 1:19, the book has to divide at 4:1 regardless of whether one combines the vision of 1:9-20 with chapters 2 and 3 or divides it into a separate section.

Section 1 - The things which you have seen (1:9-20), circumstances of the vision (1:9-11), and physical circumstances (1:9). John does not exalt himself above his fellow believers, but calls himself a brother. Patmos is an island about 15 miles in circumference in the Aegean Sea, southwest of Ephesus. The reason for his banishment was literally because of the Word of God (God's claim on men) and the testimony of Jesus (the gospel message).

Spiritual Circumstances

John, being in the Spirit, seems to indicate a trance-like state of spiritual ecstasy. "Was" is literally "became," indicating that this was something unusual. The phrase "the Lord's day" could refer to Sunday or the Day of the Lord, that is the tribulation and the millennium, which are the subject of much of the prophecy. "Lord's" is an adjective (Kuriakos) which is used only here and in I Corinthians 11:20 in the New Testament. Outside the New Testament, it means "imperial." Unless this is a reference to Sunday, there is no place in the New Testament where this expression is used for that day since the usual designation is the "first day of the week." It could then refer to that imperial day in the future when Christ will take the reins of earthly government, which was what John saw in his vision. The voice which John heard was that of Christ who is identified as "the first and the last" in verse 17. That entire vision John saw, 22:8, not just the particular letter to each church, chapters 2 and 3, was to be communicated to all these seven churches mentioned in verse 11.

Revelation.1:5. "To Him who loves us, and has washed us from our sins in his blood." He loves us continuously, always and forever. But he washed us in one great, atoning act. We are priests unto God. The priesthood of all believers is a celestial doctrine.

Chapter 1:7. "Behold he is coming with clouds."

This is the cry that shall reach to the bottom of every grave. It is the cry that shall sound in the depths of the ocean. It is the cry that shall reach to the uttermost part of the world, waking the sleeping millions of our dead, who are buried in the heart of the earth. Behold he is coming. This is the theme and the text of the book of the Revelation. The trials and sorrows, the psalms are prototypes of the return of our Lord. The uplifted voices of the prophets spoke of the golden, Millennial Age in glorious announcement of the coming of our Lord. Isaiah 2:4. 11:6. "For the earth shall be filled with the knowledge of the glory of the Lord, as the waters cover the sea", Habakkuk 2:14. Such is the sublime text of the New Testament. This theme is also the content of the preaching of the apostles. The great preacher, Paul in Philippians 3:20-22 stated the same thing. "For our commonwealth has its existence in the heavens, from which also we await the Lord Jesus Christ as Savior, who shall transform our body of humiliation into conformity to his body of glory, according to the working of the power which he has even to subdue all things to himself." Our body in its present state is called a vile body or lowly body, but the literal translation is "the body of humiliation." Our Lord will transform us until it is like unto his own body of His glory.

(See JND translation.)

Our savior had an earthly body here in humiliation; that body was like ours in all respects, except that it could see no corruption, for it was undefiled with sin. The body in which our Lord wept, and sweat great drops of blood, and yielded up His spirit, was the body of His humiliation. Our present body which is now in its humiliation is to be conformed to the glorified body of Jesus Christ. Jesus is the standard of man in glory." We shall be like him, for we shall see him as he is "1 John 3.2. Here we dwell in this body of our humiliation (tent), but it shall undergo a change" in a moment, in the twinkling of an eye, at the last trumpet, for the trumpet shall sound and the dead shall be raised incorruptible, and we shall be changed." 1 Corinthians 15:50-55. Then shall we come into our glory, and our body being made suitable to the glory state, shall be fitted, fashioned into the body of glory. What is begun in Genesis finds its concluding, consummating climax in the revelation.

Position of the Lord - (Revelation 1:12, 13)

The Lord is described as "like unto the Son of man." This means that His form was humanlike. He was in the midst of seven lampstands. These are explained in verse 20 as the seven churches of verse 11. The Lord has a direct relationship to each church. His clothing in verse thirteen is that of a priest and judge, which are the relationships of authority which He sustains to the local churches.

Picture of the Lord - (Revelation 1:14-16)

This is a picture of the risen, glorified Lord, depicted under a number of similes - the only way He could be described to finite creatures (note the occurrences of "like" and "as"). There are seven features to this picture, and the meaning of these similes may have been unexplained deliberately in order to convey more than one thing to our minds. His head, 1:14, was as white as wool or snow. This may represent the wisdom of age and the purity of holiness. His eyes, 1:14, were piercing in their fiery holiness. The true character of each Church is transparent to His eyes. There may also be a connection between this verse and I Corinthians 3:13; that is, the fire, which shall try men's works at the judgment seat of Christ. It will be the gaze of Christ which will itself consume the works of wood, hay and stubble. His feet, 1:15 were like burnished bronze. This may indicate the trials He experienced in His earthly life which make Him a sympathetic high priest (Hebrews 4:15) and an experienced judge. His voice, 1:15, was to John as the sound of many waters, like the noise of a mighty waterfall. His voice of authority stands out above all the rest. His right hand, 1:16, which is the place of honor, held the seven stars, which are explained in verse 20 as the messengers of the churches of chapters 2 and 3.

Verses 1:18. The keys of hell and of death.

This is a symbolic word that testifies to and presents the universal lordship of our great Christ. Philippians 2:9-11. Whether it is in heaven, on earth, or in hell, our Lord reigns. Our Christ is Lord; He is king over all. The imagery is this: that He is king over men in the unseen world in the vast beyond, king over men's souls; and He is king over death and over the grave.

The keys are a symbol of authority, control, possession, and government. As Isaiah prophesied in chapter 9:6, the government shall be upon his shoulder. Even hell trembles at the presence of Christ, and nothing happens by chance.

All history lies in the elective purpose of God and under the review of heaven.

Keys of Hades.

Christ is the ruler of the unseen world. He is adored in heaven and feared in hell. He also has the key of torment, of Gehenna. When we die, we are with our Lord in Paradise, in glory. But when the lost die, they fall into torment. They fall into perdition. There will never be an infidel in hell. They all will believe there. His key one day will be turned on Satan.

The key of Death.

"Death is a horrible spectacle. All the poetry of the world, all the songs of the saints, and all the flowers of the earth cannot cover the horrible, decaying, decadent visage of death. God calls death an enemy. It is an intruder. It was not planned. Death is the exact opposite of the spirit and the will and purpose of God. Death is an implacable enemy. The footprints of death and the grave seem inscrutable, unfathomable, black and horrible. Death is a horrible fortress, a castle of despair, a journey from which no traveler even returns. Death is a black camel that kneels at every gate. With impartial fate, with certain pace, death knocks at every palace and every cottage gate".

If he has not visited your house, look down the road. If he has not broken up the circle of your family, Wait a while. We shall not escape.

But does death reign forever? Is there never to be any triumph over the tomb and the sepulcher and the grave. Is death king of the universe? No, for our Lord Jesus Christ says I have the keys of Hades and of death. Death is in the hands of our Christ. Death moves only in the permissive will of heaven. The issues of death lie in the hands of the Almighty. Our lord holds the key to that mystic door of death. No man enters it unless our Christ shall open it. Even the ungodly and the unsaved owe their spared lives to Christ. No man ever dies except by the permissive will of our Lord. When you die is known to him. How you die is known to him. The circumstances under which you die are known to him. He controls them all. Death to the Christian is not death. We fall asleep in Jesus. Death to the Christian is just a falling asleep, a laying aside of this house of clay for a little while, while we wait with the Lord. In death we wait with the Lord for that great and final consummation, the full redemption of the purchased possession, soul and body. For when Christ died for us, he not only bought our souls, but he also bought our bodies. We are not wholly redeemed in soul and in body until our death. There shall not a bone be left behind, not a relic for the devil to gloat over. We shall all be raised and live in eternity. Therefore, a Christian is never to tremble in the presence of death.

In each letter, the Lord addresses "the angel." Who and what was he? The regular charges of elders and deacons are passed over in silence; nor are the gifts of the ascended Christ in evidence. But a new title at issue, with the sanctioned order hitherto, would be a strange thing on our Lord's part, when one man's decline had set in. We never hear of "angel" as an official title in the ordinary arrangements of the New Testament. "The angel" is a term for the leader that suits chapters 2 and 3 in such a prophetic book as the Revelation, just as literal angels are in keeping with the book of Daniel. Does it mean what we commonly call an angelic being? Not here surely where "angels of the churches" are spoken of. If we hear of the angel of fire and even of the angel of Jesus Christ, as of Jehovah elsewhere, there is no difficulty, though all these are outside the thoughts and language of the epistles. But it is very new to hear of the angel of this or that assembly. Again, we can understand an angel employed as a spiritual messenger from on high as the means of communication between the Lord and His servant John; but how harsh to suppose that His servant John writes a letter from Christ to a literal angel! This is one of the clear difficulties in which those are involved who suppose angelic beings to be meant here. The nature of the case precludes it.

"As "angel" is used in the sense of a representative, so in reference to the assemblies the Lord here avails Himself of this general idea. A messenger or moral representative of each assembly is implied. "Angel" was used of a human representative. For instance, when John the Baptist sent two of his disciples, there was a representation of his mind by these men when they gave the message of him who sent them (Luke 7:24). The representative force appears also in Acts 12:15 (only here it was of a spiritual character), and so in Matthew 18:10. But it assumes a different shape when it was a question of assemblies. They were His chief lights representing each of the assemblies and so became His medium in judging its state according to the divine standard. If, therefore, we look at the abstract nature of the angel of the church, what is taught by the term? Presumably this, that the Lord had in view not necessarily an elder, nor a teacher, but one who might be either or both; but before His Mind He truly represented, and was in a special way bound up with the responsibility of the state of the assembly, whoever that might be, was meant by the angel of the church." -William Kelly

The Importance of Prophecy

The entire Bible is profitable and practical (II Timothy 3:16, 17), but some Scriptures are more significant and precious. Thus it is with (Revelation 1 verse 3). This is the same commitment that confronted Mary, the maiden mother of our Lord. She did not understand the things that were spoken by the angel nor the things that were coming to pass, but the Scriptures say, "She treasured them and kept them and pondered them in her heart" (Luke 2:19). And as the days passed, the meaning of those words was fulfilled and became understandable. When Simeon, in the temple, said, "Behold, this child is destined for the fall and rising of many in Israel, and for a sign which will be spoken against (yes, a sword will pierce through your own soul also), that the thoughts of many hearts may be revealed" (Luke 2:34,35), she had no idea what that meant until the day when she stood by the cross and looked upon the Son of God, her child of promise, nailed and lifted up between the earth and the sky. But, she, though not understanding the words at the time, treasured them and kept them in her heart. II Peter chapter 1:19-21 speaks about the importance of prophecy.

In the history of the Church, the eschatological or prophetic portions of Scripture have suffered more from inadequate interpretation than any other subjects. The reason for this is that the Church turned aside from a normal and grammatical literal interpretation of prophecy to one that is nonliteral and subject to the caprice of the interpreter.

In the first two centuries of the Christian era, the church was predominantly pre-millennial, interpreting Scripture to teach that Christ would fulfill the prophecy of His Second Coming and bring a thousand-year reign on earth before the eternal state would begin. Although not always cogent, prophecy was treated in the same way as other Scripture. In the last ten years of the second century and in the third century, the heretical school of theology at Alexandria, Egypt, advanced the erroneous principle that the Bible should be interpreted in a nonliteral or allegorical sense. In applying this to the Scripture, they subverted all the major doctrines of the faith, including prophecy. The result was that there was little progress in theology, especially in the prophetic area, until this problem of interpretation was solved. Augustine (354-430) tried to change this erroneous teaching, except the prophetic Scriptures. The Reformation did not change much. For example, even Martin Luther, at one time, refused to include the Revelation in his canon of Scripture because he said no man could understand it. But with the establishment of the Plymouth Brethren movement in the nineteenth century, the literal truth of prophecy was restored. The importance of prophecy should be evident, even superficially, in examining the faith, for about one fourth of the Bible was prophetic when it was written.

Today, we live in a culture in which the Bible has been available for centuries. It is impossible for us to imagine the effect of a passage like I Thessalonians 4:13-18 as it was first read by early Christians. What did it mean to them that the dead in Christ will be raised with new bodies when the Lord comes? Think of the excitement of knowing that living believers may never see death, but could be changed instantly at the return of Christ.

Up until that time, all that the Greek and Roman civilizations told men about death was contained in such descriptive terms as bitter, ruinous, relentless, the eternal chamber of those who have withered. Among the living, hope endures, but hopeless are the dead. But Paul states in II Corinthians 5:8, "I prefer to be away from the body and at home with the Lord."

The revelation of prophecy in Scripture serves as important evidence that the Scriptures are accurate in their interpretation of the future, because half of the prophecies of the Bible have already been fulfilled in a literal way.

God has done two things here. First, He gave this great revelation to Christ. Secondly, He has given us an unsealed book. John bore record of what God said and what God did, of the testimony of Jesus Christ and of all things that he saw. Revelation 22:10 says, "Do not seal the words of the prophecy of this book for the time is at hand." Some of the great prophetic revelations that were given to Daniel were closed up. They were sealed. They were veiled (Daniel 12:4). But, Daniel shut up the words, and sealed the book, even to the time of the end. What was sealed in Daniel is unsealed in the apocalypse; what was not made known in Daniel is made known in the Revelation.

The term, Apokalupsis Jesou Christou means "The Apocalypse of Jesus the Christ." The word Apokalupsis is compounded from a verb and preposition. Apo means "away from" and Kalupto means "to cover or to hide." Apokalupsis, therefore, means, "to take away the covering, to unveil, or to reveal." This is the unveiling of our Savior in His glorious coming and appearance.

There is another word sounding like apocalypse, apocrypha. Apocrypha means "hidden, covered over." It ultimately bears the meaning "not authentic, not true." Apocalypse is the Greek word that means exactly the opposite of the Greek word apocrypha. Revelation is not apocrypha, a covering up, but an uncovering. So this book is the unveiling of our Lord Jesus Christ. If you would learn to appreciate Christ more, read this book frequently and pray fully. It reveals Him as the lamb rejected but soon to reign in glory- the lamb on the throne. Revelation is the crowning book of the Bible.

A comparison of Genesis and Revelation will readily make this truth plain and show how we have types in Genesis and the completion of the truth in Revelation. Genesis describes the beginning and Revelation describes the consummation. Genesis gives us the creation of the heavens and the earth; Revelation presents a new heaven and a new earth. Genesis shows us the earthly paradise, with the tree of life and the river of blessing lost through sin. Revelation gives us the paradise of God, with the Tree of life and the pure river of water of life proceeding out of the throne of God and the lamb. In Genesis we see the first man and his wife set over all of God's creation; in Revelation, we behold the second man and his bride ruling over a redeemed world.

In Genesis, we are told of the first typical sacrificial lamb; in Revelation, the lamb once slain is in the midst of the throne. In Genesis, we learn of the beginning of sin, when the serpent first entered the garden of delight to beguile Adam and Eve. With his deception; in Revelation, that old serpent, called the devil and Satan, is cast in the lake of fire. In Genesis, we see the city of man; in Revelation, we see the city of God. Genesis shows us how sorrow, death, pain, and tears, the inevitable accompaniments of sin and rebellion came in to the world; Revelation doesn't close until we have seen God wiping away all tears and welcoming his redeemed into a home where sin, death, pain, and sorrow never come.

REVELATION CHAPTER 2

The City of Ephesus - (Revelation 2:1-7)

Ephesus was a large city with an excellent harbor, and it was known at that time as the marketplace of Asia. Ephesus was a tremendously important political center. Above all, Ephesus was a religious city. The temple of Diana, or Artemis as the Greeks called her, was considered one of the seven wonders of the ancient world. It was also a banking center because of its great vault in the temple of Diana, which was considered the safest place in Asia Minor. The goddess of Diana was the patron of all the prostitutes, and represented fertility and sexuality. Many writers in ancient times described the immorality of the city. One pillar in the Ephesian economy was the production of silver images of Diana by the many silversmiths. They sold little gods, and people fastened them on their chariots, placed them in their houses, hung them upon the walls and carried them around their necks, arms, and ankles. The Roman church copied this by making images of saints and hanging them around their necks. Black magic was also widely practiced in Ephesus. Paul met these occultists and led some of them to Christ (Acts 19:13-19, 23-27).

The Christian assembly of Ephesus was extremely well taught, having had Paul, Apollos, Timothy, and John as elders. Paul wrote the book of Ephesians in the New Testament to the Ephesian saints while he was in prison in Rome in approximately 60 A.D. First, there was a word of congratulation. Second, there was a word of complaint. Third, there was a word of counsel.

Commendation

His word of commendation comprises seven things. As the Lord walks among the assemblies, He is intimately aware of their thoughts and attitudes. There was much in this assembly to commend and praise. It was an active and energetic assembly. It was a soul winning assembly. Soul winning begets more soul winners. The believers were zealous of good works and service for the Lord. Twice, the letter speaks of how they labored for the name of Christ. These saints knew how to trust the Lord consistently under trial, which is the meaning of the word patience. Patience does not mean passively bearing anything. No matter how the Ephesian Christians were beaten down, discouraged, or persecuted, they did not quit. They stayed with the work.

They were also sensitive to the presence of evil. They could identify the "bad apples." Doctrinally, they were competent and militant in their stand against false teaching. They examined and expelled the false apostles. A lot of so-called scholars have infiltrated the church today and they have been received. Furthermore, a present day assembly has many ministries. It is important to support and participate in our assembly activities. The little Ephesian assembly said, "We don't want numbers if they are not holy numbers. We don't want growth at the expense of holiness".

Complaint

Jesus walks among His churches with eyes as a flame of fire. He sees everything among His people. Our eyes are covered with the smoke of the world. After all these compliments, He finds a fault. The penetrating eye of the Lord found a fatal fault. "You have left your first love." The old abounding joy, gladness and the old enthusiasm was altered. It was beginning to wane. Their services became mechanical, their devotion, routine. They did not have that old flame and fire. They have become cold and regular. If prolonged activities don't produce a greater love for Christ, then they are unprofitable. Formalism crept into Ephesus.

Counsel or Exhortation - Remember and Repent

He says that the Ephesian believers are fallen because they do not have a deep devotion, love, and commitment in their hearts to Him any longer. Today, our heart is often in the world. We used to love prayer meetings and Bible studies, but now we are too busy. We are not content with just the things of God. O Lord come and probe our hearts.

Prophetic Application - 33-100 A.D.

The Ephesian church was a prophetic picture of the apostolic church. Eventually they opened the door for legalism.

Here in seven typical Churches we see the predominant characteristics of seven successive eras of church history. The seven churches represent historical periods in the history of Christ. The prophetic aspects were never understood clearly until much of church history had unfolded, but now as we look back, we can see striking similarities between the characteristics of each church in Revelation and the various periods of church history up until today.

Seven Churches in Every Age

Those periods also co-exist throughout all the ages. In every year, age, country, and denomination, there are Ephesian churches that cool off, who once had a fire and a flame and an evangelistic zeal, but have become apathetic in their drive for the souls of men. There are Ephesian churches in this age and Ephesian members in every Church. All seven churches co-exist in almost every church today.

Smyrna

Smyrna - (Revelation 2:8-11)

This is one of the ancient cities of the world. Today, it is a large metropolis in Asia Minor. It has at present, a population of 400,000 people. The name of it is Izmir, the Turkish corruption of Smyrna. Ephesus, Miletus, and other cities ceased to exist, but Smyrna has lived through the centuries. In Roman times, it was a great city. The harbor was one of the finest in the world. The gulf of Smyrna reaches back into the inland of Asia Minor about thirty-five miles. It was beautiful and spacious.

Smyrna was a great political center and it was always on the winning side. The city never lost a cause; it was always right. The conquering Romans made Smyrna a free city. It had its own government. It was the proudest of all of the cities of Asia. It was the birthplace of the great Greek Poet Homer. For them, God was not supreme. To Smyrna, worldly things were the first and the last. The Lord introduced Himself here as being the first and the last. To Smyrna, the first and the last were glories of Greek culture. Alexander wanted to make it a model city. After his death, Lysimachus, his general, built it and made it a model city. Streets were wide and spacious.

One of the Meaningful Messages in the New Testament

Three times Smyrna is used in the New Testament. The first time is in Matthew two when three wise men coming from the East, opened their treasures and presented before the young king gold and frankincense and Smyrna. The second time is in Mark 15 at the crucifixion of our Lord. He was offered wine mixed with Smyrna in order to help alleviate, anesthetically, the sufferings He bore. And the third place is in John 19. When Jesus dies, Nicodemus came with Joseph of Arimathea, and the two men, after carefully taking down the body of our Lord from the cross, wrapped it in long linen cloth in the folds of which they placed a hundred-pound weight of aloes and Smyrna. In each of these instances, the word is translated in the King James Version as myrrh. The city received its name from the trade of Smyrna. It was the port of the fragrance and perfume of myrrh. In the providence of God, the name came to symbolize that era in the story of the Christian church when it entered severe and terrible persecution. Myrrh pictures suffering, and was used in the embalming of the dead. They brought unto Him gifts: gold, frankincense, and Smyrna. The gold is a picture of the deity of our Lord. The frankincense is a picture of His great mediatorial office, interceding for us in heaven. Myrrh typifies the suffering of our Lord for our sins. This is the church of great trial, tribulation, and martyrdom. The Lord has only commendation for this church. He has no complaint against them.

There are three things our Lord states. First, "I know thy tribulation." The word contains the idea of pressure that forces the blood out of the grapes; the pressure of persecution, sorrow, and death. Secondly, "I know thy tribulation and thy poverty." The actual word is ptocheia meaning "beggary." It means absolute and utter destitution. Why were these Christians at Smyrna so destitute in the richest city? Scribes and Pharisees called the disciples, unlearned, untaught, and unschooled men of poor and deprived lives. God does not need extraordinary personalities for His work. They were plain ordinary people. They were plundered and deprived of the right to work and make a living. And thirdly, "I know the blasphemy of them which say they are Jews and are not, but are the synagogue of Satan." False Jews and false Christians wanted to practice Judicial laws. Jews encouraged authorities also to persecute the Christians. One of the most famous martyrdoms in the entire world happened in this city of Smyrna. Polycarp was the leader of the Christians in the city. Upon a festival day, when the crowds were inflammable and excitable, the cry went out from the mob about Polycarp, and they brought him before the Roman governor. He was given the choice of saying "Caesar is Lord" or "Jesus is Lord." He refused to say that Caesar is Lord. The governor urged him saying, "Swear! I will set thee at liberty. Reproach Christ." Polycarp answered with one of the famous avowals in all history, "Eighty and six years have I served Him and He never did me harm. How then can I blaspheme my King and my Savior?" The people, led by the Jews, (it was on their Sabbath day and in contradiction of their law,) gathered the wood and burned the faithful servant. In the flames, he prayed, "I thank Thee that Thou have graciously thought me worthy of this day and of this hour that I may receive a portion in the number of Thy martyrs in the cup of Thy Christ."

Lord's Words of Encouragement

Encouragement is found even in the way that He introduces Himself. The first and the last, who was dead, and came to life. Satan shall cast you into prison for ten days. The word ten refers to a fierce and intense persecution, like the ten plagues in the land of Egypt. The Lord did not promise an escape, but said, "You are to have more of the same." Some say the ten days of persecution were under ten diabolical Caesars, which dated from Nero (64-312 A.D.).

Faithful unto Death

James was beheaded by the sword of Herod Agrippa, John was exiled, and Peter was crucified. When the Lord called Paul, He said, "I will show him how many things he must suffer for my name's sake." What an amazing thing (Acts 9:16).

The Lord never said we would have the abundance of all the things that this life has to offer; about being rich, healthy, etc. (Romans 8:38, 39). Fortunately, death or anything else cannot separate us from the love of God.

Prophetic Application - (100-312 A.D.)

The suffering of the church at Smyrna was prophetic of the great era of persecution under the ten Caesars. The motives of the church were purified during this long and difficult period. Millions of Christians met cruel martyrs' deaths rather than renounce Christ or swear allegiance to Caesar as Lord. This was a period of tremendous witness and heroic faith. Even the wicked Roman Empire was finally shaken by the testimony of these Christians.

Pergamos

The temple of Aesculapius in the ancient city of Pergamos and home to the physician Galen (131-210 CE)

Pergamos - A Compromise with the World System - (Revelation 2:12-17)

On the ancient site of Pergamos, there is today a village called Bergama, which is a Turkish corruption of this Greek name, Pergamos. The original Pergamos was a beautiful and illustrious city. It was the capital of Asia Minor. The Attalid kings beautified the city. The library contained more than 200,000 books. The use of parchment, of skins of animals, as writing materials was invented in Pergamos. The name "parchment" comes from this town of Pergamos.

The letter of our Lord begins with a grim tone. The word "seat" in Greek is thronos. He is referring to the fact that these Christians live where Satan has great authority and great power. What was Satan's throne? In this capital city, there were temples to the four greatest Greek gods: Zeus (Latin - Jupiter), Dionysius (Bacchus), Athena (Minerva), and Aesculapius. Zeus was the head of all the gods. Dionysius was the god of wine and of drama. Athena was the god of wisdom. Aesculapius was the god of healing. His emblem was a serpent. Snakes roamed around in the temple. Another wonder of the ancient world was the magnificent altar to Zeus. Emperor worship (Caesar) was also prevalent. There were another three temples dedicated to Roman emperors.

Notice the word "you have not denied my faith". It refers to a thing in the past, a great persecution. In that angry day, Antipas was martyred. In his faithfulness to Christ and in protest against Caesar worship, Antipas laid down his life. The Lord says, "I know where you live. You cannot escape. You cannot run away." It is a description of our state in this present wicked world. We cannot run away. We have to stay like Antipas.

The Doctrine of Balaam

With verse fourteen, the tone of our Lord changes. The doctrine of Balaam was the teaching and counsel of a shrewd sage. He was hired by Balak to curse Israel. He could not curse Israel. God would not let Him. But he did something worse to corrupt God's people. He introduced them to strange Moabite women. Those strange Moabite women did the work. They corrupted Israel, a thing Balaam himself could not do. But they did it. That is the method of Balaam

One of the most astonishing things in the Greco-Roman world was this: With all of their magnificent philosophy and ethics and their achievements in every realm of art and science and literature, they looked upon prostitution as a needful and acceptable way of life. But believers in the church did not go along with the crowd. The doctrine of Balaam is the same today as it was then. What Christians faced concerned things sacrificed to idols, like "Halaal" meat for Muslims. The social customs of idolatry were a threat to the Christian faith on every side. So, a Christian was cut off from social intercourse with the world and the pattern of life in which he lived.

When Lucifer fell, he kept his brilliance. When he came down to this earth, he set up his throne on this planet. In the previous letter, the Lord addressed Smyrna. There, the opposition to the church was in the synagogue. In the period of ecclesiastical history represented by Smyrna, the opposition to the church was veiled under the cloak of religion. But in Pergamos, the opposition to the church takes an altogether different turn. Satan invites the church and the people of God to share with him the glamour and the glitter of all things that mammon have to offer of worldly greatness and glory. There is evil in our country and all over the world. Satan's throne is in the city where mammon dwells." You cannot serve God and mammon". False doctrine is found in the cities far more than in rural areas. What a trying, perilous, difficult place to locate God's house. But that is where it needs to be. How do we deny the faith in the city where Satan's throne is? We deny the faith by refusing to confess it. The Lord mentions His faithful martyr Antipas. Many Christians were persecuted in one part of India. A Christian could live in that place without any trouble if they remained a silent Christian, not disclosing their faith to others. We also deny the faith by preaching the wrong gospel. There is no different salvation for the first century and the 15th century Christians. Jesus Christ weeps over the great cities of the world. The population everyday presses more and more toward the cities. The Lord said, "I understand the trial of the Church in the heart of the city and I know her peril and the difficulty."

The Doctrines of Nicolaitane - Doctrine of Balaam

The reference to Balaam is an allusion to the experience of Balaam recorded in Numbers 22-25 when he was hired by the kings of the Midianites and the Moabites to curse the children of Israel for not exterminating the women of the Midianites. Here we learn for the first time that the prophet Balaam had advised King Balak to corrupt Israel by tempting them to sin through intermarriage with their women and the resulting inducement to worship idols (Numbers 1:15-16). The doctrine of Balaam therefore was the teaching that the people of God should intermarry with the heathen and compromise in the matter of idolatrous worship. This is in contrast to "the way of Balaam." That is, selling his prophetic gift for money (II Peter 2:15) and the "error of Balaam," his assumption that God would curse Israel (Jude 11).

Undoubtedly, intermarriage with the heathen and spiritual compromise, were real issues in Pergamos where civic life and religious life were so entwined. It would be most difficult for Christians in this city to have any kind of social contact with the outside world without becoming involved with the worship of idols or in the matter of intermarriage with non-Christians. Practically, all meat was offered to idols before it was consumed, and it was difficult for Christians to accept social engagements or even to buy meat in the marketplace without, in some sense, compromising in respect to the meat offered to idols. Intermarriage with the heathen was also a real problem. Social relations with the heathen world would lead in some instances to partaking of the heathen feasts which in turn led to heathen immorality which was a part of the idolatrous worship. Christ's absolute condemnation of the doctrine of Balaam as it related to the church of Pergamos is a clear testimony to the fact that Christians must at all costs remain pure and separate from defilement with the world and its religion and moral standards.

The Doctrine of Nicolaitans - (Revelation 2:14, 15)

What is this doctrine? There are even many strange explanations about them. One of them says that the Nicolaitane were the apostatizing followers of Nicholas of Antioch, who was one of the seven deacons in the assembly of Jerusalem. There is no basis, no substantiation for such a theory, either in profane or in sacred history. The doctrine of Nicolaitane was connected with the doctrine of Balaam, which included carnality, lust, fornication, and sensuality. However, the doctrine of Nicolaitane was different from the doctrine of Balaam. Twice in this chapter, the Lord speaks, concerning this doctrine. We can find the answer in two areas. The first area is in the name itself. Names have great significance in the Word of God. The second area is in the Pergamean period of church history. Consider the name itself. The word "Nicolaitane" is composed of two simple Greek words. The first is Nike, the Greek word for "victory." The other is Laos, the simple word of the Greeks for "people."

The word "laity" is derived from the Greek word laos. When these words are put together, Nike and Laos, we have in English, "Nicolaos" or "Nicolaitane." The word refers to a group, or a class, that exalt themselves above the people. They subjugate the people. They are oppressors of and conquerors of the people, "Nicolaitans."

The other area in which we can learn the meaning of the doctrine of Nicolaitans is to be found in the Pergamean period of the church. Prophetical application is from 312-590 AD. This is the church of the establishment. This is the day when the church is married to the world. Look at the name Pergamos. The Greek word for "marriage" is gamos; the word gamos also appears in polygamy and bigamy. This is the day when the church has become wealthy, popular, and lifted up. This is when the church enters the great field of power and political aggrandizement. The Church is married to the Roman government. Nico-laos, means the conquerors, the subjugators of the people of Pergamos. This movement is a rising up of a class separate, apart and exalted over the great mass of God's people. They had the power to forgive sins, and to excommunicate. They alone had the power to interpret and to mediate the word and the will of God. The Nicolaitans entered the political, imperial and governmental arena of the world. Both the Church and the government became pawns in a game of political power, and the two were married together. "The friendship of the world is enmity with God" (James 4:4).

The Early Growth

The doctrine of the Nicolaitans began early (Revelations 2:6) with the deeds of Nicolaitans. By the time of the Pergamean period of the church, however, those "deeds" had become a system and a theology.

The law of degeneration works in all areas of life, apart from the presence of power of God. Corruption, corrosion, rust, and disintegration are the common lot of all created things. The Sun, the rain and even the air itself are arms of destruction and disintegration. So it is with spiritual life. Spiritual life has a tendency to degenerate, to go down, and to lose its fresh thrust and spiritual power. Look at the life of Noah (Genesis 6:8). But Noah found grace in the eyes of the Lord. Noah was a just man, perfect in his generations. Noah walked with God. He begot three sons. Then God remembered Noah (8:1).

After the Flood

Noah built an altar to the Lord (Genesis 8:20) and God blessed Noah (Genesis 9:1). "Noah began to be a farmer and he planted a vineyard. Then he drank of the wine and was drunk and became uncovered in his tent." (Genesis 9:20, 21)

The Curse on Canaan

This was so in the churches of our Lord. They began in a miraculous and heavenly way, but fell into the hands of Satan.

Priestly Class - (III John verse 9)

Diotrephes lifts himself above his brethren and will not receive the messengers. Such, even in the apostolic days, were the deeds of the Nicolaitans. In the Pergamean period, those deeds had become a great system, a great teaching, held by churches themselves. Priest-craft was supplanting the preacher of the word of God; ceremony was taking the place of the regenerating power of the Holy Spirit; and the church had opened its heart to the love and the power and the wages of the world. This was the doctrine of the Nicolaitans.

All of these things came to pass in the days of the Pergamean church after 300 A.D. The class distinction between clergy and laity grew ever wider. The assembly was no longer a company of believers, of saved, regenerated souls; but the church became a channel through which a sacramental and hypothetical salvation was offered.

In the Old Testament in Exodus 19:5, 6, the Lord said, "If you obey me and keep My words, then you shall be a peculiar treasure unto Me above all people: for all the earth is Mine: And ye shall be unto Me a kingdom of priests, and holy nation. These are the words which thou shalt speak unto the children of Israel." What was conditionally offered to Israel was actually realized in the Christian assembly. Everyone became a priest of God, mediating the truth of the Lord. Peter said two things that undermined forever priest-craft and salvation by ritual and ceremonialism. The old day of the priest is gone. The veil is rent from the top to the bottom, and any man can go to God for himself anywhere (I Peter 2:5). That is the true Christian faith. But, in a short time, less than 300 years, the shadow had become the substance. Gone were all of the spiritual liberties and endowments of the Christian household. The church was led back to ceremonialism, the salvation by ritual that had developed in the judaistic system of the Old Testament dispensation.

The State Church

The establishment of the church, not upon the Rock of Christ, but upon governmental power and worldly favor under the oppressive hand of the ruling hierarchy was an amazing thing. It happened suddenly when Emperor Constantine became an unconverted and unbaptized Christian. Immediately, like a clap of thunder, like a meteor, like the snap of your finger, the Christians were no longer persecuted.

They became popular. The pagans turned their idol-temples into churches and they said, "These are no longer images of Jupiter or Juno or the Saints." The same rituals by which they had worshiped Astarte, Aphrodite or Venus were now employed to worship the true Queen of heaven. They bowed down in the same way, in the same ceremony, in the same temples, before the same idols; only now, the idols were named after so called Christian saints. Even the days by which the priests honored their gods were made days on the calendar to honor these saints, like Easter and Christmas. The astonishing thing took place overnight. The persecution was a thing of the past. The rags of persecution were changed for the plush silk of the imperial palace. The Pergamean period of the church had begun. Constantine was a shrewd politician. He saw an opportunity to be Caesar of the Roman Empire by employing the great might of those who were Christians, who by that time had pervaded the whole-civilized world. Was he really saved, born again? Consider this - he kept all of his heathen and pagan superstitions. Second, he planned to combine the worship of Christ with the worship of Apollo. For example, on his coins, he would put the picture of Apollo and then the name of Christ. He became prince of the Church. This isn't an ancient story, but a monstrous system of error that girdles the globe to this day and to this hour. The Lord hates this doctrine of sacramental salvation. As you are born a citizen of the state, you are christened a member of the church. The world and the church become one and the same.

Some Important Parables

The parable of the mustard seed (Matthew 13:31, 32) - This gives us the outward as well as the inward spiritual reality of the present Christian world. Daniel 4:10-12 can explain this parable. It indicates worldly power and greatness. But the strange thing in Matthew thirteen is that "the least of all seeds" should grow into such a tree (verse 19). For the seed, here as elsewhere is the word of the kingdom. Today, professing Christianity has become a power in the world. Yes, the little seed has become indeed a tree, but the "birds of the air" are in its branches. Satan himself has got lodgment and shelter in the very midst of the tree of Christendom! "The Christian world is the world still; and the whole world lies in the wicked one". (I John 5:19). The opposition to Christ and His truth is from within now instead of from outside. Successor to the tree like power is the power of old Babel. She is called "Babylon the Great" (Revelation 17:6). This is the full ripe result. The beginning of it is already seen in Corinth even in the apostle's day. Thus early was the little seed developing. Even in Paul's day, divergence started. Paul says, "All that are in Asia have departed me."

Thyatira

Ruins of Thyatira, home of Lydia. Photo by Leon Mauldin

Thyatira: The Great Counterfeit - (Revelation 2:18-29)

This city was about thirty miles away from Pergamos. It is amazing that the longest letter of the seven was written to the church in the least important of the cities. Pliny dismisses Thyatira with these contemptuous words: "Thyatira and other unimportant communities." In ancient days, it was the center of a dying wool industry. It is remarkable that Christ should single out a very small Church in a relatively obscure city for such an important letter. However, the message reaches far beyond the immediate circumstances in the church at Thyatira. One other mention is found in Acts 16:14, 15 where we read of the conversion of Lydia, a seller of purple, in the city of Thyatira. Lydia must have been a wealthy merchant princess indeed, dealing in one of the costliest substances in the Roman Empire. Today, Thyatira is a little city of about forty-five thousand people, their means of sustenance was found in the weaving of oriental rugs. There was also a temple for fortune-tellers in Thyatira, with a powerful female oracle who presided over it at that time.

Introduction of the Lord

As the Lord introduces Himself to these churches, the description of Him is always pertinent. He introduces Himself to the Church at Ephesus as the one who is walking among the seven lampstands. Then he says to Ephesus, "Except thou repent, I will remove thy lampstand." He introduces Himself to Smyrna as the One who is the First and the Last, who was dead and is alive again. He speaks this to comfort those Smyrnian Christians in their great trial and agony of persecution. He had been through it Himself. He had been slain. He had been raised victorious. Then, in His address to the church at Pergamos, He introduces Himself as the One Who has a sharp two-edged sword. To the church of Thyatira, He introduces Himself in verse eighteen as "the Son of God who has eyes like a flame of fire, and His feet like fine brass." This letter is going to be a letter of wrath because brass is a symbol of the wrath of the judgment of God. He is named the Son of God in contrast to the designation in chapter one where He is called the Son of Man. His title here is in keeping with the character of the judgment pronounced upon the church. Their diversion from the true worship of Jesus Christ the Son of God was so serious that it called for a reiteration of His deity. The description of His eyes as a flame of fire speaks of burning indignation and purifying judgment. In a similar way, His feet are declared to be like fine brass.

Christ makes a commendation of works, faith, and love. "I know thy works and charity and service and faith, and thy patience and thy works; and the last to be more than the first" (Revelation 2:19). Christ commends the church at Thyatira in a remarkable way, considering the severe condemnation. It is remarkable that the church was commended first for its charity or love, especially when none of the three preceding churches were commended for this quality. In addition, mention is made of their service, their faith, and their patience, and for the fact that their last works were greater than the former works, in contrast for instance, to the case of the Ephesian Church. In spite of these most commendable features, the Church at Thyatira was guilty of terrible sin; and with this fact, Christ deals beginning in Revelation 2:20-23.

Who is Jezebel?

Her name immediately takes us back to Israel. Ahab, the king, married a daughter of the king of Sidon, whose name was Jezebel. When she came to live in the capital city of Samaria, she brought her heathen gods with her, and she introduced into Israel its worst days of apostasy. She was a brilliant woman, an able woman, and a zealous woman. She slew the prophets of Jehovah, swept Israel off its religious feet, and subverted the doctrine of God. Jezebel even brought the mighty prophet, Elijah, down to his knees as he fled before her face for his life and prayed that he might die. But who is this Jezebel of Thyatira who claims to be an oracle of God, a prophetess, and to deliver the infallible words of heaven and who teaches and seduces God's servants? There are those who say that since this commercial city of Thyatira was organized similar to (AFLCIO, American Trade Union) guilds, and since all of the commercial people belonged to a patron god or goddess, there was opportunity for an influential woman, an able woman in that assembly, to teach the people that for them to belong to the guilds and to enter into the sacrifices and orgies that went along with oriental pagan, idolatrous worship, was altogether acceptable. A Christian could compromise and do both.

Here God is speaking of a development in the church, in the age of the Thyatiran history of His people (590-1517 A.D.). The Ephesian period was the day of the apostles, the apostolic church. The Smyrnian period represented the Church of persecution and tribulation, the Church of catacombs, when the heavy iron hand of the Roman Empire was upon it. The Pergamean Church was the Church of the establishment, when the church was married to the Roman government, no longer persecuted and no longer hated and despised, but now exalted and lifted up. Then follows the age of the Church of Thyatira. She is dressed in purple and silk, with golden chains around her neck, and she speaks as the infallible prophetess of God, subverting the Word of the Lord Himself. Thyatira is the apostate Church, who looks upon herself as the infallible oracle of the Almighty. Prophetically, the major characteristics of Thyatira fit the Church era (590-1517) that spanned the Middle Ages. During this time, the dominant Church fabricated a system that, like Jezebel, bound the people to image worship, superstition and priest-craft. These Scripture verses indicate this Church still has some adherents and some power into the great tribulation (Revelation 2:22).

There are many reasons for identification with Jezebel. The Church is always represented by a woman. The Church is always referred to as a "she" or as a "her," never as a "he" or a "him." The Him in Christianity is the great God and Savior, Jesus Christ. The Church is always described as the Bride of Christ, espoused to Christ, and subject to Christ. When we see a woman here, we see a figure of the Church, and when that woman is called Jezebel, we immediately know that the Lord is speaking of an apostate church.

The third parable in Matthew thirteen is identical in meaning to Christ's letter to the fourth church. They are one and the same. Here, the meal offering represents our Lord. He is the bread of life. He is the food from heaven, the meal offering, and the fine flour, which represents the Word of God, the bread of life, the true manna from heaven. Leaven corrupted the great truths of the doctrine of the Son of God. The leaven represents evil doctrine and teaching. This prophetess delivers not the true message of God, but her own evil, corrupt doctrine. All Christendom became corrupt, outside of the few who remained true to the faith.

The Corruption of the Woman

The dream that the gospel of the Son of God will ever convert the world is a fantastic thing out of man's imagination. It is not revealed in the Bible. In the thirteenth chapter of the gospel of Matthew, there were four kinds of soil, and it was only one of them that produced fruit for God. There we see the tares grow with the wheat, and the leaven grows in the lump until the time of the end. There is never a time without tares. It is only in the end days when God's judgment comes, that God separates the tares from the wheat and burns up the tares with unquenchable fire. They are both together until the end. There is never a time when the gospel converts the world. This, the parable of the leaven teaches. Corruption and men's false doctrine enter into the truth of God and pervade it. The kingdom of Heaven, in the thirteenth chapter, refers to the kingdom here in this world as it is administered by men. It is what we call "Christendom," the great nations of the world who are called Christian nations. This corruption works and it is furthered by this woman Jezebel. God refers to what she teaches as "the depths of Satan." She, of course, would call what she teaches "the depths of God." "You cannot learn this book by yourself," she says, "You must come to me and let me teach you the deep things of God." Man cannot read the simple gospel for himself. He cannot listen to the Word of God and repent of his sins and trust Jesus and be saved. He must come and be instructed by lectures and classes in the deep things of God.

One stands in awe before the unfolding of prophecy as it has been written by the finger of God in this amazing book. This woman subverts almost all Christendom. But there are a few, there is a minority, there are some who are faithful to the Lord and He says, " And he shall rule them with a rod of iron; as the vessels of a potter shall they be broken to shivers: even as I received of my Father" (Revelation 2:27). This is a quotation from the second Psalm: "Ask of me, and I shall give thee the heathen for thine inheritance, and the uttermost parts of the earth for thy possession. Thou shalt break them with a rod of iron; thou shalt dash them in pieces like a potter's vessel" (Psalm 2:8, 9).

There is a limit beyond which false doctrine and false teaching cannot go. Someday, God Himself shall destroy that system (Revelation 17:1-6, 16). God will not put up forever with Jezebel and the seduction of His people. God will judge her. God will give His people a great victory, a victory that is minutely delineated in the book of Revelation.

But God has a second reward to the faithful. "And I will give him the morning star" (Revelation 22:16). The Lord describes Himself: "I am the bright and morning star." When Christ gives us the morning star, we have Him. The morning star is also the announcement of the dawn. If we have Christ, then we will have been caught away unto Him and shall appear with Him in glory. Caught away with our Lord, the morning star! There, when the day dawns, with our Savior, announcing the glorious consummation of the age. "He, who has an ear, let him hear what the Spirit says to the Churches".

REVELATION CHAPTER 3

Sardis

Sardis. Artemis Temple and 5th century A.D. Church. Photo ©Leon Mauldin.

Sardis - (Revelation 3:1-6)

Sardis is the fifth Church of the seven. In the great circle of the seven churches in Asia, the messenger carried the letter to Ephesus, then north to Smyrna, then further north to Pergamos; there, he turned south and somewhat east to Thyatira and so down to Sardis. Sardis is about 30 miles from Thyatira, about 60 miles from Pergamos and east of Smyrna about 50 miles. It was an important and wealthy city located on the commercial trade route running east and west through Lydia. An ancient city with a long history, Sardis has come back into prominence under Roman rule. One time it was the capital of the kingdom of Lydia. Much of its wealth came from its textile manufacturing and dye industry and its jewelry trade. Most of the city practiced pagan worship, and there were many mystery cults or secret religious societies. The magnificent temple of Artemis, dating from the fourth century BC, was one of its points of interest and still exists as an important ruin. The Church to which the letter was addressed continued its existence until the fourteenth century, but it never was prominent. Today, only a small village known as Sart, exists amid the ancient ruins.

The Church has a name, is alive, but dead. The church was contaminated with the world, inward decay, spiritual disintegration and dry rot. In Museums of natural history certain animal which are lifelike in their natural habitat, and mounted exactly as they lived, but they are dead. Like the letter to Laodicea, it is an unmixed message of rebuke and censor. It is almost devoid of any word of commendation, such as that characterized the word of Christ to the other churches. The reason for the sad condition in Sardis was that the people were surrounded by a severe form of idolatry.

In relation to Sardis, Christ is introduced in verse one as the one that has the seven spirits of God, and is similar to the description given in Revelation 1:4. In both verses, however, the Holy Spirit is in view. Here there is an apparent allusion to the sevenfold character of the Holy Spirit as resting upon Christ according to the prophecy of Isaiah 11:2-5. There the Holy Spirit is described thus, "the Spirit of the Lord." "The Spirit of wisdom and understanding, the spirit of counsel and might, the spirit of knowledge and of the fear of the Lord." There also He is described as coming from God and resting upon Christ. A similar description is found later in Revelation 5:6. In addition to having the sevenfold spirit of God, Christ is revealed as the One who has the seven stars, interpreted in 1:20 as the angels or messengers of the seven churches. The fact that the leaders of the church represented by these messengers belong to Christ makes their leadership and transmission of the message all the more authoritative and responsible. The same description of Christ as holding the seven stars in His right hand was given in relation to the letter to the church at Ephesus in 2:1 to make clear that the leaders of the church are responsible to no human representative of Christ and must give account directly to the Lord Himself.

The church at Sardis evidently had a reputation among the churches in that area, and was considered a spiritual church and one that had an effective ministry and testimony for God. From the divine standpoint, however, it is considered as a church that had only a name of being alive, yet actually was dead as far as spiritual life and power were concerned. The searching judgment of Christ as it relates to the church of Sardis is one to be pondered by the modern church, which often is full of activity, even though there is little that speaks of Christ, spiritual life, and power.

Warning

Though the church at Sardis was classified as being dead in the sight of God, it is obvious from verse two that there were some in the church who still had true life and spirituality.

The previous history of Sardis should have warned them concerning the possibility of sudden and unexpected judgment. Although the situation of the city was ideal for defense, as it stood high above the valley of Hermus, and was surrounded by deep cliffs almost impossible to scale, Sardis had twice before fallen because of overconfidence and failure to watch. In 549 B.C., Persian king Cyrus had ended the rule of Croesus by scaling the cliffs under the cover of darkness. In 214 B.C., the armies of Antiochus the Great (III) captured the city by the same method. The city of Sardis, at the time it received this letter, was in fact, in a period of decline as compared to its former glory.

On October 31, 1517, Martin Luther nailed his "Ninety-Five Theses" on the church door at Wittenberg, Germany. The spiritual history of the church was to correspond to the political history of the city. Their works are also declared to be not perfect, literally not fulfilled, that is, not achieving the full extent of the will of God. Their works were short, either in motive or in execution, and they are exhorted to fill to the full the opportunity of service and testimony.

Prophetic Application - (1517-1750)

The church of Sardis symbolized the Reformation Era. During this period of history, the church was reformed, but not revived. Some essential doctrines were reclaimed, such as the truth that people can be justified by faith, but the changes did not shake loose the elaborate rituals and human traditions of the medieval church. Complacency and new legislation set in, and only a few tasted the power of the Holy Spirit for Christian living.

Not only are they exhorted to be watchful and strengthen the things which remain, but they are also warned to remember the truth that they have received, heard, and held fast to, and to turn away from any defection from it. If they refuse to heed the exhortation, Christ promises that He will come upon them unexpectedly with devastating suddenness and living judgment upon the church at Sardis. However, it is going to be just as unexpected, sudden, and irrevocable as that which is related to the Second Coming.

Promise to Godly Remnant

To those individuals in the Sardis church who overcame, the promise is given that they shall be clothed in white raiment. This means that the fidelity of character and service shall presently have its outward manifestation.

Further, it is promised, "I will not blot out his name out of the Book of Life." This book contains the names of all the individuals ever born. If a person does not receive Jesus Christ as Savior by the time he dies, his name is blotted out of the Book of Life.

The message is, therefore, a series of exhortations, not only to the church of the first century, but to those who need the same exhortations in every century. To such, the commands are given to be watchful, to strengthen the things which remain that are ready to die, to remember the truth and experience of the past, to hold fast that which remains, and to repent in mind and heart. As in the other churches, the message deals with the individual invitation, "He that has an ear to hear, let him hear what the Spirit says to the churches."

Philadelphia

Philadelphia - (Revelation 3:7-13)

Philadelphia was about thirty miles southeast of Sardis. It was destroyed in 17 A.D. by the same earthquake that toppled Sardis. Tiberius Caesar, the great builder of cities, reestablished it. This city was founded in 140 B.C. by the king of Pergamos, Attalus II, whose other name was Philadelphus. The city was named Philadelphia after him. It is interesting how much the letter of our Lord to this sixth Asian church reflects the topography, the history, and the situation of the city. Philadelphia means brotherly love.

Philadelphia was the last bastion of Christianity when Asia Minor was overrun by Islamic Turks. One of the most interesting commentaries upon prophecy and the Word of God is to be found in the works of the famous historian Edward Gibbon: "In the loss of Ephesus, the Christians deplored the fall of the first angel and the extinction of the first candlestick of the Revelation. The desolation is complete and the temple of Diana, or the church of Mary, will equally elude the search of the curious traveler. The circus and the three stately theaters of Laodicea are now peopled with wolves and foxes. Sardis is reduced to a miserable village. The god of Mohammed, without a rival or a son, is invoked in the mosques of Thyatira and Pergamos. The populousness of Smyrna is supported by the foreign trade of the Franks and Armenians. Philadelphia alone has been saved by prophecy or courage. Among the Greek colonies and churches of Asia, Philadelphia is still erect, a column in the scene of ruins."

It is to this day largely a Christian town. Our Lord had nothing but words of commendation for Smyrna and for this missionary church of Philadelphia. The Philadelphian church is: the church of the missionaries, the church of the evangelists, the church of the Bible societies, the church of the soul winners, and the church of world-wide preaching of the gospel of the Son of God.

Open Door

Rev.7-13

[7] "And to the angel of the church in Philadelphia write,

'These things say He who is holy, He who is true, "He who has the key of David, He who opens and no one shuts, and shuts and no one opens": "I know your works. See, I have set before you an open door, and no one can shut it;] for you have a little strength, have kept My word, and have not denied My name. [9] Indeed I will make *those* of the synagogue of Satan, who say they are Jews and are not, but lie—indeed I will make them come and worship before your feet, and to know that I have loved you. [10] Because you have kept My command to persevere, I also will keep you from the hour of trial which shall come upon the whole world, to test those who dwell on the earth. [11] Behold, I am coming quickly! Hold fast what you have, that no one may take your crown. [12] He who overcomes, I will make him a pillar in the temple of My God, and he shall go out no more. I will write on him the name of My God and the name of the city of My God, the New Jerusalem, which comes down out of heaven from My God. And *I will write on him* My new name.

[13] "He who has an ear, let him hear what the Spirit says to the churches."'

Rev.3:7. "And the 'key of the house of David' will I lay upon His shoulder; so He shall open, and none shall shut; and He shall shut, and none shall open." This quotation is from Isaiah 22:20-22, which itself is a characterization of Eliakim, the steward of King Hezekiah. The noble, trusted man was given the key to the palace. No one came to approach the king except through Eliakim. So it is with us in Christ. There is an open door to God in our Savior and no man can shut it. In the time of Philadelphia, many famous preachers were raised. In 1792, William Carey went to India.

Philadelphia has developed outside of the Reformation from the spiritually dead state churches. Although there always have been Philadelphian believers, a Philadelphian movement is another matter. From the addresses of the Lord to the seven churches, everyone must ask himself where he fits into this. If I don't belong to the group of Thyatira, and if I don't belong to the state churches of reformation or these churches similarly constituted, then I must find my place either in Philadelphia or Laodicea. The Lord will lead Christians to seek out their own company of brethren - the meaning of the word Philadelphia.

Philadelphia stands for a well-defined movement in the history of the professing church. J. N. Darby spoke of the historical churches: "Outside of Scripture, the historical church never was, as a system, the institution of God or what God had established, but at all times, from its first appearance in ecclesiastical history, the departure as a system from what God established and nothing else. And as to doctrines, it is quite certain that neither a full redemption nor a complete possessed justification by faith, as Paul teaches it, a perfecting forever by Christ's one offering, a known personal acceptance in Christ, is ever found in any ecclesiastical writings after the Scriptures, for long centuries."

Out of the deadness of the state churches, over and over again came forth companies of believers energized by the Holy Spirit (The Brethren Movement). It is a complete return to the first principles. The message makes this clear. They receive only praise, for they pleased the Lord. It is a revival and turning back to their first love. The Lord Jesus Christ is once more the all-absorbing object before their heart. Philadelphia repudiates all that dishonors Him. It is a faithful remnant gathering in His name, around the table. The unity of believers and brotherly love was established. They walk in the path of separation in self-judgment and in lowliness of mind. They have a little strength, which means weakness; they are a feeble few. Twice, the Lord speaks of obedience to His word. Thou hast kept My word. Thou hast kept the word of my patience, and the Philadelphian does not deny His name. These are the two characteristics of this phase of Christianity during the closing days of Christianity.

Obedience to His Word and Devotion to His name

The Word and the name are denied in the last days. The apostasy of Christendom exists in the rejection of the written Word and the living Word.

Christ's Word and His Name

The Lord speaks of Himself in a distinct way from that in which He spoke of Himself before.

The Holy and True One

The way the Lord presents Himself in these epistles is always in accordance with the state of those to whom He speaks. It is for warning or encouragement, or perhaps both, as in the address to Smyrna. He that lives and was dead, enforced by the words, be thou faithful unto death, and I will give thee the crown of life. Here, He that is holy and He that is true is a solemn admonition, and yet it surely has its blessed comfort too. This personal title in conjunction with the whole epistle seems to show the final breakup of the ecclesiastical system, with an individual Christian walk becoming the whole matter. Holiness and truth have seldom been the attributes of bodies of men.

Features of Philadelphia

(1) Thou hast kept My word (2) and hast not denied My name. (3) Thou hast kept the word of My patience.

(1) My word in opposition to all other. Everywhere through this writing, "My" is remarkably emphasized, and the person of the Lord is exceedingly prominent. Today, the Word of God

is in special question everywhere. Modern world organizations and philosophies try to lower and take away the authority of this word. The voice of the church (clergy) is substituted for Christ's voice. Religion is an earth born thing - not heaven born, an aspiration, but not an inspiration. What an immense thing it is to be keepers of Christ's word. Philadelphians are exemplifying a spirit of true obedience.

(2) Thou hast not denied My name. Names in Scripture have significant meanings. They are not as in the present day, put upon people for their prettiness, or because they run in the family. God did not think it an unworthy thing often Himself to interfere and change or give a name, and so the Lord did with His disciples. There was a reason for the name. It was the expression of what the person was, most generally, or would be, as in Abraham, Israel, Peter, and such like, especially with the names of God or of Christ.

When God took the special name of Jehovah with Israel, it meant that He was going to approve Himself to them in that character, as the immutable God, the "I AM" upon whom they could rely upon to keep the covenant. So Christ is Immanuel, "God is with us" and in order that that prophecy may be or shown to be fulfilled, He is called 'Jesus,' His people's Savior from their sins. God could not be with us except our sins were met, and none but a divine person could meet them - salvation must be of God, and this is all expressed in the name "Jesus."

Christ is the Greek form of the Hebrew "Messiah," which speaks of Him as the one anointed of God to be the deliverer in three necessary ways: a prophet to bring out of error, a priest to open the way to God, and a king to govern for God. Thus, Christ's name is a remarkably explicit declaration of Himself. And this name of His, with the facts which it implies, is what is committed to His people to hold fast and maintain as His, in the midst of a world which has rejected Him. To confess His name involves thus the confession: of His absolute deity, His true humanity, His salvation of His people, and His being their only and sufficient Teacher, Intercessor and Lord. The name of Christ expresses what He is. The truth of what He is, is what is committed to us, what we have to confess in the face of the world.

Christ is the truth; Satan is the liar from the beginning. By a lie of his, man was first seduced and fell. By the truth, he is brought back to God and sanctified. Satan's effort is therefore by counteracting lies to destroy the power of the truth. And his most successful method is not so much direct denial as perversion of the truth, knowing man's heart but too well by long experience. He knows how to combine truth and error so skillfully, that the truth shall give only the mere speciousness to the error, while the error in the guise of truth shall appeal to the lusts and passion and enlist them upon its side. (For example, a mere 10% of cyanide in a glass of milk can kill you.)

Thus Satan seduces as an angel of light, and Christendom, with its profession of Christ's Lordship, can worship many lords under the profession. Not denying His name, may, in this way, be given as a signal mark of approbation in the midst of Christendom, even more than in the midst of heathenism.

If we look further into Scripture for the association in which we find the name of Christ, we shall soon see that it is connected with the whole standing and walk of the individual believer, as well as with the practical gathering together of His people. We are justified in the name of the Lord Jesus. Our prayers are to be presented in His name, our every word and work is to be done in His name. Our gathering as Christians is to be "to His name." Jesus represents us in heaven; we represent Him on earth. We represent Him before the world. Whatever we do in word or deed, we are to "do all in the name of the Lord Jesus" (Colossians 3:17). Are not these truths which God has been graciously restoring to us in those days (Brethren Movement) afresh? No doubt the revival of justification by faith is as old as the Reformation, and was then brought out with simplicity and power. There was one thing to which the Reformation did not attain, and of which the common evangelical doctrine, so called, has fallen entirely short.

Even the full manhood of the Lord, as a present thing in heaven, has become misty and indistinct, and the resurrection side of the gospel is nearly absent from the evangelical systems. They stop short with Christ's death for us.

The word Philadelphia means "brotherly love." Not association merely, as brothers, but having brotherly love. So it is to be with us: love, wherever there are "brothers," love to all children of the Father as His children, but a love which consists, with deed full maintenance, of what is due to the Father. "This commandment have we from Him that he who loves God loves his brother also." In II Peter 1:5-7, we find the order of divine growth. "Brotherly love" comes in a very different place from what we should naturally imagine. From "faith," the beginning of everything is in us. Brotherly love is the sixth stage on towards perfection, and only short of the full maturity of "love" itself. We are first of all to add to our faith "virtue." For as faith's walk is against nature and through a hostile world, the very first requisite for it, next to faith itself, is courage.

In Philadelphia, there is a revival of prophetic truth, an earnest waiting for the coming of the Lord. Philadelphia is a description of a loyal remnant. In the mid-1800's, Scripture has been opened to us more as a whole than at any former time since the apostles. Furthermore, this has been in connection with a movement that has all the features of Philadelphia. Certain great truths, having been recovered to the church, have helped to open up in a new way both the Old and New Testaments. The dispensations have been distinguished. The gospel has been cleared from Galatian error (law keeping). Our place in Christ as we learned, is in connection with our participation in His death and resurrection. The real nature of eternal life and the present seal and baptism of the Holy Spirit, in contrast with all former or other spiritual operations and gifts, has been learned, and the Rapture has been distinguished from His appearing.

"For where two or three are gathered together in My name, there am I in the midst of them" (Matthew 18:20). What is His name? His name is above all names; Wonderful. The main test for a Philadelphian movement would be the confession or denial of the name of Christ as the center of gathering. Philadelphia is mentioned seven times in the Bible, but only as a city: Romans 12:10, I Thessalonians 4:9, Hebrews 13:1, I Peter 1:22, I Peter 1:7(twice), and Revelation 3:7.

In the winter of 1827-1828, four Christian men came together on the Lord's Day for the breaking of bread as the early Christians did. They were J.N. Darby, Dr. A.J. Cronin, Mr. Bellett, and Mr. Hutchinson. The first meeting was held in Dublin. They had been studying the Scriptures and comparing what they found in the Word of God with the existing state of things around them. But they could find no expression of the nature and character of the church of God, either in the national establishment, or in the various forms of dissenting bodies. This brought them into the place of separation from all these ecclesiastical systems, and led them to come together in the name of the Lord Jesus, owning the presence and sovereign action of the Holy Spirit in their midst (Matthew 18:20; Ephesians 4:3,4).

Prophetical teaching, especially the teaching of the rapture, electrified the whole Christian world, and great revivals were started. The church, with little strength, will be blessed and made strong when He appears. The true church suffered. You are weak now, but you are going to be His in heaven.

The Lord's Promises to Overcome

Because thou hast kept the word of My patience, I also will keep thee from the hour of trial (temptation) that is coming upon the entire world. "I will make him a pillar in the temple of God." This of course is a figure of speech. The entire heavenly city is considered a temple. In keeping with the symbolism, the Philadelphian Christians will be permanent, like a pillar in the temple, and speaking figuratively, they will stand when all else has fallen. This perhaps had peculiar significance to those who were in Philadelphia because of their historic experiences with earthquakes, which frequently had ruined their buildings and left only the pillars standing.

The church is called the pillar and ground of the truth. Peter, John, and James (the Lord's brother) in Galatians two were called "pillars of the church." So, in the New Jerusalem, we are the adornment of God forever. "We are to be pillars and we shall go no more out." In the courses of the Old Testament priests, death took them out of their ministries. Even our first "parents" were driven out, beyond Eden to water the ground with their tears and their sweat and to be buried beneath its sod. But in the New Jerusalem, we shall "go no more out."

"And I will write upon him the name of my God, and the name of the city of my God, which is the New Jerusalem." In the Revelation, as he looked on the saints in glory, John said, "And His name was written in their foreheads." Like the high priest of old, we also shall have the dignity of His high office, carrying with it the right of access to God forever. We shall see His face and live. And we shall be citizens of the New Jerusalem. In the eleventh chapter of the book of Hebrews, Abraham saw the city, which has foundations whose builder and maker is God. And in the same chapter we are told, "Therefore God is not ashamed to be called their God, for He has prepared a city for them" (Hebrews 11:16).

"And I will write upon him My new name." He has many names: "And His name shall be called Wonderful, Counselor, the Mighty God, the Everlasting Father, the Prince of Peace" (Isaiah 9:6). In the glory that is to come, the Lord does not lay these names aside. He will continue to be known by His old names (Philippians 2:9). We see "therefore God also has highly exalted Him and given Him the name which is above every name." John sees the Christ as conqueror and calls Him "the True and Faithful" (Revelation 19:11). Verse 12: He had a new name written that no one knew except Himself. Verse 13: And His name is called "the Word of God." Verse 16: And His name is written KING OF KINGS, AND LORD OF LORDS. "And he will be given each a white stone, and in the stone a new name written, which no man knoweth except he himself" (Revelation 2:17).

There are worlds and universes and infinite areas in which our Lord Jesus Christ shall live and reign triumphantly beyond anything that man can imagine. These conquests are also ours. We are hidden with Christ in God, from grace to grace and from glory to glory, until the fullness of our Lord becomes the fullness of His people, and He and we are one, a world without end. Oh the blessedness of it all. Amen.

Laodicea

The Laodicean Church - (Revelation 3:14-22)

In the great circle by which the messenger carried these seven letters from our Lord to each one of the separate congregations, we have come to the last, the most southeasterly. The background, the topography and the history of the city are most evident in this letter. The very name "Laodicea" is rich in meaning. It was founded by Antiochus II, who named it after his wife, Laodicea. It was founded because it controlled the entrance into the interior province of Phrygia. At the end of Colossians, we can see the name of this church mentioned. So this assembly and the valley in which it was located belong to a famous group of ancient Christian churches.

The City Reflected in the Church

Our Lord draws from the topography of the country when He says, "You are neither cold nor hot, because you are tepid (lukewarm). I will spew you out of my mouth." In the district around Laodicea and Hierapolis were hot mineral springs. Lukewarm mineral water is very nauseating and ill tasting. So our Lord uses the background of those hot mineral springs, cooled off and making the drinker sick. Then He says, "You say I am rich, have become wealthy, and have need of nothing, and do not know that you are wretched, miserable, poor, blind and naked."

From the beginning, Laodicea was a success story. Jewish merchants made this province very rich. Laodiceans had a breed of sheep raised in that district that was different from any other in the world. The wool of the sheep was black and its glossy, raven-colored beauty was superior to any other to be found in the world. Laodicea manufactured four different kinds of garments, one being an outer garment. One other thing our Lord refers to in the background of the city. "Anoint your eyes with eye salve that you may see." There was a medical center in Laodicea, and one of the things manufactured and exported among other medicinal products was a "tephra Phrygia," which was a tablet bought all over the Roman Empire. The users crushed it and put it on their eyes in order to heal any eye ailment.

In 62 A.D., a Roman governor prohibited the export of gold. They were running out of gold and they needed to keep it in order to bolster their currency. Once a year, every male Jew above 21 years of age sent half a shekel to the temple in Jerusalem to support the worship of Jehovah there. In order not to have too heavy a package, the money was sent across the sea in gold. However, the Jews in Laodicea proposed to disregard the ban of the governor against the export of gold and to send their contributions in gold anyway. The governor promptly seized it and confiscated it. It weighed 20 pounds.

Christ the Eternal and Faithful Witness

"And to the angel of the church of the Laodiceans[a] write,

'**These things say the Amen, the Faithful and True Witness, the Beginning of the creation of God**" (Revelation 3:14). As in His introduction to other churches of Asia, Christ describes Himself in an unusual way as the "Amen" in addressing the angel of the church in Laodicea. The frequent use of Amen, meaning, "so be it," is a feature of the declarations of Christ, and is usually translated "verily," or used as an ending to a prayer. As a title of Christ, it indicates His sovereignty and the certainty of the fulfillment of His promises. As Paul wrote the Corinthians, "For all the promises of God are in Him, yes, and in Him Amen, to the glory of God through us" (II Corinthians 1:20). When Christ speaks, it is the final word, and His will is always effected. Christ is called the faithful and true witness in contrast to the church in Laodicea which was neither faithful nor true. Christ had been earlier introduced as the faithful witness in 1:5 and as He that is true in 3:7.

Laodicea means the "judging or rights of people." It is the opposite of Nicolaitanism. In Protestantism, the people (the laity) arise and claim their rights and do the judging. This condition was also foreseen by Paul in II Timothy 4:3. We see in Laodicea the final religious and apostate conditions of Protestant Christendom and the complete rejection of the professing body.

Not Cold, not Hot, but Lukewarm

The Laodicean church is a lukewarm church, not cold, not hot, but lukewarm. It is vastly indifferent. It is indifferent to doctrine, to truth, and to the teaching of God. To the Laodiceans, one church was about as good as another. For them, Christianity was a sort of civic betterment program, a sort of "pay your debt and don't kill anyone," etc. Such Christians are lukewarm and indifferent to the great fundamental truths that God reveals in His Book.

The Laodicean Church was not only lukewarm and indifferent about the great truths and doctrines of God, but its members did not even know the truths and the doctrines of God. So today, ask any so-called Christians some simple questions about God, about the Bible and about the revelation of Christ, and he has no idea what to answer. The Laodiceans were untaught and mostly did not care. What does the church believe? What does it stand for? What is its teaching? What is its goal? They worshiped Baal and Jehovah at the same time. They worshiped God and mammon at the same time. Today, men try to worship Christ and the world at the same time. The lukewarm church lives in the world, is a part of the world, worships and loves the same things that the world does. One cannot tell the difference between such a church and the world. Another characteristic of the Laodicean Church is that it was self-deceived. They said, "We are rich." Christ said, "You are poor." They said, "We don't need anything." Christ said, "You are wretched." They were filled with self-contentment and self-satisfaction. Today's Humanism and the New Age teach these philosophies; that we can do without God.

Christ Outside

The Philadelphian Christian, who is separated from the Laodicean state, whose heart is filled with the love of Christ, can learn a lesson here. If our Lord stands outside and yet knocks and waits in patience, we too with Him outside of the camp, where He is disowned, can try to gain admittance into the Laodicean hearts. Epaphras did this (Colossians 4:12-13). Laodicea consists in a proudly boasting spirit with total indifference to the Lord Jesus Christ and to His name. It is religiousness without any truth, nor the power of the Holy Spirit. He is on the outside, what a tragedy and sadness.

When the Lord makes an appeal, it is always addressed in the singular, to the individual. "If any man hears my voice..." It is the duty of the individual Christian to hear. We cannot cover ourselves or hide ourselves under the great blanket of the vast congregations of Christendom. The faith is individual. That fact is the very genius of the Christian religion. What is said to the churches and what is addressed to the congregations must be individually heard by the people.

Promise

To him who overcomes, I will grant to sit with Me on My throne, as I also overcame and sat down with My Father on His throne. There are two thrones. First, there is the Father's throne, the throne of the invisible. Christ as God and co-regent with the Father is sat down in the Father's throne, unapproachable, awesome and removed. But there is another throne. There is Christ's throne, the throne of our Lord. He shall be our visible King, our reigning Lord, and all the power of the kingdom and empire will be in His hands. And in that day, we shall reign with Him, according to the Word of God (Revelation 22:3).

Taken as a whole, the messages to the seven churches of Asia constitute a comprehensive warning from Christ Himself as embodied in the exhortations to each of the churches. In summary, there is a warning for the churches of today to "hear what the Spirit says unto the churches." The church at Ephesus represents the danger of losing our first love (2:4).

The church at Smyrna representing the danger of the fear of suffering, was exhorted (2:10). "Do not fear any of those things which you are about to suffer." The church at Pergamos illustrates the constant danger of doctrinal compromise (2:14, 15). The church at Thyatira is a monument to the danger of moral compromise (2:20). The church today may well take heed to the departure from moral standards, which has invaded the church itself. The church at Sardis is a warning against the danger of spiritual deadness (3:1, 2), of orthodoxy without life, a mere outward appearance of being like the Pharisees, white sepulchers. The final message to the church at Laodicea is the crowning indictment, a warning against the danger of Luke warmness (3:15, 16), of self-sufficiency, and of being unconscious of desperate spiritual need.

REVELATION CHAPTER 4

After considering the failures of the Church in all ages, we might be inclined to think that Christ would give upon it. But just the opposite is true. As the centuries have rolled by, Christ has been preparing a place in heaven for his bride, and each passing year has brought nearer God's appointed day for our happy reunion with him.

The Old Testament saints looked forward to spending eternity with the Lord, but they knew they would have to face death before they could see their Lord. They did not know, because it wasn't revealed until the New Testament, that someday Jesus would return to the sky and take a whole generation of believers to heaven without dying physically. There would be no "Valley of the shadow of death" for them. In each of the seven phases of Church history that we looked at in Chapters 2 and 3, earnest believers longed to be in that select group who would witness the coming of Christ. But God has a perfect time schedule for His program, and the long interlude between Jesus's first and second coming has given the opportunity for countless millions more to receive his love and forgiveness of sin.

The apostle John was granted the unique privilege of leaving the earth and recording for us the future events in heaven and on earth. Jesus told John to write about three things: First, the things he had seen in the glorified person of Jesus; second, the things that were spiritually significant in the Churches of John's day, Churches whose experiences would typify conditions throughout Church history until Jesus returned for his people; Third, things that would take place "after all these things". Revelation 1:19

Although John didn't comprehend many of the things he saw, he faithfully recorded it all. In chapter one, we see his description of Christ in his glory. Chapters 2 and 3 witness the spiritual condition of the Church through the ages.

These visions were given to John while he was still in Patmos.

It is important to note that the Church has been the main theme of the revelation until chapter 4. Starting with this chapter, the Church isn't seen on earth again until chapter 19, where we suddenly find it returning to earth with Christ as He comes to reign as king of kings and lord of lords... The big question is, where is the church during the earthly devastation described in Chapter 6 through 19, and how did it get where it is?

Mystery

The apostle gives us the prophetic answer to the question, calling it a "Mystery". When the word "Mystery' is used in the Bible, it usually refers to a secret that no one can know until God chooses to reveal it. Since the Church itself was a mystery to the believers of Old Testament days, its final destiny was also unknown. After Christ's resurrection, after the Church was established, God revealed His secret to Paul... In first Corinthians 15:51-52, Paul writes "Behold I show you a mystery "We shall not all die, but we shall all be changed from mortal to immortal, in a moment, in the twinkling of an eye, at the last trumpet".

The mystery revealed here is the promise that a certain group of people wouldn't have to die before going to be with the Lord, but will be changed from mortals to immortals without going through Physical death. Paul further amplifies this in first Thessalonians 4:15-17.

The Great Snatch.

It is obvious from these verses and others, that Paul predicts a time when Jesus will raise the bodies of dead believers and simultaneously change living believers to immortals. The word for caught up actually means to "snatch up". It is usually referred to as the "Rapture' from the Latin word rapture, which means to "take away" or "snatch out." Why would Jesus promise that a special group of His people would be taken from earth to heaven without first dying? The answer is clear. God will take his beloved Church before the great tribulation starts on earth.

Will the Church go through the tribulation?

This question has caused a great deal of controversy among true believers. The Bible teaches the church will escape the great tribulation. Although believers may well experience severe persecutions the day of Christ's return draws near.

Part of the confusion on the issue rises from a failure to distinguish two stages in Jesus's second coming. One passage, of scripture speaks of Christ's coming in the air and in secret, like a thief coming in the night. Another part of the scripture describes Christ's coming in power and majesty to the earth, with every eye seeing him. It is also interesting that in chapters 2 and 3 we read "He who has an ear, let him hear what the spirit says to the Churches" repeated seven times while in chapter 13 we see: "If anyone has an ear, let him hear". This is the same warning except that the Church is left out. Jesus answered three questions by His disciples. When would the temple be destroyed? What would be the sign of the end of the age? He gave his reply in a parable and an historical allegory. (Matthew 24:32-44). From these we can deduce when He will return to catch up the church.

The parable involved a fig tree sprouting its first leaves. Jesus said that as new fig leaves indicate the nearness of summer in Israel, the accumulation of certain signs on the earth and in the skies would signal the arrival of God's judgments upon the generation which saw all the signs begin to appear. Matthew 24:34creates a lot of problems for interpreters. Reformed and covenant expositors try to discredit the futuristic interpretation based on this verse.

John Macarthur and Charles Ryrie have given the most sensible interpretation to this verse. Matthew 24:34. "Assuredly, I say to you, this generation will by no means pass away till all these things take place."

This cannot refer to the generation living at that time of Christ, for "all these things'- the abomination of desolation (v.15), the persecutions and judgments (v v.17-22), the false prophets (...v v.23-26), the signs in the heavens (v v.27-29), Christ's final return (v.30), and the gathering of the elect (v.31) - did not take place in their lifetime. It seems best to interpret Christ's words as a reference to the generation alive at the time when those final hard labor pains begin. This would fit with the lesson of the fig tree, which stresses the short span of time in which these things will occur See verse 32.

According to Ryrie, this generation means that "No one living when Jesus spoke these words lived to see "all these things' come to pass. However, the Greek word can mean "race" or family, which makes good sense here; i.e., the Jewish race will be preserved, in spite of terrible persecution, until the Lord comes."

The sign of Noah:

To illustrate this, Jesus gave a historical allegory about the great flood of Noah's day. He said the people were going about their business as usual eating, drinking, and marrying but paying no attention to Noah's warnings about God's impending judgment. They had no idea God's prophetic time of judgment had come until the flood destroyed them all.

Jesus said His coming would be exactly like that. The flood was a judgment on everyone who rejected God's prophetic warning and offer of forgiveness.

The flood symbolizes a judgment which is coming upon the unbelieving world. Jesus pointed out that first there was a prophetic warning and God removed His people to safety, and then judgment fell.

We are also told that Jesus' coming will have similarities to the destruction of Sodom. God's angel came to save Lot and his family (Luke 17:20-36).

This is a pattern. First a prophetic warning, then God removes His people and judgment falls on unbelievers.

Rapture before Judgment:

We are now living in a period of prophetic warning about God's impending judgment. Books, the internet, preaching, the media – messages about Jesus' return are having a wider dissemination than any other time in history.

After the Rapture We Face the Judgment Seat of Christ

We shall stand at the Bema, the judgment seat of Christ. (2 Cor 5:10; 1 Cor 3:11-15).

As we are leading a hectic and busy life, we get less and less time to spend for our Lord. We are busy building and making more money and one fine morning you will no longer be on this earth. In our calendar there is a lot of unfinished work.

Have you ever stopped to think, when your life's work is ended, when all further opportunity to serve the Lord on earth will have gone by forever, then you will stand in your glorified body before the Bema seat? Jesus will go back all the way from the day of salvation and will give His own estimate of all your service.

Sometimes He may say to many like this "You had a very good opportunity to glorify me, but you failed because you were so self-occupied, you were so much concerned about what people would think of you, instead of being concerned about pleasing me, I will have to blot all that out, I cannot reward you for that; for there was too much self in that service".

We may think at that time like this "Why didn't I do more when I had the chance. I was well aware of the Lord's command. Why did I spend so much time on foolish things? How could I have allowed my service for the Lord to be so minimal"? All these thoughts would be useless.

24 Elders

JND: "The number 24 represents twice 12. 12 patriarchs and 12 apostles – the saints of the two dispensations"

When the millennium commences, the tribulation martyrs will also have been raised from the dead. The marriage takes place in heaven.

The elders are now under the sea of Glass waiting the "catching away". John himself will be one of those elders. Rev 4:6.

As a glass sea, like crystal. It was the paradise side within the earth where Christ had taken the thief on the cross who had accepted the Lord Jesus Christ.

When Christ arose from the dead, He led captivity captive (Eph 4:8-9). That is, those in paradise were taken out and transported to the sea of glass directly beneath the throne of God. That was when Christ moved paradise from within the earth to heaven. They are at rest, at peace. They are awaiting resurrection (Heb 4:9-11). At the rapture of the church, this sea will be emptied. Afterward the Sea of Glass will be used for the keeping of the souls of those martyred during the tribulation period. They will be restless souls, yet at rest (Rev 6:9-11).

The Four Living Creatures Rev 4:7-9

John Nelson Darby says in the synopsis, "Besides these, four living creatures are there in the circle of the throne itself and around the throne. They may be moved as forming the throne, or apart from it, though connected with it as a center. They have some of the characters of the cherubim, some of the seraphim's, but somewhat different from both".

Prophecy to occupy their allotted place. The next time we see the church is in chapter 19 at the end of the age she is there, the bride of Christ, coming with her Lord in glory.

A door opened in Heaven

The opening of the door indicates that John had to enter into heaven in order to understand the prophecy. The trumpet voice summons John from earth to heaven. Prophecy has its source in heaven, and hence John must go to heaven to receive the complete vision.

Chronological order

The "after this" inverse reflects only what John saw after receiving the messages to the churches, not that a complete chronological order of events is maintained. The Bible never gave a chronological order of events.

Immediately I was in the spirit; and behold, a throne set in heaven, and one sat on the throne, and He who sat there was like a jasper and a sardius stone in appearance; and there was a rainbow round the throne, in appearance like an emerald. The divine summons "come up here" took him to heaven. The vision of Christ as son of man in transcendent glory in the midst of the seven golden lamps was a sight too much for mortal gaze. John, for the time being was under the absolute control of the Spirit; he lived and moved in another mode of existence. He became in the Spirit (chapter 1:10). But this cannot in the nature of things be prolonged. The state had lapsed. Now fresh visions and of the future, are to be witnessed and written. Visions of things in Heaven were witnessed by certain prophets on earth, but to the distinguished prophet of the New Testament alone were visions beheld in heaven itself. The Spirit once again laid hold of the human vessel, and entirely occupied it. John for the time lived in a new mode and sphere of existence in which human weakness and frailty had no place. The Spirit filled and controlled him.

Throne in Heaven

This was the first sight beheld by John in the new vision. The throne is the central subject in this heavenly scene. It is the sign and symbol of God's universal government. The throne set in Heaven is in contrast to the mutability of all earthly governments. The sitter upon the throne is unnamed, but is described in general. Two precious stones are named: the jasper and sardius, and by these the glory and majesty of God are reflected. His essential glory cannot be communicated even by the most exalted of creatures. God dwells in light unapproachable; whom no man has seen, nor can see (1 Tim 6:16). But what can be witnessed by creatures is displayed. The jasper and sardius are mentioned in the last of precious stones adorning the breastplate of the high priest of old (Ex 28:17-20). The sardius being first named and the jasper last; they are also named among those to describe the glory of the typical king of Tyre (Ez 28:13), the sardius again coming first and the jasper sixth. We again meet with those precious stones in the description of the holy Jerusalem governmental authority and glory towards the millennial world (Rev 21:19-20), the jasper first and the sardius sixth. The brilliance of the jasper and the deep red hue of the sardius reflect the glory and surpassing splendor of God. The glory of God, too, as symbolized by the jasper is the light (Rev 21:11), the security (v18), and the foundation (v19) of the church or bride in future governmental display.

Jasper may be today's diamond. The sardius stone is a familiar stone in color like a ruby, a beautiful red.

The significance, however, goes far beyond the color. Though the clear jasper might refer to the purity of God and the sardius stone to His redemptive purpose, according to the Old Testament, these stones had a relationship to the tribes of Israel. Each tribe of Israel had a representative stone, and the high priest had stones representing each of the twelve tribes of Israel on his breast plate when he functioned in his priestly office before the altar. This symbolized the fact that he as the high priest was representing all twelve tribes before the throne of God. Significantly, the jasper and the sardius stone are the first and last of these twelve stones (Ex 28:17-21).

Both the Father and the Son are properly on the throne as Christ himself mentioned in Revelation 3:21. We see Christ on the throne in chapter 4 and the Father on the throne in chapter 5. Another point of view is that both chapters picture God the Father on the throne in the special character of the God of Israel. The seeming contradiction may also be resolved in the doctrine of the trinity as Christ expressed it in John 14:9. Apart from the fact that He is said to sit on the throne, no description is given except the colors which impressed John.

The controversy of 24 Elders

Rev 4:4 Some think that the 24 elders represent the church only. And some who reject dispensational truth assert that "Darby and the Brethren taught this interpretation. However, they didn't read Darby's works." For example, O.T. Allis, an Amillennialist, erroneously claims that JND taught that the 24 elders represent the Church.

JND said: "the number 24 represents twice 12. One might perhaps see the twelve patriarchs and the twelve apostles – the saints of the two dispensations". (Collected writings

11:22). Kelly wrote that the 24 elders represent "the full complement of those whose mortality was swallowed up by life, the saints of both old and new changed at Christ's coming and caught up."

In Rev 19 we hear of the bride and guests. The figure of the 24 elders is there dropped because the church is seen in distinction among the heavenly saints as the bride. The OT saints are guest at the marriage, but not part of the bride. They are there because they will have been resurrected and caught up when the saints composing the church are resurrected, or changed, and caught up (Heb 11:40). The marriage takes place in heaven. The 24 elders are not angels. In the description of these who give praise to God, they are always separated and separately delineated from the angels. For example, in chapter 5:11 "and I beheld, and I heard the voice of many angels round about the throne and the cherubim and the elders".

Hebrews 12 refers to an innumerable company of angels. But, angels are never numbered. The elders are numbered. Angels are never crowned. The Greek word for "crown" here is stephanos. There are 2 Greek words for crown: diadem, which is a crown of a Potentate, a king; then throne is the word stephanos – which is the crown of a Victor.

The twenty-four elders represent the glorified OT saints and the saints of the present period, which have been changed and caught up. The OT saints and we Christians will be made perfect at the same time when Christ arrives. (Heb 11:40), (1 Cor 13:10), at the coming of the Lord for this saints. Christ is the first fruits of the resurrection (1 Cor 15:23). As first fruits, He has part in "the first resurrection".

His resurrection was phase one. Phase two will occur at the time of the rapture of the saints.

Those raised from the dead at that time will have a part in the resurrection of the "just". The OT just ones will also be raised then. Heb 11:40. When the millennium commences, the tribulation martyrs will also have been raised from the dead, for at that time the entire "first resurrection" is seen reigning (Rev 20:4).

The first resurrection states its priority before the resurrection of the unjust after the thousand years (Rev 20:5), while the resurrection of the just describes the character of the those who participate in the first resurrection. Moreover, the resurrection of life describes its result and blessedness. The first resurrection then is not a point in time but a class of persons. Phase two of the resurrection of the just will occur at the time of the rapture and the OT "just" will not be left in the grave. The objection that the godly Israelites must be raised after the tribulation not only flies in the face of Heb 11:40, it fails to deal with the OT "just" who are not Israelites. "The resurrection of the just does not distinguish among saints preceding Israel, Israel, or the church.

The lamb's marriage takes place before He comes forth from heaven as the lion of the tribe of Judah. The marriage takes place (Col 3:4). It is morally fitting that this marriage is consummated before the display of glory, for it is part of Christ's glory. Then follows the coming forth of the rider on the white horse and His armies in His train.

Some have thought that the elders represent only the church because we are priests. But Rev 20:6 shows that all who are included in the first resurrection, i.e.; all of the redeemed that had died and were raised from the dead, will be priests. This includes the three classes noted in Rev 20:4

which comprise the heavenly saints. Earth will have its own order during the millennium (Ezk 40-48).

Some have thought that only the church has been promised co-enthronement (Rev 3:21) and therefore these elders, who sit on thrones, cannot include OT saints. This is an incorrect conclusion, even supposing the premise is true. The elders are not co-enthroned according to the sense of Rev 3:21 because Christ does not take His own throne until after the appearing in glory (Psa 110:1; Matt 25:31; Rev 3:21). Thus the thrones indicating association with Christ in His reign are not seen until Rev 20:4. The thrones of Rev 4 are not reward thrones.

The elders are, however associated with the throne of Rev 4:4. "And round the throne were 24 thrones..." JND explained in a footnote to his translation why he used the word round and not around. I use 'round' for what is connected with anything (not necessarily united to it) as a center, as the tire of a wheel, but 'around' is used for detached object encircling.

The throne is the throne of God's judgment (Rev 4:5). Rather than signifying co-enthronement in Christ's reign, the 24 thrones round this throne signify association with the pouring out of God's judgment and with the wrath of the lamb. There is nothing in this, that precludes OT saints from participation in what is figured by 24 elders.

Some have thought that only the church can sing the new song. This is another assumption without proof. Rev 14:3 is not the new song of Rev: 5. the Song of Revelation 5 is sung by some who form no part of the church; and, at any rate, it is a new song. So the fact that the song is new does not mean that it can only be sung by the church. Nor does the subject of the new song exclude OT saints.

It has been noticed that in the Revelation we find no addition to the 24 elders, yet God will have others in glory. The symbol of the 24 elders is not a symbol that in itself distinguishes the church from others.

Where distinction is required, as in Rev 19, the symbol of the elders is dropped. The souls under the alter (Rev 6) are disembodied souls of martyrs during part of Daniel's 70th week and are not, of course, added to the 24 elders who symbolized the heavenly priesthood composed of raptured and resurrected saints who are in their new bodies. The tribulation martyrs will be resurrected at the end.

Why are there 24 elders? William Kelly says "the number of this is 24, corresponding the 24 courses of priesthood in Israel. When the forerunner of the Lord was to be born, his father Zacharias was a priest of the course or order of Abia. In 1 Chronicles 24 we must look to see these divisions, and we find the 8th was one in question. The priesthood was divided in to these courses in order that each in succession might take up the work of the priesthood, every course having its own chief priest. The high priest is not named here. We all know who he is; but we have the 24 elders and answering to these 24 courses of priesthood, or rather to the chiefs who represented them. (Verse 4). The elders are characteristically "round" the throne but the angles form the outer circle.

The same system of numbers is given in John's description of the beautiful city, the New Jerusalem. There are 12 gates, and on those gates are the names of the 12 tribes of Israel and on the 12 foundations are written the names of the 12 apostles of the lamb. The 12 of Israel and the 12 of the church make up the 24 elders.

After the Rapture those 24 elders are in heaven. They are in heaven as they watch the lamb take the sealed book in chapter 5. They worship God and fall down and praise Him forever as He receives the Book to open the seals thereof. These 24 elders, mentioned 12 different times in the Revelation, are in their places as they watch the mighty accession of those who are coming out of the great tribulation, their robes washed in the blood of the lamb, entering through the gates of glory, tribulation saints, the martyred of the Son of God. These elders are in their places, in the chapter 11 of the Book of the Revelation, when the seventh angel sounds and the kingdoms of this world become the kingdoms of our Lord God and His Christ, and they glorify Him who is to reign forever and forever.

They are in their places and in their positions when, in the fourteenth chapter of the Revelation, 144,000 are gathered unto the Lord upon Mount Zion. They are in the 19th chapter, verse four where they are last mentioned, where they last appear. They are there rejoicing over the conquest of Babylon and the fall of that awful system that blasphemes the name of God. They rejoice in singing Alleluias to the Lord God, world without end. These are first in heaven; then all of these things transpire in the days of the great tribulation upon the earth. `

In the prophetic vision of the future, John saw these 24 thrones occupied. The thrones, at the present are empty. The elders are now under the Sea of Glass awaiting the "catching away". John, himself, will be one of those elders after the resurrection. Remember that this is a vision of the future, after the Rapture and involves saints of both the OT and NT.

Lightening, Thundering and Voices 4: 5

John saw a great sight. He also heard thundering and voices coming from the throne. This reveals the awesome power which proceeds from the throne of God. His great power illuminates even from the seated position.

The lightenings, thunderings, and voices which proceed from the throne are prophetic of the righteous judgment of God upon a sinful world. They are similar to the thunders, lightenings and voice of the trumpet which mark the giving of the law in Exodus 19:16 and are a fitting preliminary to the awful judgments which are to follow in the great tribulation as God deals with the earth in righteousness.

John's attention is also directed to seven lamps of fire which are seen burning before the throne. They are identified as "the seven spirits of God" mentioned earlier in 1:4 and 3:1. These are best understood as a representation of the Holy Spirit in a sevenfold way rather that seven individual spirits which would require that they be understood as seven angels. Ordinarily the Holy Spirit is not humanly visible unless embodied in some way. When the Holy Spirit descended on Christ on the occasion of His baptism, the people saw a dove descending. If it had not been for the dove, they could not have seen the Holy Spirit. In a similar way on the day of Pentecost, the coming of the Spirit would not have been visible if it had not been for the "cloven tongues" like as of fire (Acts 2:3). The seven lamps of fire therefore are the means by which John is informed of the presence of the Holy Spirit. The number seven is characteristic of the perfection of the Spirit and is in keeping with the Revelation (Isa 11:2-3). In the heavenly scene it may be concluded on the basis of both chapters 4 and 5 that all three persons of the trinity are in evidence, each in His particular form of revelation.

Sea of Glass 4:6

"And before the throne, was a glass sea, like crystal. And in the midst of the throne, and around the throne, four living creatures, full of eyes, before and behind."

It was to the paradise side within the earth that Christ had taken the thief on the cross who had accepted Him.

When Christ arose from the dead, He led captivity captive. That is, those in paradise were taken out and transported to the "Sea of Glass" directly beneath the throne of God (v6). That was when Christ moved paradise within the earth to heaven. He led those captive in the paradise of Heaven, a place of perfect tranquility(Ephe.4:8) They are at rest, at peace; they are awaiting the resurrection (Heb 4:9-11). At the Rapture of the church, this sea will be emptied (1 Theses 4:16-17). Afterward, the Sea of Glass will be used for the keeping of souls of those martyred during the tribulation period. They will be restless souls yet at rest (Rev 6:9-11).

The Four Living Creatures 4:7-9

JND states in the synopsis of the Books of the Bible: "Besides these, four living creatures are there in the circle of the throne itself and around the throne. They may be viewed as forming the throne, or apart from it, though connected with it as a center. They have some of the characters of the cherubim, some of the seraphim, but somewhat different from both."

The four living creatures are not in the same class with the "elders", for they have no "thrones" or crowns or harps or golden vials. They are the guardians of the throne of God, and accompany it wherever it goes Ezekiel 1:24-28. They have eyes before and behind and within, which reveals their intelligence and spiritual insight of things past, present and to come, and they are tireless in their service; for they rest not day or night, saying Holy, Holy Lord Almighty, which was, and is and is to come.

The first time these living creatures are mentioned in the Bible is in Genesis. 3:24; where they are called "cherubim", but are not described. They were placed at the entrance to the Garden of Eden to prevent the re-entrance of Adam and Eve, and to keep the way of the "Tree of Life".

When Moses was given on the Holy Mount the pattern of the Tabernacle, he was instructed to make the "ark of the covenant" with the cherubim upon it (Exodus 25:10-22). These cherubim were guardians of the mercy seat or the place of God's presence when He in His "Shekinah Glory" visited the tabernacle. But it is not until Ezekiel had his vision of the cherubim (Ezekiel 1:28; 10:1-22) that we have a description of what they are like. Ezekiel describes them as having the likeness of a man, with 4 faces, and 4 wings, and feet like a calf's foot, and hands like a man's hand under their wings on their 4 sides. Their four faces were different. The front face was that of a man, the right side face was that of a Lion, the left side face was that of an ox, and the rear face was that of an eagle, and their whole body, back, hands, and wings, were full of eyes round about (Ezekiel 10:12). In John's vision of the "cherubim" or living creatures they are described like animals; the first was like a lion, the second like a calf, or a young ox, the third had the face of a man, and the fourth was like a flying eagle. John's Living Creatures had six wings, while Ezekiel's cherubim had only four. In Ezekiel's vision, the cherubim or living creatures were accompanied by the Holy Spirit (Ezekiel 1:12) and traveled on wheels, which shows that they were on some tour or mission, attended by the Lord, who sat on His throne over their heads (Ezekiel 1:25-28). We see the wheels are absent in John's vision, for the scene is in heaven, the permanent home of the throne of God.

In the camping and marching order of Israel in the wilderness, there was a fixed relation of the twelve tribes to the tabernacle. In camp the tabernacle rested in the middle. The camp of Judah, composed of 3 tribes, rested on the east, with its standard bearing the figure of a lion. The camp of Ephraim composed of 3 tribes rested on the west, with its standard bearing the figure of an ox.

The camp of Reuben, composed of 3 tribes, rested in the south, with its standard bearing the figure of a man. The camp of Dan, composed of 3 tribes, rested in the north, with its standard bearing the figure of an eagle. Thus the tabernacle in the center of the camp, the place of God's presence, was surrounded and protected by standards that bore the figures of Ezekiel's and John's "Living Creatures".

The dissimilarity between Ezekiel's living creatures and John's living creatures can only be explained on the supposition that there are different orders of living creatures or cherubim, each adapted to the service he is created to perform.

In Isaiah's vision in the temple of the Lord seated on His throne, he saw a heavenly order of beings that he called the "Seraphim". They had 6 wings, like John's living creatures, and cried "Holy, Holy, Holy, is the Lord of Hosts, the whole earth is full of His glory" (Isa 6:1-4), but they stood above the throne while Ezekiel's cherubim supported the throne, and John's living creatures were in the midst or round the throne.

Whatever significances there may be in the different forms the "cherubim" or living creatures took, it is clear that they do not represent the church, but are attendants or officials attached to the throne of God, for they summon the four horsemen to appear (Rev 6:1-8), and one of them gives to the "seven vial angels", the golden 'vials' filled with the wrath of God (Rev 15:7).

The Judgment Seat of Christ

There are two great events that transpire when we are resurrected or transformed, (those who are living.)

The first is that we shall stand at the Bema, the judgment seat of Christ. The Greek Word Bema is the word for "a step", and it came to refer to the raised step upon which the judge would sit when he crowned a victor in a race or when he gave the rewards of state. Finally, of course, the word came to refer to a tribunal, a judge's seat. Now the scriptures are very plain in teaching that all of us some day shall stand at the Bema of Christ (2 Corinthians 5:10). In 1 Corinthians 3, there is delineated in detail what will happen when God's children before the Bema, the judgment seat of Christ.

Now the Bema of Christ is not the judgment as to whether we are saved or not (damned). That judgment is here, in this life. That judgment is in your heart and in your soul. You are judged now according to the damnation or salvation of your soul. For those who will accept Jesus, the judgment and the wrath of God against our iniquities fell upon Him. His sufferings, His agony and His blood made atonement for our sins. But to those who refuse the overtures of mercy and say "NO" to God and "NO" to Jesus, that judgment is now. They are lost now. They are not someday going to perdition; they are on the way to perdition now. There is an awesome judgment going on now in the hearts of all mankind.

But this judgment at the Bema of Christ is an altogether different kind of judgment. When we are taken up in into glory, this judgment has to do with our rewards. We receive the fruit of our hands and of the labor of our lives at the judgment seat of Christ. That judgment is always connected with resurrection and with the return of our Lord.

The reward for a man's life for the good that he does is always at the time of the end, at the resurrection. That, of course, is connected with the return of our savior (2 Tim 4:7-8). The great reward is not when man dies, but when Jesus comes again, at the resurrection. In Revelation 22:12 "Behold I come quickly; and my reward is with me, to give every man according as his work shall be." Our reward is at the resurrection day; it is at the return of our savior.

It is very plain, why this should be. No man could be given the reward of his life when he dies, because when he dies, he does not die. The influence of his life goes on, it lives on and on and on and it continues until Jesus comes again. Only God, at the Bema of Christ, is able to unravel the influence of a man's life and make it all one, that the man may receive the reward he deserves. A man that does good – think of the illimitable reward that will come to a man like the apostle Paul, a man like the disciple John or the great reward that will come to some of those mighty preachers of other days and the sainted of God throughout the years. Their lives live on and on in others. But also think of the tragic reward that will come to those who have sown seeds of death and destruction.

Think of those who have precipated these horrible wars. If the influence of a man died, when he died the greatness of his reward or the terribleness of his reward might not be so much. But it goes on and on until the end of time. The Lord's people will appear at the Bema of Christ where we shall receive all of God's goodness to us. However, the wicked and the unbelieving will appear at the great white throne judgment of God where they will receive the bitter results. The shadow of our lives extends beyond the grave when we are resurrected, when all of us are changed, we shall appear immediately before the Bema of Christ, there to receive the rewards of our lives. In a thousand ways it is possible for a Christian to reap and to sow and to work for God now and until Jesus comes again.

The Marriage of the Lamb

Now the second great event in heaven is the marriage of the lamb and the marriage supper of the Great King. It is described in the 19th chapter of revelation. At the wedding God has already given us our rewards. At the Bema of Christ, God's people are prepared to be married to the Lamb of God. All of our filthiness has been taken away.

The Bride of Christ is the Church. It is not Israel, nor is a remnant of Israel. There is a special blessedness to us who have been saved and who love Jesus in this day of Grace. All of the saints, from the day of Pentecost until the resurrection and translation are the Bride of Christ – and there is a special blessing for us (Eph 5).

But there is also a great marriage supper prepared to which there are guests invited. The bride is married to the Lamb. The Church is married to Christ. These 24 elders are referred to the last time in this chapter 19. After that the term is never used again. The 24 elders divide into the twelve representing the church are married to the lamb. While the other twelve represent the saints of the old dispensation. They are the guests at the marriage supper of the lamb.

Our Lord said about John the Baptist "of those born of women there has never been a greater than he." John said in the gospel of John 3:29," He who has the bride has the bridegroom; but the friend of the bridegroom, who stands and serves him, rejoices greatly because of the bridegroom's voice. Therefore, this joy of mine is fulfilled".

John the Baptist was martyred before the Church was formed, and it is the church that is the Bride of Christ. The least child in the church is greater than John. Again let me quote the last verse of the eleventh chapter of Hebrews. "And all these having attained a good testimony through faith, did not receive the promise, God having provided something better for us, that they should not be made perfect apart from us."

But what of these OT saints? Is there a blessing for them? Rev 19:9 "Then he said to me," write "Blessed are those who are called to the marriage supper of the lamb." And he said to me, these are the true sayings of God." Among the guests, the greatest may be John the Baptist. When John comes, he will be the most honored of all the guests. Then will come in Abraham, who rejoiced to see his day and he saw it and was glad. Abraham rejoicing in the voice of the bridegroom. Do you belong to this household of faith? Is your name written in the Lamb's Book of Life? Have you given your heart to Jesus?

REVELATION CHAPTER 5

Chapter 4 and 5 in the Revelation go together. They record the greatest event in the history of the universe. The scene, as it develops, brings into focus an all-important scroll that is laid upon the hand of God.

There are several books mentioned in the Revelation. There is the book of life, a register of the names of all those who have been redeemed by the blood of the Lamb. There is another book, the Book of Works, wherein God writes down all the deeds that are done in this human life. Again in the tenth chapter of the Revelation, there is a book of the testimony that is given to John by which he speaks in prophecy to the peoples and the nations.

But this is a unique book. Remember, when we use here the term "book" we refer to the book as it was in an ancient day, a scroll. The Christian people took the long roll and cut it into leaves and tied the back part together, like this book you are reading. The book we read in modern times was invented by the first Christian preachers, martyrs, missionaries and evangelists, as they took the scroll of the scriptures and preached to the people, showing out of the Holy Scriptures that Jesus is the Christ, the Son of God. It takes time to unroll a scroll; so the Christian people cut it up and bound the backside of the leaves together into what was called a "codex". That was done so the Christian could testify and the preacher easily turn to a place in the Bible where he could show God's word presenting the Son and our Savior. But the scroll was the only kind of a book known when the Bible was written.

This scroll that lay in the hand of God was sealed with seven seals. Literally it was sealed down with seals seven. Now the vision that John saw was this: There was a scroll rolled up, then that part sealed, then rolled again and sealed, and rolled again and sealed; so through all six seals, and the seventh seal, sealed the entire scroll. When it was unsealed, the process was reversed. When the first seal was broken, a portion of the scroll could be unrolled and could be read. When the second seal was broken, another portion of the scroll was unbound and could be read; and so on down until, when all seven of the seals were broken, the entire scroll was opened and could be read. There is immeasurable significance in that book.

The Content of the Book

God gave Adam dominion over the earth, including every one of its creatures (Gen 1:26). In a moment of weakness, Adam lost that dominion to the arch-enemy of God, the Devil (Gen 3:1-19).

The shift of dominion was clearly seen in the wilderness temptation of Christ. The devil tempted Christ by offering Him the power and glory of the kingdoms of the world (Luke 4:5-6). Christ did not submit to the wiles of the devil, but caused him to flee by quoting scripture (Matt 4:1-11).

The devil, in the Garden of Eden, in the form of a serpent,

won a major battle against mankind. The lost dominion of Adam is like the OT law concerning the surrender or sale of land. The loss of dominion and control is part of such a transaction (Lev 25:25-27). This law also afforded the opportunity to redeem the lost possession.

Adam's disobedience involved more than just eating forbidden fruit. It was a surrendering; a selling-out to the devil. Adam's sin of disobedience not only severed man's fellowship with God (Rom 5:12), it was a surrendering of earth dominion as well. We have the great privilege of restoring fellowship with God by personally accepting Christ as our Lord and Savior (1 Tim 2:5; Rom 10:13). This is wonderful; however, if earth's dominion is not redeemed and restored, we will never receive our promised inheritance.

Possession Redeemed

The apostle Paul tells us that the possession of our inheritance shall be redeemed. It is a promise from God (Eph 1:13-14).

The inheritance of this purchased possession is for those who have heard and believed the gospel. These are the ones who have accepted salvation and are thus sealed with the Holy Spirit of promise. The seal or stamp is the promise; the pledge of an inheritance yet to come (Eph 1) The Holy Spirit has given his guarantee of our inheritance.

The inheritance belongs to the devil now. There is a usurper who possesses it. There is an interloper, there is an intruder, there is an illegal alien, and there is a stranger who has destroyed God's world.

The possession was purchased at Calvary, but it has not yet been redeemed (1 Corinthians 6:20; 7:23), however, earth's dominion was not. God owned the earth already. God does not have to buy it back. God created the earth, all that has to be done is to redeem what has been lost.

The Title Deed

The seven seals express the perfection with which the hidden counsels of God are securely wrapped up in the divine mind till their open disclosure by the Lamb. The prophet Daniel (Chapter 12:4) was instructed to 'shut up' the words and seal the book even to the time of the end; whereas the seer at Patmos (Rev 22:10) is told the exact opposite, seal not the sayings of the prophecy of this book, for the time is at hand. The former was to seal; the latter was not to seal.

Now, we have reached "the time of the end", not exactly the end. All is open. The book of prophecy is completely and openly revealed.

According to the custom of the ancient law, the estate, the land and possessions of a Jew, a Hebrew, in God's land, Palestine, could never be sold or given away. Forever it belonged in that family and in that household.

We see in the scripture that at the year of Jubilee (the fiftieth year was a Jubilee), the trumpet was to sound and every man was to return unto his possession (Leviticus 25:8-13, 23-25). We have an instance of such redemption in the fourth chapter of the Book of Ruth. Boaz, a kinsman, a kinsman redeemer, redeemed the lost inheritance of Naomi and of Mahlon, the dead husband of Ruth. How they did it is beautifully told in the story of Ruth. The story of Ruth is a story of redemption.

Also we see the event in the book of Jeremiah chapter 32. The prophet Jeremiah lived in a day just before the fall of Jerusalem under Nebuchadnezzar. He had been telling the people of Israel that they were going to be carried away as slaves to Babylon. They would be in captivity for seventy years, but, at the end of that time, they would be restored and would build again the waste places (Jeremiah 29:10). Hanameel, Jeremiah's cousin, who had a piece of ground, knew well that it was soon to be absolutely worthless, and he was anxious to get it off his hands and realize what he could from it. He decided to try to sell it to his prophet-cousin, who was in prison for the truth's sake at the time. The Lord said to Jeremiah to buy the field. So Jeremiah 32:8 says that Hanameel came and besought him to buy the land. Jeremiah acquiesced. The title deeds were made out, sealed, and hidden. Jeremiah purchased the land, but he was not going to enter into possession of it. He too was to be driven out, to be rejected and set to one side. But some day that sealed roll would be of great value when the restoration took place. He gave it to his secretary to hide with a view of making known to his heirs the location of the deed that was to give them the title to the land. The sealed book was the title deed to Jeremiah's inheritance, and when the people of Israel came back from Babylon a man could go into court and say, "This deed belongs to me. I am Jeremiah's heir. I have the right to break the seals and take the property".

With these illustrations from the Old Testament before us, we have no difficulty in seeing what the seven-sealed book in Revelation means. The question was not, who is willing? but who is worthy.

The book that John saw in the hand of Him that sat upon the throne is the title deed to this world; when God says, "Who is worthy to take the book and to loose the seals thereof? It is just another way of saying, who is the rightful heir? Who can say, I have title to break those seals, title to claim that world, it belongs to me who is worthy to take possession of that world and subject it to himself?

The Lord never created Adam to die. Death is an enemy, God says, an interloper. God never made the earth to groan and to travail in agony and in pain, a place where the animals eat one another, where the earth is blasted with desert and with the burning of the sun and the cold of the winds. God never intended this earth to be bathed in tears and in blood. An enemy has done this. The sign of that forfeiture lies in the hand of God. The book represents the instrument, the mortgages, and the bonds, of our lost inheritance. The completeness of that forfeiture and the terrible encumbrance upon it is signified by seven seals. Adam's race has forfeited the inheritance altogether. The breaking of those seven seals represents the restitution of the creation of God and to Adam's fallen race. If the breaking of those seven seals is the restitution of the inheritance to the seed of Adam, then the sealing of those seven seals represent the vast encumbrance that lies upon Adam's inheritance. It is lost; it is completely lost. That sealed book represents the forfeiture of our lost inheritance.

The Whole Creation to be Redeemed

The record of our lost inheritance is written within and on the backside. Inside is the story of how we lost it, the distress, and the agony and the tears and the sorrow by which we lost our father's inheritance. Written on the outside are the terms of its redemption waiting for a kinsman-redeemer to buy us back to God. That book represents the entire creation of God. Everything you have ever seen, everything you have ever read about, everything that your eye could behold at night, everything that your heart has ever experienced the whole earth around us, the whole creation of God, all of it is lost to us. Galaxies, planets, stars all have been lost.

Adam was cursed in death. The curse that fell upon Adam falls upon us, and the death that fell upon him falls upon us. When Adam was cursed, he lost the glory and the beauty of his soul. He lost the perfection of his mind and character. He became a prey to every evil thing, every wind of violence, every disease in death and age and senility, all of which fell upon Adam and upon us. The house in which we live is cursed, the mind with which we think is cursed the heart with which we feel is destroyed.

The ground was cursed. Great desert wastes, all things that are sterile and barren on this earth. The ground was cursed for Adam's sake. The vegetable kingdom was cursed. 'Thorns also thistles shall it bring forth to thee". The vegetable kingdom lost its glory and its beauty.

The animal kingdom was cursed. The stars and the planets were cursed; the whole creation of God lost to an interloper, lost to an intruder, lost to Satan. That evil messenger reigns. Death seems to be supreme, and the grave seems never to be satiated. The whole earth seems forever to burn in its blistering heat in the summer time, and to die in its frigid cold in the winter.

2 Corinthians 5:4. But there is a decree of God and there is a purpose of God to redeem the whole purchased possession. Just for a while we wait, just for a while in agony and tears now, just for a while in death, but there is coming a day, there is coming a time when He is going to make everything right. This is the story of the little book.

When God restores to us our inheritance, He is going to redeem our bodies. 2 Corinthians 5:1-8. Second, there is the redemption of this earth. Oh, the promises in this book! Isaiah Chapter eleven.

Finally, there will be the redemption of the whole creation.

Rom 8:21-22.

Revelation 5:1-10
The worthiness of the Lamb

These messages concern one great solemn, supreme and sublime, celestial theme: the redemption of the creation of God. It is the substance of the seven sealed book. The vision begins with these words 5:2.

Then I saw a strong angel proclaiming with a loud voice, "who is worthy to open the scroll and to loose its seals". The whole universe and heaven turned their focus upon the sealed book. The voice of the strong angel calls, saying that the time has come, if there is a legal representative, if there is a qualified Goel, (a kinsman-redeemer) who is worthy and able to buy back the inheritance, "come forward to redeem the purchased possession". The voice of that strong angel penetrates to the farthest corners of glory; it searches the entire earth, and it reaches down into the realm of the departed dead. Where is one thus worthy? The search is made in heaven. The search is made in the nether-world. Where is one who is able to come and lift these title deeds, to retrieve this mortgaged inheritance and to buy it back from the interloper, the intruder, the alien, the enemy who now possesses it? Verse 3 "And no one was able in the heaven, or upon the earth, or underneath the earth, to open the book, or to look at it".

When the angels, the principalities and powers, and the archangels, and all of the order and ranks of heaven looked at that sealed book and read on the backside the qualifications of those who were worthy and able to break the seals, they shrank back in unworthiness and inability (shuddered). They were mute. All heaven turned silent. Not even one could be found in the whole realm of the spirit world, not one could be found who was worthy.

The Lamentation of John

From the way that sentence is framed, "Who is worthy to open the book"? it would seem that there were those who had attempted to do so, who had sought to achieve it. For during the ages since Adam lost his inheritance, there has been the constant attempt on the part of men to buy it back, to win it back, to find that ultimate good, to give to us our last inheritance, the utopia for which our souls long. The arts of civilizations have sought to do it. Philosophy, and man's finest thinking has sought to think it through, man-made religions have sought to buy it back. Through the centuries and all the story of mankind, that attempt has been made. Who is worthy, who is able to buy back, to give us back the lost inheritance. Verse 4. John says "And I wept much". The emphasis is upon the distress and the agony of his heart and the great sorrow of the seer (John) as he breathlessly waited for someone out of heaven, or out of the nether-world, or out of the earth, to come forward to redeem this lost inheritance, God's destroyed creation. John, as he waited and as no one came forward, burst into audible lamentation and tears. Those represented the tears of all God's people through all the centuries. Those tears of the apostle John were the tears of Adam and Eve; driven out of the Garden of Eden, as they bowed over the first grave, as they watered the dust of the ground with their tears over the silent, still form of their son, Abel. Those were the tears of the children of Israel in bondage as they cried unto God in their affliction and slavery. Those are the tears of God's elect through the centuries as they cried unto heaven. Those are the sobs and tears that have been wrung from the heart and soul of God's people as they looked on their silent dead, as they stand beside their open graves, as they experience, in the trials and sufferings of life, heart aches and disappointments indescribable. Such is the curse that sin had laid upon God's beautiful creation. "And I wept audibly", for the failure to find a redeemer meant that this earth in its curse is consigned forever to death.

"And one of the elders said to me," weep not". Notice it is not a strong angel, but it is one of the elders. One who himself had known what it was to be regenerated, one of the redeemed. That has been the cry of the Church throughout all the centuries. "Weep not". Lift up your eyes. Lift up your hearts. Behold, the lion of the tribe of Judah, the Root of David has prevailed to open the book, and to break the seven seals of encumbrances and to lift the mortgage and to buy it back and to redeem it to Adam's fallen race.

The Lion is the Lamb

Every syllable of the book, every word and sentence, is written with unfathomable meaning. We know who that refers to. Genesis 49:8-10. Judah, you are he whom your brothers shall praise; your hand shall be on the neck of your enemies. Your father's children shall bow down before you. Judah is a lion's cub; from the prey, my son, you have gone up. He bows down, he lies down as a lion; And as a lion, who shall raise him? The scepter shall not depart from Judah, nor a lawgiver from between his feet, until Shiloh comes; And to Him shall be the obedience of the people". (Rev 22:16). Rev 5:6. John saw a Lamb. Now the Greek word for lamb is amnos. The Greek word for a little pet lamb, a baby lamb, is arnios. It is used only twice in the New Testament. The first time is in John 21:15. Jesus says to Simon, then take care of my arnios (my little pet lambs) Secondly it is found in Rev 5:6. The Malayalam translation also says baby lamb.

Remember, in the directions for the Passover, the people were not to go out and slay just any lamb. The lamb was to be carefully chosen from the firstlings of the flock, for its beauty and perfection, and it was to be placed in the bosom of the family for four days; that is until the children loved it and it was looked upon as a member of the family, a pet lamb, held next to the hearts of those who lived in the household. That little arnios was identified with the family, loved, cuddled, and petted. John saw it slain; the word means violently slain. The little pet lamb was violently slain. The signs of its suffering are its body. In His body were the marks of His passion; in His hands, the print of the nails; in His side, the scar of the terrible spear thrust; in His body, the signs of His suffering. A lamb as it had been slain.

The Redemption by the Lamb

The Lamb that John saw is standing. Standing, slain, destroyed, with blood poured out onto the earth. There Christ, the lamb of God stands, in the midst of the throne, preparing to receive the sovereignty of God's universe; standing, on the basis of His sacrifice, having identified himself with us as our kinsman-redeemer; standing; to take the purchased possession and to cast out the interloper, the dragon. The picture of the lamb is the picture of our Lord Jesus Christ in His first coming as He stood and they spit upon Him. Ah, His face and His beard were covered with vile spittle. And they plucked out His beard and they smote Him in the face and they said who smote you. What is my name? They placed a crown of thorns and they mocked Him with a reed for a scepter and a filthy, cast off, dirty robe in the place of His raiment as a King.

They nailed Him like a common malefactor to a cross, raised Him up for the whole world to see. He stood as a lamb slain, with its throat cut, with blood pouring out unto death. That is the basis of redemption, the blood that washes sin away, the sacrifice that paid the price and the penalty of our iniquity. But now the time has come when God's suffering servant who paid the price of our sin, who redeemed us and bought us back to God, the time has come for the lamb of God to take us out of the hand of the interloper, out of the hand of death, out of the hand of that grief, out of the curse and the damnation of sin; the time has come when, in the majesty of the lion and as the King of Glory, He will receive us back and bestow upon us our lost and defiled inheritance. And the Lord has laid on Him the iniquity of us all.

Chapter 5:5

He has prevailed, He is victorious. He prevailed in the day of temptation in the wilderness. He prevailed in the cross. He prevailed when he broke those bonds asunder and was raised from the dead.

He prevails now when He opens the seals and takes from the hands of the intruder our purchased possession to bestow it back and to give it to us, Adam's fallen race and Adam's seed.

Do you know this blessed Lamb of God? Are you acquainted with Him? Is He your own Savior? Have you cast yourself on His mercies?

And I beheld, and lo, the lamb slain as he stands, having seven horns and seven eyes. The seven horns are representative of the fullness of power that has been placed in His hands; and the seven eyes of the vigilance, the intelligence by which Christ takes care of His people, watching, directing, counseling, marshalling, against the final day of which the Revelation here speaks, when He shall take unto Himself His great power and shall reign in the earth.

"And He came and took the book out of the right hand of God. That is the greatest act in the story of God's creation. That is the greatest act in the history of mankind. He came and took the book. In that act is the answer to the prayer of all of the saints throughout all the ages. In that act is the judgment of God upon sin and upon Satan and upon death and upon the grave and upon hell. What right Christ had to act like this? He took the book, because He went to the cross to pay the great debt of sin thus to redeem this forfeited inheritance and free it from Satan's dominion. The Lamb has the title to the book. It was His because He created it. He gave it to man, but man forfeited it through sin. And the Lord Jesus Christ bought it all back when he hung on Golgotha's tree, more than 2000 years ago. He has been waiting patiently up there in the glory until the appointed time for claiming his inheritance; so this book of the title deeds has been sealed. In this interval, man has been having pretty much their own way down here; the devil has been running things to suit himself. But in a little while Christ is coming again. He is going to put everything right, but He will have to act in judgment to do so because the very world in which the Lord Jesus died is going to be the sphere in which the glory of God will be displayed, not only in the millennium, but also afterward in the new earth and the new heaven.

The Song of Heaven Rev 5:9-14

The moment that the Lamb takes the book, in verse 8, the four living creatures and the 24 elders fall down before Him, every one of them having a harp and golden bowls full of odors, which are the prayers of the saints.

Note the great throng suggested by the words of the song. Far more people will be in heaven than will ever be lost in hell. All the children that died in infancy will be there. What a throng will fill that home. Oh, how wonderful the fellowship! But notice carefully what they sing up there. They ascribe their redemption entirely to the Lamb and His work. Those are the saints of God. Then you find another company in the next two verses, but they are angels. Notice that you have an inner circle composed of sinners who were redeemed. That will be the glory of heaven.

You often hear of the angels singing, but it is remarkable that in the Bible there is only one place where you read of angels singing. In Job 38:7, They are called the "morning stars". They are angels, and they sang together when this world in its pristine beauty sprang from God's hand. But that ancient song was stilled. Sin came in and marred that beautiful creation, and from the time that sin came in we never read again that angels sang. At the birth of our Lord Jesus a multitude of heavenly hosts praised God, saying "Glory to God in the highest" (Luke 2:14), but we do not read that they sang. It is the redeemed who sing, and they sing a new song. It is the song of redemption. Will you be able to sing that song? Angels will praise the Lamb.

The angels stand in an outer circle. In other words, the angels stand off and look on and say "The Lamb deserves all the honor He is receiving. Then there is a third company a third circle, embracing all creation. John looks throughout the universe, and he sees every creature extolling the Lamb. The day is coming when all created intelligences will join in saying "Glory to the Lamb". Rom 8:19-22.

The Worship of Angels

Everywhere in the Word of God angels are unnumbered. They are innumerable. In the center of the throne is the Lamb of God; and round the throne are the 24 elders; and then beyond, innumerable celestial hosts of glory. It is significant that they are introduced here according to William Kelly. "The angels take up, not the new song in view of the Lamb's purchase, but His worthiness to receive power, and riches, and wisdom, and strength, and honor, and glory, and blessing. They do not sing of His purchase, because they were not so bought; they have not to do with it, though they are sustained by the power of God; but those who have known their need as poor sinners can well sing the new song. The angels speak of His worth and His death, but they do not chant the deep and joyous notes of the blood-bought".

When the elders sing, they sing directly to the Lamb. The angels, in keeping with their inferior stations of service, do not address the Lamb directly when they speak of Him. They speak about Him, not to Him. They say, worthy is the lamb that was slain to receive power, and riches, and wisdom, and strength, and honor, and glory and blessing.

JND in his synopsis says "Here the angels come into praise, not in the fourth chapter. I can hardly doubt that a change in administrative order takes place here until the Lamb took the book, they were the administrative power; they were the instruments through which what the four living creatures symbolized was exercised in the earth. As soon as the Lamb appears and takes the book, as soon as the idea of redemption is brought in the living creatures and elders are brought together, and the angels take their own place apart. Like the living creatures before, they give no reason for their praise. As the heads of creation as to their nature, they celebrate with all creatures the title to glory of the Lamb and His own worthiness, ascribing praise to Him that sits on the throne and to the lamb forever and ever."

Why do angels not sing the song of redemption? W.A. Criswell concludes like this "Music is made up of major chords and minor chords. The minor chords speak of the wretchedness, death and sorrow of his fallen creation. Most of nature moans and groans in a plaintive and minor key. The sound of the wind through the forest, the sound of the storm, the sound of the wind around the house, is always in a minor key. It wails the sound of the ocean moans in its restlessness, in its speechless trouble. Even the nightingale's song, the sweetest song of the birds, is the saddest. Most of the sounds of nature are in a minor key. It reflects the wretchedness, the despair, the hurt, the agony, the travail of this fallen creation. But an angel knows nothing of it. An angel knows nothing of the wretchedness, nothing of the despair, nothing of the fall of our lost race.

The major key and the major chords are chords of triumph and victory. Surely God has taken us out of the miry clay, He has taken us out of the horrible pit, He has set our feet upon the rock and He has put a new song in our souls and new praises on our lips. But an angel knows nothing of this. An angel has never been redeemed. An angel has never been saved. An angel has never fallen and been brought back to God. This is the reason angels never sing".

The Heavenly Doxologies

There are three doxologies in this chapter. There are other doxologies in this book. The first doxology is in the first chapter of Revelation verse 6. It is a twofold doxology. Verse 5 and 6. "To Him who loved us and washed us from our sins in His own blood and has made us Kings and Priests to His God and Father, to Him be glory and dominion forever and ever. Amen".

The next doxology is threefold. Rev 4:11. You are worthy, O Lord, to receive glory and honor and power; For you created all things, and by your will they exist and were created". The next doxology that the redeemed sing is four fold in Rev 5:13.

" And every creature which is in heaven and on the earth and under the earth and such as are in the sea, and all that are in them, I heard saying: "Blessing and honor and glory and power be to Him who sits on the throne, and to the lamb, forever and ever".

"Blessing and honor and glory and power. Here is a fourfold doxology" saying: Amen! Blessing and glory and wisdom, thanksgiving and honor and power and might, be to our God forever and ever. Amen. As the revelation progresses and as the redeemed are made more aware of what God has done for them, the doxologies grow and grow in glory, in majesty, in adoration, in wonder, in reverential awe and worship.

Now we will examine three doxologies in Revelation chapter 5. Rev 5:9. JND and Kelly Translation. They sing a new song. Present tense, emphasizing the intensity of that singing, and they sing a new song. They sing a new kind of a song. They sing a song the world has never heard before. There are three Greek words for "song". The Greek word psalmos is a psalm. The Greek word hymnos is a sacred song. The Greek word ode is a song in general or a poem.

"And they sing a new ode, they sing a new song, saying-and there are four things in their song. First they speak of our redemption for the glory of God, "redeemed us to God". That is the thought in the first chapter of Ephesians. Second, they speak of our redemption by the blood of the cross. Third, they speak of our redemption as illimitable. "Out of every kindred and tongue and people and nation. And fourth, they speak of our redemption as resulting in our actual reign in an actual kingdom in this actual earth. Some people think it is absurd to think of a real resurrection and a real body, a real redemption, a real earth, a real Christ, a real kingdom and God's people living in His presence a real life. Yes, we are going to be real people. We shall live in a redeemed body like the body of our Lord and we shall be real people. We shall reign upon the earth. Rev 5:13. The number four is the number of the world. These four ascriptions here are very significantly and signally set apart. And I heard all creation saying, and praising God. "And every creature which is in heaven, and on earth, under the earth, and under the sea, heard, I them saying- Blessing and honor; and glory, and power, be unto him that sits upon the throne, and unto lamb forever and ever".

Hereafter in the Book of Revelation, the Lamb and the Lord God Almighty will be together. In the next chapter they are together in wrath; in Chapter 7, together in consolation, Chapter 9, together in triumph; Chapters 21 and 22, the Lamb and the Lord God are together the light of the New Jerusalem; they are the temple of it. The only God we shall ever see is the Lord Jesus; the only God we shall ever feel is the Holy Spirit, and the only God there in heaven is the one Great Lord God Almighty. When you go to heaven you will see the Lord God Almighty, Jesus Christ. We are going to worship Him and adore Him.

REVELATION CHAPTER 6

The Beginning of Tribulation.

In chapters 6 through 19 of the book of Revelation we are given an unfolding chronological picture of a future seven-year period of the greatest tribulation this earth will ever experience. This period is God's final countdown for mankind, culminating in the personal, visible return of Jesus Christ to this earth to reclaim it as His own possession.

The "Tribulation", as this period is called, is well named, for there will be sorrow and suffering on this earth such as man has never known before and will never know again. These are the days Jesus spoke of when He said that if He didn't return to end the tribulation there wouldn't be anyone left alive.

Men who have studied Bible prophecy all their lives are startled by the fact that right before their eyes, the entire setting for the events of the tribulation are coming into focus.

We are bombarded daily by accounts that bear witness to the fact that despite our professed civility, we are in a period as barbarous and perverse as any in human history.

The scripture tells us that the end will come like a flood. While the Apocalypse looms and Armageddon sucks all of fallen mankind into its vortex, the time will resemble the days of Noah and the days of Lot.

God's holy righteousness demanded that the generation alive in Noah's time be destroyed. The contamination that sin brought had finally so corrupted mankind physically, mentally, and spiritually that the earth had to be cleansed. Noah and his family were the only people perfect in their generation, and were spared.

Sodom and Gomorrah, of Lot's day, were similarly affected and infected. The thoughts of the people, according to God's word, were only on evil continually. Homosexual activity was not an alternate lifestyle; it was the predominate lifestyle. Society fostered as well with all other manner of reprobate human interaction. Man had reached the point of incorrigibility that demanded a just and righteous God to destroy them in order for cleansing to take place. Jesus said in Luke 17:26. "And as it was in the days of Noah, so it will be also in the days of the Son of man." In verse 28, Jesus said it will be as it was in the days of Lot".

The final Diagnosis

Exactly how, then will things be in the period just before Christ returns? According to God's word, how will man be conducting human affairs at the time of the end?

The apostle Paul delineated the precise societal symptoms of man's last gasp of living death. God, who loves man and wants to give him the life and freedom that is in His Son Jesus Christ, must in the final analysis, give God - rejecting man up to his vile affections. The symptoms are clear, unmistakable in their presentation, as the apostle minces no words in outlining them.

Jesus said in Luke 21:28 "And when these things begin to come to pass, then look up, and lift up your heads; for your redemption is near."

The major symptoms of fallen humanity's end-time societal disorder are given in 2 Tim 3:1-5.

Symptom #1

Lovers of Self

Today we are told by sociologists and by psychologists that, at the root of practically every personality problem, there is a lack of self-esteem.

Psychologists say people should be taught to acquire higher self-esteem; then they will become useful, productive citizens. Self-esteem is another expression of self-love. When people think first and foremost of themselves, others whose lives they affect inevitably suffer from their self-indulgence.

One of the most blatant forms of self-love, and one of the greatest detrimental effect of egocentricity is found in the problem of teenage sex and the havoc it wreaks upon individuals, families, and society at large. Young people are shown by example that it is a natural thing to indulge in sexual activity apart from the bonds of marital commitment. The body is to be enjoyed. They see in movies, TV sitcoms, and their adulterous parents the "If it feels good, do it" philosophy. Teens are now told by public school systems that sex is a natural act to be enjoyed, just as eating is to be enjoyed. After all, we are but a higher form of animal life, according to public education's adoptive religion, the theory of evolution. The only concern seems to be that teens engage in "safe sex".

Revelation 6

For two breathtaking, soul-inspiring chapters, we have been in heaven. The scroll has changed hands, and Jesus took our forfeited inheritance out of the hands of the usurper, the interloper, the intruder, the stranger and the illegal alien. Now we must come down from the mount and out of the ivory palaces.

The first Seal is opened (Rev 6:1-2)

Who is this mysterious rider on the great white horse? In the scripture, a horse is often used as a symbol of war. The white color of the horse suggests that the rider wins victories without bloodshed. Peaceful victory is implied. He is a conqueror, a victor. He has a crown and a bow. In ancient processions of triumph, the victor rode on a white horse; and in the 19th chapter of Revelation, when our Lord comes again out of heaven, He comes, riding on a white horse. Who is he? He represents the blasphemous philosophers of the last days, those anti-Christian ideologies that prepare men's minds for the devil's gospel and the ultimate reception of the strong delusion and the great lie (2 Thessalonians 2:3-12).

The temporary triumph of Antichrist Matt 24

Our Lord has outlined the time of the end. If the Revelation is a picture of the time of the end, then it ought to fit exactly with the outline that our Lord gave in Matt 24. The outline that our Lord Jesus Christ gave in His great apocalyptic discourse in Matt 24 corresponds to what occurs in the visions given to John in the Revelation.

Mathew 24:4-5

First, Jesus says in answer to the question of the disciples as to what shall be the sign of His coming and of the end of the world." "For many will come in My name, saying I am the Christ, and will deceive many." (Verse 5)

Many will come saying "I am Dear Fuehrer; I am the great savior; I am the deliverer of the people; I am the great Stalin. There will be many deceivers, and self-styled saviors. There will be false Christs. Current dictators or evil men are just shadows of that final world dictator, who is yet to come. The final dictator is Satan's masterpiece imitator. In the court of Pharaoh, when Moses and Aaron showed their signs before the king, Satan had his sorcerers and his witch doctors and his necromancers, performed those same marvelous signs. There is nothing original about Satan. So he imitates the Lord Christ here. Satan is a fabricator and calumniator, and is a quintessential master of deception.

The Antichrist will finally appear when God's people are taken away and the days of that terrible tribulation begin. In the restlessness of nations and in the revolution of the masses and in the prospect of catastrophic war, the first thing that will happen is the appearance of this great, final world-tyrant. He will promise peace, and he will bring with him every token of affluence and prosperity; and the nations of the world and the peoples of the earth will flock after him.

He comes riding on a white horse, 'conquering and to conquer". The entire military, economic and political resources of the world are at his disposal and in his hands.

When we make this identification, we find that it will fit every prophecy in the Bible precisely. For example, in the second Thessalonians letter the second chapter God says that after the falling away, after the apostasy, and after God's people are taken away, the man of sin will be revealed. That is the first thing that happens-the coming across the horizon of history, this white horseman. The first development is the appearance of this man of sin, the son of damnation, who opposes and exalts himself above all that is called God. Satan's masterpiece cannot be revealed; the tribulation cannot come. The fire and the flame and fury cannot fall upon Sodom until Lot be taken out. First God's people have to be taken out.

There is in this world that which prevents the final judgment. It is God's people.

The Seventy Weeks of Daniel

The ninth chapter of the Book of Daniel is one of the most significant of all the prophecies in the Word of God. It is the prophecy of the Seventy Weeks. It says that this prince, this antichrist, this masterpiece of Satan, this false deceiver, will come in peace and will make his covenant with the people. The Roman church is going to endorse him, just as it did Mussolini and Hitler. And the Jewish people will find in him a marvelous refuge from the terrible afflictions that beset them on every hand.

He is going to enter into a treaty with the Jewish nation, according to the ninth chapter of the Book of Daniel. For a while he is truly the savior of the world.

Then according to Daniel 9:27 and the 13th chapter of Revelation, in the midst of his rise to power and to conquest, the deceiver reveals himself for who he really is. He is the friend of hell, he is the masterpiece of the devil, he is the great Antichrist, the opposer and blasphemer of God. In the midst of his career he turns and becomes the enemy of the

Jewish nation, which following there is a wave of anti-Semitism such as the earth has never known before.

Then he turns on the Roman Church, and according to the seventeenth chapter of the Book of Revelation, he destroys her (Babylon the Great). That leader, that beast, that ruler, shall take the whore and he shall make her desolate and naked and shall eat of her flesh and burn her with fire. All the dictators followed the same pattern throughout history. First he is the liberator of his people. He is the conqueror in the name of the great nation he represents. He leads his people to conquest and to victory. Then, the fiendish spirit of hell appears in him and the world is plunged into blood.

The Tragedies that Follow the World Deceiver.

But such a world tyrant never rides alone. What inevitably follows him is depicted here in the Revelation. The second of the Cherubim said, "Come" "go", "proceed". Then there came a red horse: and power was given to him to take peace from the earth, and that they should kill one another: and there was given unto him a great sword". This is not the normal sword. This is a knife with which to cut the throat of an animal or of a man. Recently, there is an explosion of beheading by Islamo-fascists all over the world. This is a harbinger of the method of execution at the time of the tribulation. The red horseman represents not only nation rising against kingdom, but more nearly, the terrible slaughter of class fighting class and party fighting party as in the civil war. The fighters ambush in the night; they assassinate in the day; they murder in twilight and at noontime, and every one lives in the fear of his life. There is murder and bloodshed everywhere. The red horseman bathes the earth in blood.

The Second Seal 6:3-4

During the first three and one-half years of the tribulation the Antichrist will bring a pseudo-peace to the world. Everyone will be singing his praises as the greatest leader in all human history.

But at the midpoint of the tribulation, the second seal is opened and, according to Ezekiel 38 and Daniel 11, Russia, the rider of the red horse, snatches peace from the earth. With her Arab allies she invades the Middle East and attacks Israel. The war escalates until it involves all the major powers on the earth and becomes the greatest battle in the history of mankind-the battle of Armageddon. This is developed fully in Revelation chapter 16.

The Third Seal Economic Catastrophe (Rev 6:5-6)

The judgment symbolized by the rider of the black horse seems to be a worldwide financial catastrophe. With war raging across the world-from the Middle East, food, fuel, and other life-supporting commodities will become more and more scarce.

The frightening thing is that a day's ration for wheat will cost a denarius, the Bible equivalent of an average worker's entire daily wage. During the tribulation the average man will have to payout his entire day's salary just to purchase food for his family. There is not much chance that the Antichrist will be issuing food stamps either.

Olive oil and wine were the luxury foods of John's day. The horseman was told not to tamper with these items.

What about the numbers of aged people, women and children unable to work? If the denarius can only procure the necessary food for one, what about the multitudes who through infirmity or other incapacity are unable to work? Must starvation be their bitter experience, and death anticipated as a happy release from the agonies of hunger.

The living creatures are not themselves the source of this providential chastisement. God employed them as agents in accomplishing His purposes.

The Rich Spared

"Do not injure the oil and the wine", is by some supposed to signify a mitigation of the famine as intimated in the preceding declarations. But that can hardly be. People could not subsist on oil and wine. Wheat and barley are essentials. Oil and wine were regarded as luxuries found only on the table of the rich (Proverb 21:17, Jeremiah 31:12, Psalms 104:15). Hence the chastisement under the sea falls especially on the working classes. The rich, the wealthy, and the governing classes are markedly exempted, but they shall not escape. For under the sixth seal judgment, is impartially meted out to all alike, from the monarch down to the slave.

Socialism appears in another form. An ominous sign of the times is the spread of tolerance and diversity, the gospel of equality among the nations of the world. The time-honored distinctions of master and servant, of rulers and ruled, are scorned; wealth and social position, with their respective claims, are treated with contempt; and labor and capital are regarded as opposing forces. The spirit of insubordination and contempt of authority is prevalent.

The Fourth Seal (Rev 6:7-8)

Following close on the heels of the second and third horsemen is the pale horse. He brings death on a massive scale. It staggers the imagination to realize that one-fourth of the world's population will be destroyed within a matter of days. Overnight world civilization will turn into a primitive civilization.

Pestilence is another word for epidemics. Whenever you have a combination of poverty and famine, disease is close kin, as the situation in Africa so vividly portrays.

The Fifth Seal (Rev 6:9-11) Mass murder of believers

"When He opened the fifth seal, I saw underneath the altar the souls of them that had been slain for the Word of God, and for the testimony which they held; and they cried with a loud voice, saying, how long, O Sovereign ruler, holy and true, dost thou judge and avenge our blood on them that dwell upon the earth?". JND.

The Revelation is a book of judgment. The OT describes the days of the law. The NT describes the days in which we now live, the days of grace. But the Apocalypse is a revelation of the days of the visitation of the wrath of God. It is described as such in Revelation 4:5 "And out of the throne proceeded lightnings and thunderings and voices". The four Cherubim, who stand before God to administer His decrees, are instruments of the wrath of God upon this earth. Law-Grace-Judgment.

As they speak, there appear on the horizon of history the four horsemen of the apocalypse. The four horsemen are themselves, the instruments of judgment upon this earth. The first seal brings on the state of human history the ultimate Antichrist, which the world receives with open arms. The opening of the second, the third and the fourth seals are the judgment of God that follows the acceptance of that tyrannical world dictator.

The sixth seal is a seal of the judgment day of God, when

the heavens are rolled back like a scroll, when the great men of the earth cry for the rocks and the mountains to fall upon them, when the great day of God's wrath is come.

The fifth seal is also a seal of judgment. The fifth seal is different from the rest of the seven in that we see not the action itself, but the result of action. This is a picture of the result of what has happened. John sees under the altar the souls of those who have already been slain.

Who are these martyrs, whose souls John sees under the altar of heaven? As they cry to God they say, "O lord, how long dost thou not judge and avenge our blood on them that dwell on the earth?" These are the martyrs who have lost their lives under those first four seals, in the first half of the tribulation. At the end of the tribulation and at the beginning of the millennium, in Rev 20:4, we find all the martyrs standing in the presence of God and preparing to enter into the millennium kingdom, where they will reign with the Lord for a thousand years.

The Altar of Sacrifices

John says, "I saw them under the altar". That is unusual, however the whole book is unusual. The Book of Hebrews describes the heavenly tabernacle, the heavenly temple. The Book of Hebrews says what Exodus says, that Moses saw the pattern of the tabernacle, the temple, the form of it in heaven, so he made a material copy of it down here on earth. So, the heaven of God's throne, where the Lord now dwells, has a temple. In the eleventh chapter of the revelation, John sees the temple of God in heaven, the pattern of which was given to Moses, who made a material copy on earth. Therefore, like the earthly tabernacle, the heavenly one has two altars, both of which are described in the book of the

Revelation.

There is the altar of brass which is the altar of sacrifice, mentioned several times in the Revelation. There is the altar of gold, which is the altar of incense and prayer, which is mentioned several times in the Revelation. This altar in our text is the altar of sacrifice, the brazen altar that stood in the courtyard of the tabernacle and of the temple.

The Word of God always presents the devotion of the lives of children as being sacrificed upon the altar unto God. We find that idea all through the Scripture. For example, in Romans 12:1, Paul exhorts us to offer our lives a living sacrifice on the altar of God. In the passage of 2 Tim 4:6 Paul says, "For I am now ready to be offered", the word 'offered' being a technical word for sacrifice. As he anticipated his approaching martyrdom, he looked upon it as a sacrifice unto God in the altar of heaven. That is the way God beholds all of His children who pour out their lives unto him. If it is pleasing to Him that the sacrifice be a living sacrifice, wonderful and well. The martyrs were slain for the Word of God, and for the testimony which they held.

The great troubles that face America are due to the sins of her people. Our country is more debauched every day. The fear and anxiety in which we live is a part of that judgment. When the bombs rain upon the cities in America, the leftists will blame America first. But it will happen because of them and their atheistic policies. But the prophets (Gospel Preachers) of God will say that, this is the visitation of the judgment and the wrath of the Almighty. At the tribulation the restraining power of God which we feel today has been taken out of the earth in that day and these prophets are mercilessly slaughtered and massacred who cry unto God.

Wherever there is a true prophet of God, he will preach judgment. The modern so-called ministers speak all things nice. Modern pedagogical methods admonish never to mention things which are negative.

So they stand up and they speak of the love of Jesus, and they speak of peace, and all things that are pretty and beautiful, but remember, these other things are also real. The same book that tells us about the good, tell us about the bad.

The same revelation that speaks about heaven, speaks about hell. The two go together. If there is not anything to be saved from, we do not need a savior, and if we can evolve into angels, just give us time and maybe we shall be archangels by and by. We love to hear things beautiful and encouraging. Do you ever notice what these modern pedagogues say to them? Let us always teach our children the positive side and never the negative. All the Ten Commandments are" thou shall what"? Thou shall not. These modern pedagogues say that such negative approaches give the little divinities inferiority complexes and damages their self-esteem.

The state of recalcitrance and rebellion of juveniles is beyond anything the world has ever seen, and it came from their modern approach.

The Cry to God

The text continues, "And they cry unto the Lord". This is the only place in the Revelation where this word, translated here "Lord" is used. In the Greek it is 'ho Despotes'. Our English word 'despot' is exact the Greek word. Look for the correct translation by John Nelson Darby "O Sovereign Ruler", holy and true, dost thou not judge and avenge our blood on them that dwell upon the earth? And there was given to them, to each one a white robe; and it was said to them that they should rest yet a little while, until both their fellowbondmen and their brethren, who were about to be killed as they, should be fulfilled." (Rev. 6:9-10).

The Soul After Death Rev 6:9-11

This is a message on the intermediate state. The sermon concerns the fact of living, the existence, the conscious life, of those souls that John saw in heaven. The difference between soul and spirit is this: pure spirit has no relationship to a body. God is a Spirit. He has no body. Angels are spirits and they have no bodies. Satan is a spirit and he has no body. But a soul must have a body. If a soul is separated from the body if the soul is disembodied, it may be referred to us as a spirit. But the word 'soul' always implies a body.

John says though these martyrs were slain, though they were dead, their souls still live. John says, "I saw their souls in heaven and I heard their cry. One might say that this is an unusual situation, that it is merely a vision. But it is a vision of reality. It is a supernatural vision of facts before the time, but it is a vision of the facts themselves.

It is a reality that John sees before the time. If the martyrs still live, then death is not the end of them. Their bodies lie moldering in the ground, corrupting in the grave. Their blood has been spilled out on the earth. But their souls are still alive, in conscious existence in heaven. They speak and know what is happening here on earth. Human eyes, eyes of the flesh, cannot see them. But they are known to the eyes of God.

It is a common revelation throughout scripture that death is not the end of life but rather that there is a conscious existence beyond the grave. Whether one be saved or unsaved, righteous or unrighteous, good or bad, wicked or holy, the soul lives beyond death.

There was a certain rich man and a certain beggar. It came

to pass that the beggar died and was carried by the angels in to Abraham's bosom. It also came to pass that the rich man died and was honored with a funeral. The poor man did not have a funeral. They just dumped him out in some potter's field. But the rich man died and was buried sumptuously. But there is more to the story. In Hades the rich man lifted up his eyes, being in torment, crying for Abraham to send Lazarus, the poor man, to minister unto him. He had been in the habit of ordering people around all his life. Why not continue to do so beyond the grave? Send Lazarus, "he cried" that he may dip the tip of his finger in water and cool my tongue for I am tormented in the flame". These men are what you call dead. But they are in a conscious existence in another world.

The State of the Unrighteous

The unrighteous also live beyond death. The rich man spurned the Word of God. He would not listen to the prophet or Moses. In his affluence, he lived and fared sumptuously. But he was like the Book says: He did not repent, he did not turn, he did not look to God. Then he died, as all inevitably die. He went to the netherworld. Thus the soul of any unbeliever falls into torment. He is in misery, pain, and agony. They are imprisoned somewhere in the nether world - awaiting the great white throne judgment Day of the Lord. 1 Pet 3:19-20 describes lost souls as being imprisoned. Those referred to in this passage are those who laughed at Noah when Noah for 120 years preached righteousness and called a vile and blaspheming world to repentance. Those blasphemers are imprisoned, awaiting the great judgment day of the Lord. Such judgment is referred to again in 2 Pet 2:3 and verse 9.

The State of the Righteous

First, the righteous will enter immediately into paradise. Luke 23:43 Paradise is a Persian word meaning "park", that beautiful park of God. In 2 Corinthians 12:2, Paul was carried into paradise.

Scriptural observations concerning the dead.

1) There is no such thing in the Word of God as soul sleep. Even those passages in the OT that appear to indicate it, are describing the rot and the ruin of death. They are speaking of the appearance of the body. When we die, we go to be with our Lord in heaven.

2) There is no such thing in the word of God as purgatory. For one thing, this supposition is inconsistent with the all-sufficient satisfaction, and adequacy, of the atonement of Christ. We are saved by the grace of God, not by Works.

REVELATION CHAPTER 7

(144,000 Evangelists)

This passage, this whole chapter seven, is plainly an interlude, a parenthesis. It is placed here between the opening of the sixth seal and opening of the final seventh seal. The first six seals were opened in chapter six. The seventh and final seal is opened in chapter eight. Between the two, between "the beginning of sorrows" and the beginning of the great and final tribulation, there is this parenthesis, this interlude. These four angels who have in their hands the storms of Almighty God, to wither to blast, and to destroy, but who in this chapter seven are held back, are in chapter 8 turned loose. As they sound the first four trumpets, there is vast waste and destruction and judgment in the earth. But before that judgment falls and before this visitation comes from an Almighty God, the Lord says, "Wait, wait stay thy hand; for first, before that judgment falls, we must seal the servants of God. Care must be taken to protect those who belong to God before that terrible judgment falls. It is thus in all the story of human history. God's elect is precious in His sight, and for their sakes judgment is stayed. The reason this world stands, the reason government exists, the reason civilization endures, is because of the elect of God. Were it not for them, the world would be destroyed like a withering branch. Had there been ten righteous men found in Sodom, it would not have been destroyed. For the lack of ten, it was wasted and judged. So it is on this earth. The reason judgment does not fall and the reason condemnation does not come is because of God's elect in the earth. For their sakes the storm is stayed and destruction waits. In between these awful visitations from heaven recorded in the sixth and eighth chapters of the Revelation, the veil is pulled aside in this seventh chapter and the mercy, grace, and love of God are revealed to His elect.

 The Seventh-day Adventists say that these 144,000 pertain to their communion, who is observing the Jewish Sabbath when the Lord comes again, and they are raptured up to glory. The Jehovah's Witnesses say that these 144,000 belong to them. They are to be saved at the end time. They are the great overcomers, and each one of these Jehovah's Witnesses is trying to be one of that select number. That is why we see them on the street corner, that is why we see them knocking at the door from house to house. Each one of these Jehovah's Witnesses is striving to be one of that elect group in order that he might be caught up to heaven and might be saved. The 144,000 were of all of the tribes of the children of Israel. Now, where are those tribes of the children of Israel? A Jew does not know. But God knows.

 12,000 from each one of the tribes of the children of Israel are to be sealed. The word "12" in the Bible with reference to the people of the Lord, always refers to Israel. Twelve is their number. There were 12 tribes. Matt 19:28, our Lord says that the 12 apostles will sit on 12 thrones judging the 12 tribes of Israel. The High Priest has a breastplate on which were 12 precious stones representing the 12 tribes. In the great city, the new Jerusalem, there are 12 gates. On each of the gates is written the name of one of the tribes of Israel. All through the Bible, from its inception until its ending, the number 12 refers to the children of Israel.

Rev 7:2 states "Then I saw another angel ascending from the east, having the seal of the living God". (NKJV). "And I saw another angel ascending from the sun rising, having the seal of the living God". JND.

That sealing is not a unique or peculiar thing. All through this book, we find the Lord placing a mark or sealing those that belong to Him. In the days of Abraham, the mark was in the flesh. He set the rite of circumcision. These so marked belonged in a special way to God. In the days of the judgment of Egypt, the mark was in the form of a cross, on the lintel above the door as the destroying angel of death looked for the mark, the seal, and passed over those who possessed it. In the days of Rahab, it was a scarlet line hanging in the window. She was to be preserved from the wanton destruction that wasted the city.

The Sealing of the Servants of God

Why are these 144,000 marked? Why are they sealed? Is it because they are Jews? No, not at all. This is an election, morally conditioned. God never does anything adventitiously, summarily, arbitrarily. There are great spiritual reasons why

God does what He does, and there are great spiritual reasons why God sealed the 12 thousand out of each of the tribes of Israel. In the 14th chapter of Revelation they are called "virgins". No virgin ever has a child. These are men chosen for a separate and elect purpose. They have no predecessors and they have no successors. They are called "servants of our God". These are men of unusual spiritual stature. They live in purity in the midst of an impure world. They are fearless and brave in their testimony for God.

These 144,000 are called "the first fruits unto God and to the lamb" and while He is calling them that, there stand the elders representing the Church. They could not be first-fruits in time or the first fruits of all God hath done, because the elders are the raptured, enthroned Church, the first fruit of Christ in the earth. In 1 Cor 15:23, Christ himself is called the first- fruits, followed by those who are raised from the dead at His coming. Yet, these who are called "the first- fruits unto God and to the Lamb-what could the name mean? They are the first- fruits unto God in another order and in another calling.

What is meant by the sealing of these 144,000? What is the seal of God? Rev 14:1 states it is their Father's name written in their forehead. We have much mention of that seal in the Bible. Eph 1:13 "You were sealed after that you trusted in Christ, you were sealed with that Holy Spirit of Promise and in Eph 4:30 "Grieve not the Holy Spirit of God, whereby you we sealed unto the day of redemption". The same reference occurs in 2 Cor 1:22.

The Holy Spirit is the soul of God. If a man has the seal of God upon him, he has the power and unction and presence of the Holy Spirit in his heart and life. In the sealing of the 144,000, they were endued with Pentecostal power; and the Holy Spirit of God, in unction and in glory, came upon them.

How would that kind of a seal appear? If you were to meet one of those men who had been sealed of God, how would he appear? He may be like Moses, when the Israelites saw him coming down from the mount after he has communed with God for forty days and forty nights. There was unction about him and his face shone like the sun. They are endued, and glorified of God, and their eloquence, their witness and their testimony to the truth of Christ are beyond compare. Just to see them and to hear them is to be moved by the presence and the glory of God in their lives. Such is the seal of the Holy Spirit of God.

In Rev 7:1, we see God stops the wind. Although the subject of angels is usually associated with fairy tales or myths, these creatures play a very important part in the judgments of God on the earth. The Bible speaks of three categories of angels. First, there are the angels of God who remained faithful to Him when Lucifer (who later became known as Satan or the Devil) rejected God and led a rebellion against Him.

The second category are the angels who followed Lucifer in the rebellion but are still free to work against God's purposes. These are fallen, unbound angels and are usually called demons. The third group are fallen angels who are bound and imprisoned. Apparently these are a particularly vicious group who overstepped their authority, thus God cast them into a place called "the abyss" to wait the final execution of their sentence-to be cast with Satan and the other demons into the Lake of Fire (2 Pet 2:4).

Because angels have superior power and intelligence, the four mentioned in verse 1 have apparently been given authority over the weather conditions of the earth. If the wind patterns are changed, radical effects will occur in all the rest of nature because of its delicate ecological balance.

Verse 1. This harm will be upon the earth, the sea, and the trees. Have you ever thought about how much destruction has been caused by wind? If you have ever experienced the terror of a great hurricane, typhoon, dust storm, or tornado you would understand the power of nature.

Many of the prophecies relating to the tribulation indicate freak weather conditions and storms of unprecedented intensity. In fact, Jesus himself predicted that strange phenomena would occur regarding the relationship of the earth to the sun, moon, and stars. (Luke 21:25-26)

Grace Before Judgment

Before the four angels are allowed to execute their judgment of shifting the wind patterns, another angel appears, coming up from the rising sun. The angel has the seal of the living God with which he seals the special servants of God who will be His witnesses during the tribulation period.

God has never allowed Himself to be without witnesses on earth to proclaim His way to receive forgiveness and acceptance. The spiritual vacuum that will be left by the removal of all true Christians at the Rapture will be quickly filled with these 144,000 Jewish "bond-servants of God".

Two Tribes Omitted

In Rev. 7: 5-8, Dan and Ephraim, are missing, and two others are substituted in their places. The tribe of Dan is missing because the Jewish Antichrist, will come from it. Read ancient prophecy about Dan (Genesis 49:17).

Ephraim is left out because it led the way in causing the civil war which divided the ten tribes of the North from the two in the South. The tribes of Dan and Ephraim were the first to lead Israel into idolatry. The priestly tribe of Levi is substituted for Dan, and Joseph (Ephraim's father) is substituted for Ephraim.

The Blood Washed Multitude (Rev 7:9-17)

The perplexity of John

Who are the uncounted numbers of this multitude and where did they come from? "One of the elders answered saying unto John". John had not said anything. There is no recorded conversation before, yet "one of the elders answered saying unto John". That is, he recognized John's perplexity and astonishment and ignorance as to who that great multitude was. The elder places in language John's questioning spirit. John saw the Church enthroned, crowned glorified, resurrected, immortalized, and raptured. He saw the redeemed throng under the form of the 24 elders. Those elders represent the Church. At the end of the church age, when John is caught up into heaven, he sees the church enthroned before God. Now he sees both of them here, elders and the church and the vast, blood-washed multitude. Who are these after comers, the congregation of the after-born, who are they and where do they come from.

Notice the great distinction between this group and the Church, and enthroned elders. This great multitude has no thrones. They stand in the presence of the thrones. They have no crowns; they have palm branches. They have come after the resurrection, and after the Rapture and after the Church has been taken up into glory.

John, from his vantage point in heaven, sees them as they are coming out of the Great Tribulation. They have washed their robes and made them white in the blood of the lamb. These, then, are tribulation saints. They are those which God has saved in His mercy during those dark, dark days. No wonder John did not know who they were.

Most unbelievers, after the church is taken away, become more confirmed in their defiance of God, until finally the waves of hell roll over them forever, and the smoke of their evil deeds ascends up throughout the endless ages. But even in those dark and tragic days, in wrath of God remembers mercy. He elects the 144,000, and He seals them. These are from among those who were left behind. Most of the professing church will be apostate and will be left behind. When the Lord comes, so bad will be the evil and the blackness on the face of this earth that Christ Himself asks, "When the Son of Man comes, will He find faith in the earth"? Two shall be in a field, one taken and the other left; two sleeping in a bed, one taken and the other left; two grinding at a mill, one taken and the other left. Matt 24:40. 1 Thess 4:16-17. The ones taken will be taken to judgment and death. The ones left will be left to enter the blessing of the millennial kingdom.

Many will turn to Christ in repentance. Their stained garments, they wash in the blood of the Lamb. They were sinners and now they are saints. They were lost, and now they are found. They were rejecters, and now they are accepters.

They hold palm branches in their hands. That is an OT reference to the Feast of the Tabernacle. (Nehemiah 8:17). The Feast of the Tabernacles, when the people sat in booths and when they carried palm branches called to remembrance the deliverance of God out of the darkness of the servitude of Egypt. Now they are free unto God. In Nehemiah, the people also are rejoicing over the deliverance from

Babylonian captivity. They are triumphant and praise the name of God with palm branches in their hands.

Judgment of Living Gentiles

Joel 3:11-16 Matt 25:31-46. Sheep and Goat. Brothers of Christ. Israel especially 144,000.

REVELATION CHAPTER 8

The Seventh Seal (Rev 8:1-5)

When the Lamb of God opened the last and the 7th seal, there was silence in heaven. That is unusual, because heaven is never silent. It is filled by day and by night and through all the unending ages with the worship, praise and adoration of the heavenly hosts, offered unto God our Father and unto God our Savior and unto God our Holy Comforter and Keeper. But at the opening of the 7th seal, all heaven was mute. All motion in heaven stopped. All praise and adoration ceased.

Why this silence? It is, first, the silence of awe and of intense expectancy. There is a second reason for the silence in heaven. It is a silence of ominous foreboding. There is a calm before the storm. This is like the eye of the hurricane.

Seven Angels

The silence in heaven at the opening of the seventh and last seal brings to view the drama of the Great Tribulation. After that silence, the first thing John sees is the seven angels who stand in the presence of God and to whom were given seven trumpets. They are septumvirate of celestial arch-regents, described here as "angels of the presence". They are designated as the seven angels who stand in the presence of God. In the 15th chapter of the Revelation, we are introduced to seven angels who are given the seven bowls of the vials of the wrath of the Almighty, but they are just as in regular angels.

The article here in chapter 8:2, is distinct and emphatic. "The", "the" seven angels of the presence. 8:2. "And I saw the seven angels who stand before God." JND.

There are ranks of preference, administration, and creations. Paul names some of those ranks of the angels of the hosts of heaven. Some of them he calls "principalities", others "dominions" and others "powers". The prophet Daniel spoke of princes among the angelic hosts. Paul and Jude refer to arch- angels in glory. So these seven are a distinct, and select group. In Luke chapter 15, it is written that Gabriel, whom Zacharias saw on the right side of the altar of incense, said, "I am Gabriel who stands in the presence of God".

To these seven distinct, highly favored, marvelous, celestial arch-regents of the Almighty there are given seven trumpets, to each one a trumpet. Why a trumpet? Because it is the most used of all of the instruments of the Holy Scriptures. If there is a war declared, there is the blowing of the trumpet. In the great convocations of the people, there was the sounding of the trumpet. All of the great festival days of the Lord were introduced by the sound of the trumpet, as at the year of jubilee. In the crowning of a king, there was the sounding of the trumpet.

The Angel-Priest

After the introduction of the special seven angels there follows as interlude, and intermission. "Then another angel came and stood at the altar, having a golden censer in his hand, and there was given unto him much incense, which came with the prayers of the saints, ascending up before God out of the angel's hand". Who is this angel? Another Angel. At least four times in the Apocalypse the identical designation is used always with reference to a mighty, indescribably glorious personality in heaven. For example, in the seventh chapter, second verse, "And I saw another angel ascending from the east, having the seal of the living God: and sealed the 144,000".

In the 10th chapter, the first verse, similarly "And I saw another mighty angel come down from heaven, clothed with a cloud: and a rainbow was upon his head; and his face was as it were the sun, and his feet as pillars of fire". Once more he is referred to in 18:1. "And after these things I saw another angel come down from heaven, having great power; and the earth was lightened with his glory". Here in 8:3, this angel stands at the altar and in his hand is the golden censor which alone belongs to the priest. Because of these descriptions and especially because of his priestly ministry, many students of the Book say He is the Angel of Jehovah, which in the OT is the pre-incarnate Christ. All of us acquainted with the tabernacle worship are familiar with this scene. Outside the court was the great brazen altar of sacrifice, the fire upon which never died by day and night, and on which all the sacrifices were offered up unto God. On the inside, in the Holy Place, before the veil, was the golden altar of incense with its four golden horns, one at each corner. Once a year, on the Day of Atonement, the High Priest, with blood shed by an animal offered on the sacrificial altar, went inside and sprinkled the blood of atonement on the four horns of that golden altar. Twice a day throughout the year, at the time of the morning sacrifice and at the time of the evening sacrifice, the Priest went in and offered incense on the golden altar while the people prayed outside. Remember the story of Zacharias in the first chapter of Luke. Each day a priest chosen by lot went into the Holy Place, there to offer incense on the golden altar of prayer, while the people outside waited in intercession before God. These are the two altars: the brazen altar of sacrifice mentioned six times in the Apocalypse and the golden altar of prayer mentioned twice. The prayers of all God's people are forwarded, they are perfected, they are made beautiful and acceptable to heaven by the merit, worth and virtue of the sacrifice, resurrection, and intercession of our glorious High Priest in glory. There is imperfection in all we do in the presence of God. This angel-priest adds to our prayers the incense, the sweet savor. No prayer is ever lost. It is kept before God. It is the prayer that Christ placed in our hearts. "Thy kingdom come and thy will be done in this earth as it is in heaven".

Now the time has come for the prayers of the saints to be answered. The time has come when God will cast out Satan, will dethrone the usurper. The time has come when iniquity and death and hell and the grave will be destroyed forever. The time has come when God's kingdom shall be established in the earth. At that time God has brought before Him the remembrance of all the prayers of His saints through the ages. The next step is, the angel-priest takes the golden censor and fills it with fire from off the altar. The brazen altar is the judgment of God.

7th Seal

God gave Adam dominion over the earth (Gen 1:26.) In a moment of weakness, Adam lost that dominion to the arch- enemy of God, the Devil (Gen 3:1-19). Adam's disobedience involved more than just eating the forbidden fruit. It was a surrendering, a selling-out to the Devil. The possession was purchased at Calvary, but it has not yet been redeemed (1 Cor 6:20; 7:23).

The book John saw is the title deed to this world. The breaking of those seven seals represents the restitution of the creation to God and to Adam's fallen race. The record of our lost inheritance is written within and on the backside. Inside is the story of how we lost it. Written on the outside are the terms of its redemption waiting for a kinsman-redeemer to buy us back to God. That book represents the entire creation.

Rev 8:5-13

We have come to the point in apocalyptic history where all things are in readiness for the climatic consummation of the age, the coming of our Lord and the establishment of His kingdom in the earth. The 7th and last seal has been opened. There is silence in heaven. The prayers of all the saints of all the ages are brought before God in remembrance, "Thy kingdom come, thy will be done".

Under the fifth seal, the cry of the saints of God whose blood had been shed in the earth was for vengeance.

The day has come for the answer to that cry. The angel-priest fills the golden censor with fire of judgment from the altar and flings it into the earth, a picture of the wrath, and the doom, and the judgment of God upon this unbelieving and blaspheming world.

This is the signal for seven angels of that judgment, of that visitation, to sound. When the seventh angel has sounded, the final day has come. The day of the great battle of Almighty God that ushers in the visible appearing of Christ, and the establishment of His millennial kingdom in the earth.

The first four trumpets 8:7

The first angel sounded and there followed hail and fire mingled with blood, and they were cast upon the earth and a third of the trees was burned up, and all green grass was burned up. The devastation seems to be a massive nuclear attack much larger than the first one described in the sixth seal of chapter 6.

Sometimes the trumpet judgments are referred to as "the judgment of thirds", since one-third of several kinds of things is destroyed by them. With this massive loss of vegetation will come soil erosion, floods, and mudslides. Air pollution will be immense; the smoke of the fire will fill the atmosphere.

(Rev 8:8-9) Notice that this verse specifies "something like a great mountain burning with fire". Again John describes this phenomenon in terms of how it looked to him. This is probably either an enormous meteor or, more likely colossal H-bomb. A hydrogen bomb exploded in the ocean would look like a huge flaming mountain smashing into the sea.

One of the reasons why such devastation occurs on the ocean may be that thermonuclear missiles are targeted toward large arms of naval vessels. Rev 8:9 says in effect, one third of all ships on the world are destroyed.

Third Angel (Rev.8:10)

This may be another thermonuclear weapon which is a part of a series of exchanges between nuclear powers.

Fourth Angel (Rev 8:12)

Here we have all natural light diminished by one-third: sunlight will be reduced by one-third and the night will be one-third darker than usual. This is the result of the mushroom cloud reached in the atmosphere due to multiple nuclear exchanges. Researchers call it "Nuclear Winter". Within a few weeks of an all-out nuclear war, a devastating freeze would settle on the northern hemisphere. Massive amounts of soot from burning cities and forests would diffuse through the atmosphere, blotting out the sun. High noon would look like the dead of night. The North American temperature might be 15 degrees. The freeze would last several months.

Revelation 8.13

At this point God interrupts the quick succession of trumpet judgments with a pause and a warning. His flying messenger informs men that the worst is yet to come. Most men, however, will ignore this warning too. Thus they must face the full fury of the last three trumpet judgments. These judgments are called "Woes" because of the intensified suffering which they unleash.

REVELATION CHAPTER 9

Holocaust from the East

The sounding trumpets are divided into two parts, into four and three. The first four trumpets are sounded in the eighth chapter of the Revelation. The last three trumpets are so terrible and so horrible that they are set apart.

The first four trumpet judgments were directed toward the earth's ecology, but the last three judgments increase in scope and magnitude as it unfolds. It appears that God is putting the pressure on man, a little more each time, to try to get him to repent and turn to Jesus for salvation.

Fifth Angel

Rev.9:1-11. The fifth trumpet of woe dissolves the demarcation, the wall of separation, between earth and hell. Here John saw the star fall, NO, John saw the star fallen. It had already fallen. It could be Satan.

Satan receives the key from Christ Himself, since Christ is the possessor of the key of hell. (Rev: 1:18)

The opening of the bottomless pit unleashes a judgment that is unparalleled in its torment. The 'locusts' of Rev. 9:3 are said to be possessed by hell's worst demons – fallen angels so vicious, ferocious and nefarious, and insidious and perfidious that God has kept them bound since the days of Noah.

[1 Peter 2: 4,5] Jude 6: Their leader is apparently a demon of almost the equivalent to power and authority of Satan himself. He is described in Rev. 9:11 as "Abaddon" and "Apollyon", meaning destroyer.

God permits the release of these vicious beings because men have failed to heed the judgments against their unbelief and have not taken advantage of the lull in the storm to cry out to God for mercy.

The locusts described in this chapter are unlike any known to man today. These locusts have a scorpion like stinger in their tails with which they relentlessly torment men for five months. The sting will be so painful that men will wish they could die. These locusts are not permitted to kill anyone. They can't even touch believers, for they will all have "the seal of God on their foreheads."

Sixth Trumpet or Second Woe

Rev. 9:12-19. 200 million Orientals attack.

Verse 13 begins with the second woe (6th trumpet). It is a terrifying judgment. Four of the most wicked and powerful of all fallen angels are released to inspire the destruction of a third of all remaining mankind. Remember that one-fourth of the world population has already been destroyed by the judgments described in Revelation 6:8.

The poisoning of fresh-water sources killed many more. Now the remaining population is reduced by still another 33 percent.

These four angels at the River Euphrates are very significant. They were bound by God because they were tremendously powerful emissaries of Satan. Their confinement at the River Euphrates is especially momentous.

The first human sin was committed right at this Euphrates region, in the Garden of Eden. In this area the first murder and the first great revolt against God also took place. It was in nearby Babylon that the first world ruler set up his kingdom. The Euphrates region is truly the site of many significant events of human history.

The Romans, Greeks, and Babylonians always considered the Euphrates River as the boundary line between the East and the West. Rudyard Kipling put it succinctly: "East is east, and west is west, and never the twain shall meet". But they are going to meet in the tribulation! The four angels of Revelation 9:14, 15 will mobilize an army of 200 million soldiers from east of the Euphrates. Revelation 16 will provide more details about this, but in essence these 200 million troops are Chinese soldiers accompanied by other Eastern allies.

The Yellow Peril

Revelation 9:20, 21, "and they repented not"

These two verses have to be among the most incredible in the whole Bible. After all the foregoing supernatural events, men are still unwilling to repent and turn to Christ. These two verses also reveal another remarkable prediction – that men will once again turn back to worshiping demons and idols.

The Big Four

Revelation 9:21 lists the four most prominent sins of the tribulation. The significance of these particular sins is great in the light of present trends in the world. It's no coincidence that the four major sins listed here are four of the most serious problems facing law enforcement today.

The first of these characteristic sins is murder. Over a century ago, before America groaned under the present crime wave, Joseph Seiss, the writer of The Apocalypse, predicted on the basis of Revelation 9:21 that capital punishment would have been largely abolished by the time of the Tribulation. He foresaw the day when murderers would be spared punishment because society, rather than the individual, would be held responsible for their crimes. Pacifists – appeasers – would be in control of most of the western society.

Once upon a time there was an ascetic (Sanyasi) who did not want to hurt a fire ant that got onto his beard. So he went to the den of the fire ants, and simply placed his beard so that the solitary fire ant on his beard might get out. What happened is just the opposite. A thousand new ones got onto his beard and bit him. Modern day liberals are living in such a utopian mindset that they have lost all practical wisdom. Today Western Europe has become a victim of Islamic terrorists because of the follies of the leftists.

Collapse of Personal Responsibility

Freudian theory paved the way for the collapse of responsibility in modern American society. Psychiatrists have been trying to dull, if not actually extract, the teeth of the Law – and this is on the distinctively Freudian assumption that it is entirely natural for the criminal to act as he does, and quite unreasonable for society to make him stand trial for being his antisocial self. People are no longer themselves responsible for what they do wrong. They claim that their problems are all ogenic (other-engendered) rather than autogenic (self-engendered). Instead of assuming personal responsibility for their behavior, they blame society.

It is easy to blame society, since what is everyone's responsibility is no one's responsibility. This is socialism of psychology or psychology of socialism. Some blame the Church, or any one of the family members. Freudian psychology turns out to be an archaeological expedition back into the past in which a search is made for others on whom to pin the blame for the patient's behavior. The fundamental idea is to find out how others have wronged him.

1) Post Traumatic Disorder (Psalms 58.3, Mark 7.20)

Parents and Churches have failed to teach children and adults the sinful nature of man and God's remedy for it which is a new birth in Christ. The breakdown in the home and the failure of fathers to assume their roles of leadership have also been strong contributing factors to the increase of violent crimes. A child who is never taught discipline in the home will grow up with destructive anxieties and frustrations, and too often he takes out his hostilities on society.

2) Another prominent sin of the tribulation era will be drug related occultic activities. The word "sorceries" in Revelation 9:21, comes from the Greek word *Pharmakia*, which means "pharmacy" and refers here to the practice of the occult with the use of drugs.

In our day, drug addiction – touted and flaunted by many rock stars – has swelled into a flood across the nation. While the 1970's saw an abatement toward use of mind-altering drugs such as LSD, the punk and heavy metal teenagers of the 1980's are once again experimenting with this dangerous drug, as well as heroin.

Use of these drugs has led youngsters to demon worship at heavy-metal concerts. The biggest hook to Satanism is the music. The kids are getting all kinds of messages in the music. Some concert kinds chant "Natas," that is Satan spelled backward. Demons and drugs are very similar to their effect on the human mind. They can take over a man to the point where he is completely altered in personality and would think nothing of committing the crimes in America today of grave robbing and animal mutilation of sacrificial purposes – or even murder.

3) The third prominent sin of tribulation will be rampant immorality. Porneia, the Greek word used in this verse, refers to all kinds of sexual activity outside of its Biblically-sanctioned function between a married man and woman. The marriage vow will be virtually unknown at this time, and there will be a complete breakdown in family relationships.

We live in a day when the impact of the rejection of Biblical morality and absolutes is beginning to be seen at every level of society, but especially in attitudes toward sex. The world is in a head long plunge downward to the morality of Sodom and Gomorrah and, unfortunately, to their same judgment as well.

4) Crime on the Increase

The fourth characteristic of the tribulation will be thievery of all kinds, including burglaries and robberies.

When a society's family unit breaks down, the whole society falls apart. Many of our world's people are without moral conviction because they have been set adrift on the sea of life without any compass, rudder or destination. Theft received a new meaning in 2008 and 2009. We saw the collapse of the Wall Street titans such as AIG, Freddie Mac, Fannie May, Lehman Brothers, Bear Stearns, Wachovia Bancorporation, Washington Mutual, City Group, Merrill Lynch, and the Bank of America etc. Greed played a part in Bernie Madoff's sixty billion Ponzi scheme. **Modern day corporations are headed by greedy thieves who care about instant profit by using multiple sales gimmicks. Employees are pressed hard to sell to whoever walks inside a financial institution. Most of the senior managers don't have stable families and are wedded to the company.**

REVELATION CHAPTER 10

This is a parenthetical portion that comes between the sixth and seventh trumpets. We have already noticed that similar parentheses are between the sixth and seventh seals and the sixth and seventh vials. This is an evidence of divine order not to be overlooked.

Like the shining through of the sun in the midst of an earth-shaking storm, this chapter brings us relief and hope. Actually this chapter is in two parts: first we turn our eyes upon Jesus, and then we turn our eyes upon John. Both exercises are refreshing indeed.

Rev. 10:1-3. All the troubles in the world stem from the act that men have lost sight of Him. At this point in the Apocalypse, men have ruled out Christ as a factor in world affairs, and the devil has provided them with a more exciting Messiah.

The world today is hastening in this direction. Men are leaving the Lord out of their calculations and the result is that little, if anything makes sense. An illustration will help us see this. For centuries men believed the theories of astronomy as propounded by Greek philosophers. The writing of Aristotle and Ptolemy were scientific gospels, and to challenge them was the worst of heresies. Men were expected to believe without debate that the earth was the center of the universe, for example, and that the heavenly bodies moved in perfect circles. Astronomy was in a hopeless muddle. Men simply did not have the key, for they ignored the centrality of the sun.

Then came Nicholas Copernicus and Johannes Kepler. The sun was put in its proper place as the center of the solar system. It was established that the earth and the planets revolved around the sun and that the true path of the planets is an ellipse, not a circle. Then everything fell into place. Copernicus and his followers won lasting fame simply by giving the sun its rightful place.

Thus it is in the affairs of men. The world has forgotten the centrality of the Son of God and that He is the Center of everything. It is no wonder that human affairs are in such a muddle. Men have postulated, in the place of Jesus as Creator, [a fortuitous concourse of atoms!] the blind workings of chance or evolution. Behind the working of history, men see some form of dialectic. The Prince of Peace has been banished from men's minds, and a grandiose United Nations organization has been put in His place. The world has lost sight of the Lord Jesus, and since everything revolves around Him, the resulting chaos is evident everywhere. So John begins by turning our eyes upon Jesus.

This angel is not an ordinary angel, for no created being, however lofty, however high, has prerogatives, powers, and attributes like these. This is the Lord who accompanied Israel in the wilderness. Here He is again coming to deal with Israel's enemies. Once He hung the rainbow in the sky. Now He wears the rainbow on His brow, a diadem of light.

When He was born, He put a new star in the sky. When He died, He put out the sun. Now His face is as the sun.

He claims dominion over all the world – river, sea, and shore; the Gentile nation and Israel. There is an open book in His hand. What Daniel was told to seal until the time of the end (Dan. 12:4) is now to be opened up to full view, for the end time has come. The Lord is about to act, but He will act in compliance with the mind and will of God. All unfulfilled prophecies and promises will now come to pass. He claims pole to pole and from sea to sea, to the end of the earth.

Next His cry.

There are few sounds that compare with an angry lion's roar in its own unfettered domain. The lion's roar is calculated to chill the stoutest heart, give pause to its most dauntless foe, and petrify its prey. Thus, the Lord, the mighty lion of the tribe of Judah, sounds forth His cry.

The angel who is possessing all creation swears that the time had come and there would no longer be delay. But in the days of the voice of the seventh angel, when he shall sound, the mystery of God is intended to be finished. It is God's predetermined, foreordained, elective purpose that in the days of the sounding of the seventh angel, the mystery of God shall be finished, as he evangelized through his servants the prophets. The mystery of God is the long delay of our Lord in taking the kingdom unto Himself and establishing righteousness in the earth. The mystery of God is seen in these thousands of years in which sin and death run riot. The pages of history, from the time of the first murder until this present hour, are written in blood, tears and death. The mystery is the delay of God in taking the kingdom unto himself. For these thousands of years, God has allowed Satan to wrap his vicious, cruel tentacles around this world. That mystery of evil has brought more stumbling to the faith of God's people than any other experience in all life. The infidel, the atheist, the agnostic and the unbeliever laugh and mock us, and God lets them mock and laugh. When evil and wickedness abound, we wonder where God is. Missionaries are slain, our churches are burned to the ground, millions of people are oppressed, living in despair and God just is forbearing. He seemingly does not intervene. Oh, the mystery of the delay of the Lord God. But in the days of the voice of the seventh angel, the mystery of God shall be finished. The forbearance and long suffering of God shall end.

The Delayed but Inevitable Victory

This universe was not only created by Christ, but this whole, vast world around us was created for Christ. The history of the world ultimately moves to that great consummation when God's people shall reign with their Lord in the earth. According to Revelation 10:7, these are the good tidings that God has evangelized to his servants the prophets. Good tidings were always announced in the message of the prophets.

But this final triumph is not now, not yet. We live in the days of the delay. We live in the day of tears, heartache, strife, and conflict. These are our days of suffering and sorrow. When the Lord closed His Apocalyptic sermon in the 24th chapter of Matthew, He closed it with a parable concerning this delay. (Matthew 24:45-51). The parable is about a servant who said in his evil heart: "my master is delaying his coming". Verse 36 says no one knows the time of His coming.

<u>2 Peter 3:3</u> "...scoffers will come..."

The whole creation groans and labors with birth pangs. <u>2 Corinthians 5:4</u> "For we who are in this tent groan, being burdened..." we wait for immortality. <u>Romans 8:21</u> "The creation itself also will be delivered from the bondage of corruption..."

The "mystery of iniquity" works its woes in this world; empires wax and wane, kingdoms rise and fall, man's cruelty to man goes on and on, and nations subjugate other nations. Suffering and sorrow, war and famine, oppression and injustice, misery and woe inundate the planet from pole to pole and from sea to sea. But God in His mercy sets limits to it all. Evil men like Stalin and Hitler and Mussolini die. In time, oppressors like Saddam Hussein and Pol Pot are overthrown; in the end, God wins.

<u>Rev 10:8-11</u> The prisoner of Patmos again hears the voice from 'the heaven,' the dwelling of God. The legs of John may have been fettered, and the wild waves of the sea dashed against his rocky prison; but the island was no lonely place for the man whose soul was wrapped up in the visions of God, whose ears heard the songs of the redeemed, and the spoken worship of angels, and who was personally addressed out of Heaven again and again.

Now John is told to go up to Him and say, "please give that book to me." Because of his prompt obedience to God's will, John is given a fresh comprehension of God's word. He learns how that word is to be personally experienced in his life.

Eating is an easily recognized symbol for receiving knowledge. For example, we ourselves speak of digesting a piece of information. Why bitter in the belly and sweet in the mouth? (Rev.10:9). Prophecy is both bitter and sweet. In Jeremiah 15:16 we see the prophet eating the words of Jehovah. To eat is to make the thing one's own, to incorporate it into one's being (John 6:49-58). The Christian prophet eating the scroll, and finding it both sweet and bitter, reminds us of a similar symbolic action by the Jewish prophet. (Ezek. 2:8-10, 3:1-3). the first effect of prophetic communication, the scroll in the mouth, was sweetness, the sweetness of honey; but as the revelations were weighed, the judgments they announce were considered, the next effect was to cause bitterness and sorrow. Prophecy is both gladness and sadness, as it contains announcements both of joy and of grief.

REVELATION CHAPTER 11

Two Witnesses

In the long parenthesis we are considering, we are looking on the bright side of a very dark picture. Mention has already been made of the completion of the mystery. Now we see the coming of the messengers, for God never leaves Himself without a witness. The more degenerate the times, the more definite the testimony. In the days before the flood, God raised up Enoch and Noah. In the days of Israel's darkest apostasy, He raised up Elijah and Elisha. He will do the same again. God is now about to unleash His wrath. The cup of human iniquity is almost full, but not quite. A few more drops need to be added. The lie must be consummated, blasphemy must be crowned, and then God will act in wrath.

Revelation 11 anticipates Revelation 13 and has its roots in Revelation 9. In Revelation 13, the Beast's coming is described. This part of the parenthesis shows how the sixth trumpet affects the Jewish world. The scene is Jerusalem and the rebuilt Temple. John, who was a passive onlooker and reporter during the previous judgments, is now spurred to action. He is told to measure the Temple and its courts. The reed was a measuring instrument, and is frequently mentioned by the prophets of old. The temple, altar, and worshipers measured by the seer intimate their appropriation, preservation, and acceptance of God. Like a staff or firm rod signifies the strength, stability, and firmness of the emblematic action referred to.

The temple, the altar, the worshipers, all are measured. Christian worship comes in- between the suspension of Jewish worship in the past and its resumption in the future. Christians have no place of worship on earth; they enter no earthly temple. The holiest in the Sanctuary above is their one and only place of worship. (John 4:21-24; Hebrews 10:19-22). Their sacrifices are praise to God and practical benevolence to men. (Hebrews 13:15-16) But this is different from Jewish worship both in the past and the future. A temple and altar are essential to Jewish worship.

The vision clearly involves Jerusalem and the future temple in the last days. When God speaks of measuring anything, the thought is implied that He is marking it off as that which belongs to Himself. When purchasing a piece of ground, it is very common to measure it and mark off its lines. In Zechariah 2, we are told that the prophet beheld a man with a measuring line in his hand, to whom he puts the question, "where are you going?" and the answer was, "To measure Jerusalem to see what is its width and what is its length." (Zechariah 2:2). And in the fourth verse, the angel who is interpreting the visions of Zechariah says to another angel, "Run, speak to this young man, saying: Jerusalem shall be inhabited as towns without walls, because of the multitude of men and livestock in it. For I, says the Lord, will be a wall of fire all around her, and I will be the glory in her midst." (Zechariah 2: 4-5). Then, in the rest of the chapter, we have a very distinct prophecy of the future deliverance of God's earthly people from all their foes, when they will be brought from the land of the north and from all parts of the world where they have been carried in the days of captivity. This will not be fully accomplished until the Lord Jesus Himself has appeared in glory. Zechariah 2:8-9 reads "For thus says the Lord of hosts: 'He sent me after glory, to the nations which plunder you; for he who touches you touch the apple of His eye.'" Read verses 11-12 also.

Clearly it is this very restoration that God had in mind when He gave John the vision of this eleventh chapter. Here John is instructed to leave out the court that is outside the temple, and measure it not because it is still to be given to the Gentiles, and the holy city shall they tread underfoot 42 months; that is, for the last 3 ½ years of the final seven that compose Daniel's 70th week, has not yet been fulfilled, nor can be until Jerusalem and the Jews are again owned by God as His own. (Luke 21:24). The "times of the Gentiles" began with Nebuchadnezzar and the captivity of Judah; it has continued until this day and will not be consummated until the downfall of the Beast, the last Gentile ruler on earth.

Daniel's 70th week (Daniel 9:27) coincides with the seven-year pact between the Beast and Israel. During the first half of the period, the Beast will honor his treaty commitments, no doubt because it is in his interest to do so. But halfway through the period, there will be a change of policy, possibly connected with the downfall of Russia and Islamic alliance. The Beast would become prominent and more powerful (Revelation 11:7). The persecution of

Revelation 7 relates to this period, commonly called the "Great Tribulation". The Beast has already moved his armies into Jerusalem, presumably under the terms of the pact that promises protection for Israel against the Islamic alliance and Russia. After the annihilation of Russia and the Arabs, the Beast becomes the unquestionable leader of the world.

The Third Temple, The Place and Time

By Dr. David Reagan

"The Bible clearly teaches that a new temple — which will be called The Third Temple — will be built in the future. The First Temple was the one that Solomon built and which was destroyed in 586 BC. The Second Temple (516 BC to 70 AD) was built after the Jews returned from Babylonian captivity. The platform on which it sat was greatly expanded and beautified by King Herod, as was the temple itself, but since the sacrifices were never stopped during this renovation and expansion, the new temple was still considered to be The Second Temple.

The Third Temple will exist during the Great Tribulation. Daniel refers to this temple when he says that "the prince who is to come" (the Antichrist) will enter it and stop the sacrifices in the middle of the Tribulation (Daniel 9:27). The Apostle Paul mentions it when he declares that the "man of lawlessness" will profane the temple by entering it and declaring himself to be God (2 Thessalonians 2:3-4). The Third Temple is also mentioned in the book of Revelation when John is told to measure it — a symbolic way of telling him to assess its spiritual condition (Revelation 11:1-2).

This raises the question as to precisely when the temple will be rebuilt. The Bible does not reveal the answer to this question. All it says for certain is that the temple will be in existence when the Antichrist reveals himself (2 Thessalonians 2:3-4), and that will be in the middle of the Tribulation (Daniel 9:27). Since this will be only three and a half years into the Tribulation, many have concluded that the temple will likely be rebuilt before the Tribulation begins, because how could such a magnificent building be constructed in such a short period of time?

But this conclusion overlooks the fact that the temple can be literally resurrected overnight! That's because the Jews plan to erect a tent temple like the Tabernacle of Moses, and they are ready to do so at any moment. Everything has been prepared. Once this temporary temple is set up, they will resume the sacrifices, and then start building a more permanent structure around and above the temporary one.

Currently there are two major obstacles to the reconstruction of The Third Temple. One pertains to its location. The next temple can only be built where the two previous temples stood, because the Holy of Holies must be on the exact same spot. But no one knows for sure where the previous temples were located on the Temple Mount. Most scholars believe that they stood where the Dome of the Rock currently stands. That conclusion may be wrong, but there is no way to prove the exact location without conducting archeological excavations on the Temple Mount, something which is currently prohibited by the Muslims. If The Third Temple is to be built where the Dome of the Rock now stands, then that Muslim structure must first of all be removed either by man or God. It could, of course, be burned to the ground by a saboteur, or it could be destroyed by an earthquake.

The second obstacle is the attitude of the Jewish people and their leaders. Currently, there is no desire among them to build a third temple. The average Israeli is very secular. He knows that any attempt to build a third temple would result in immediate war with the Muslims. Only a handful of ultra-Orthodox Jews have a passion for The Third Temple. They are the ones who have made all the preparations. But they have no popular support. Something will have to happen to create a surge of nationalistic pride that will demand a new temple. This catalytic event could be the discovery of the Ark of the Covenant.

There is a distinct possibility that the ancient temples were not located where the Dome of the Rock currently sits. There is strong evidence that their location was to the north of the Dome and that the sacrificial altar inside the Dome was the one that Solomon built in "the middle of the court" to handle the thousands of special sacrifices which he offered to the Lord on the day The First Temple was dedicated (2 Chronicles 7:7). If that is so, then The Third Temple could be built north of the Dome of the Rock, putting the Dome in the Court of the Gentiles. This may well be the solution the Antichrist will come up with when he negotiates peace between the Jews and the Arabs (Daniel 9:27).

To summarize, there is definitely going to be a third temple. It will most likely be erected at the beginning of the Tribulation in the form of a tent temple, like the Tabernacle of Moses. A more permanent structure will then be built around and above it. The Antichrist will desecrate this temple in the middle of the Tribulation.

The Third Temple will be destroyed at the Second Coming of Jesus. The great earthquake at that time will radically change the topography of Jerusalem and all the earth (Revelation

6:12-17). In Jerusalem it will result in the provision of a very large level area where the Millennial Temple will be constructed. This is the temple from which Jesus will reign over all the earth. It is described in detail in Ezekiel 40-46."

Two Jewish Witnesses

We are told that the testimony of two witnesses will last 1,260 days, or three and a half years using the biblical 360-day calendar as the basis for calculation. God, who numbers the very hairs of our heads, is much more specific, detailed, and minute in recording the ministry of His two faithful witnesses than He is in mentioning the duration of the Beast's rage. He describes the ministry of His two witnesses as a day-by-day ministry and counts up the exact number of those days.

There are two periods of 3 ½ years involved here, and while they are the same in length, they do not run concurrently. The end of the 3 ½ year period connected with the two witnesses is marked by their martyrdom and by the outbreak of the Great Tribulation. The ministry of the two witnesses would seem to be during the first half of Daniel's 70th week.

The two witnesses that God will raise up at this time will preach so effectively that no one will be able to plead ignorance about the facts of salvation. The truthfulness of the two witnesses will stand in sharp contrast to the hypocrisy of the reconstructed temple. The two witnesses will make it a point to prove that everything in the temple has already been fulfilled by Christ, and that this magnificent new building is nothing but a nationalistic sham! As a result, the Jewish people will rejoice when the Roman Antichrist kills these two prophets by a great demonstration of Satan's power. In addition to exposing the falsity of the new Temple and preaching the true way of salvation, the witnesses will identify the new world leader for what he really is.

The miracles of Moses when Israel was in subjection to the Gentiles (Exodus 7:12), and of Elijah (1 Kings 17:18) when Israel was apostate from God are again to be witnessed in like character. If any man will hurt these two witnesses, fire will proceed out of their mouth, and devour their enemies. It was the very thing the Son would not do when He was upon the earth, and He rebuked James and John for desiring it. (Luke 9: 54-55). Here God is about to take the place of the judge on earth.

Rev. 11:7-10. The two messengers are immortal until their work is done. Then, like John the Baptist, they will fall before their foes. The Antichrist will dazzle men with his miracle again. His own resurrection amazed the world, but his conquest over these two miracle workers, will be the capstone of success. He becomes the false messiah. Jerusalem, one of the cities of the Beast, has become the center of all that is degrading and defiling. The television cameras of the world will be focused on this event. It will be the gossip of the globe. News of it will filter into every nook and cranny of the earth. And as in olden days when the bodies of criminals were hung up to rot in public view, so the bodies of these two witnesses will be left on public display in scornful ignominy for half a week.

God calls their witness a testimony (11:17). The world will call it a torment. A new festival will be provided, one much more meaningful and relevant for a pagan world.

Rev.11:11-13 Picture the scene – the sun-drenched streets of Jerusalem, the holiday crowds flown in from the ends of the earth for a firsthand look at the corpses of these detested men. There they are, devilish men from every kingdom under heaven, come to dance and feast at the triumph of the Beast. And then it happens! As the crowds strain at the police cordon to peer curiosity at the two dead bodies, there comes a sudden change. Their color changes from a cadaverous hue to the blooming, rosy glow of youth. Those stiff, stark limbs – they bend, they move! Oh what a sight! They rise! The crowds fall back, break and form again. They also have a triumphant rapture. But will these evil men repent when faced with this, the greatest of all miracles? Not at all. "Father Abraham" cried the rich man from the flames of a lost eternity. "Father Abraham, if one went unto them from the dead, they will repent." The solemn reply was "If they hear not Moses and the prophets, neither will they be persuaded though one rose from the dead." (Luke 16:30-31). And here not just one, but two arise, and repentance is the furthest thing from the minds of men. And we read, "And at the same hour was there a great earthquake..." The last woe that ushers in the end of the age follows fast.

The Last Trump. The Final Woe

Rev.11:14-19 The third woe is none other than the seventh and last of the trumpets, which ushers in the world kingdom of our God and His Christ. The whole question of sovereignty is now settled. "The kingdom (singular) of this world has become the kingdom (singular) of our Lord." That is what the devil has been after for centuries – to unite the world into a single kingdom – but all his attempts fail. He can no more overcome the disruptive, divisive power of sin than he can escape the ultimate judgment of God.

Back in the beginning of human history, when men first began to organize their rebellion against God, Satan attempted at Babel to build a world society from which God was to be excluded. Men planned a city and a tower – the city was to symbolize their political unity and the tower their religious unity. They had a common tongue as well, which emphasized their cultural unity. God came down and confounded the whole thing. **When the motive is evil, the unity is catastrophic.** Man united without God, was the form taken by the first apostasy after the flood. It will be the form of the final apostasy as well.

We are entering here into the final agony of the earth, its travail, its pain, and suffering, and its judgment in the hands of a furious and wrathful God. The modern preacher speaks only easy and soft messages; we don't know where they get their messages. The revelation of God in this book from beginning to end is always the announcement that there is a final day coming in which God shall deal with this world in wrath, when His judgment shall fall upon sin, unbelief, rejection, and unrighteousness.

In the second letter to the Corinthians, chapter 4:4, Paul refers to "the god of this world" as Satan. When we read the Bible, we find that the portrayal of the governments of this world is in terms of vicious, savage, wild beasts. Daniel chapter 7 depicts 4 empires as 4 beasts.

As God in His righteousness, from the third heaven, from the heaven of heavens, looks down onto this earth, there are governments and rulers but it is the kingdoms of death and darkness.

As God looks down onto this earth, He sees endless cemeteries. This whole planet is no other thing than a place in which to bury people, people created in the image of the Lord God Almighty, made in the likeness of the Lord. This earth is full of death and the dead. There is iniquity, darkness, unrighteousness, violence, and savagery everywhere. But God says enough is enough.

The great voice from Heaven will declare that, "the kingdom of this world has become the kingdom of our Lord and of His Christ, and He shall reign forever and ever". (Verse 15).

The Praise of the 24 Elders

Rev.11:16-19 The scenes that follow this announcement are in keeping with that glorious, triumphant promise. The immediate verses describe the response of the 24 elders. The 24 elders represent God's resurrected, immortalized, raptured, taken away, transfigured saints in Heaven. The 24 elders fell down upon their faces and worshiped God. It is the only place in the Bible where we will find that clause, "and they fell on their faces." In the 5th chapter of the Revelation, for example, these four and twenty elders fall down and worship Him. But at the announcement of this amazing and heavenly promise, "they fall upon their faces." The 24 elders worshiped God (v 17) saying (NKJV), "we give you thanks, O Lord God Almighty, The One who is and who was and who is to come." (V 17, JND). "We give thee thanks, Lord God Almighty, He who is, and who was, that hast taken they great power and has reigned."

The Lord is here at the sounding of the voice of the seventh trumpet. He is here at the sounding of the voice of the seventh trumpet. "O Lord God who is, and who was" not the one who is coming, but rather the one who is already here. Is not that an amazing thing that you and I shall live to see a day when the Lord God in presence, in personal appearance, in actuality, will be here and we shall look upon Him? It is beyond human power to comprehend that these mortal eyes should ever see God. Such has been the faith taught in the Book from the beginning, it is not just an opinion voiced by someone. "Yes," said Job, "though worms through my skin destroy this body, yet in my flesh shall I see God whom mine eyes shall behold." We, creatures of the dust, worms of this earth, moving toward the grave, shall live in that hour, in that day we will see God, 'who is,' who is present, the Lord God Almighty.

The words of praise of the 24 elders continue. The nations are described as being savage and full of iniquity and sin, full of violence and wars. If they are not in war, then they are getting ready for war, beating their plowshares into swords, sharpening their implements for destruction. The 18th verse covers the entire millennium and carries us onto the judgment of the wicked (The White Throne Judgment), to the end of time because, to the Lord Jesus Christ, all judgment has been committed.

The Rewards of God for His People

Following the text, we learn that when the 7th angel sounds, God will reward His servants, the prophets, the saints, and those who tremble before his presence. There may be no reward for God's people here on earth. Read the 11th chapter of the book of Hebrews. The heroes of faith were severely persecuted. God says that down here we do not have our reward, and the books of history say the same thing. How the world has treated God's people? Some of them were burned at the stake! Some of them were crucified upside down; some of them were thrown into boiling cauldrons of oil; some of them were made to rot in dungeons. It is so today, even as the Apostle Paul says, "all who will live godly in Christ Jesus shall suffer persecution."

Before God, all things are either right or wrong. The Lord looks down from heaven and says, "I have a day of reckoning." Some things are right and some things are wrong, and all the extenuating circumstances that a man can conceive do not make wrong right or right wrong. In our sight things may be gray, but not in God's sight. To God they are either black or white, either right or wrong. God judges according to rightness and wrongness. The destiny of a country does not lie in armies or navies or air forces or nuclear power, but it lies in the hands of the Almighty God who judges the nations.

The inequalities and injustices in this life are endless. The final settlement and judgment will be carried out by Our Lord Jesus Christ. Jesus is going to make all wrongs, right. The Lord says, "When I come, I will have my reward with me." Paul says, "We shall all stand at the bema of Christ, at the judgment bar of the Lord, and there we will receive our rewards." When that time comes, then Paul shall receive his crown of righteousness which he says God has in store for all those who love His appearing.

At that time Moses shall receive the recompense to which he had respect, when he chose to suffer affliction with the people of God rather than to enjoy the pleasures of sin for a season. At that time Daniel will stand in his lot, and at that time the apostles will be seated upon their twelve everlasting thrones.

In this world we suffer tribulation, we have conflicts, and agony and war in our souls. The world is much opposed to Christians. The text closes with the words, "and shall destroy them which destroy the earth." The final destruction of the wicked will take place.

"And the temple of God was opened in heaven, and there was seen in his temple the ark of his covenant." In the midst of the lightnings, voices, thundering, earthquakes and great hails, there appears the ark of the promises of God. In that golden ark are all the promises of God. Not one of those promises will fail.

REVELATION CHAPTER 12

The Radiant Woman

This passage represents a great division in the Apocalypse. The first eleven chapters, concluding with the sounding of the seventh trumpet, bring the consummation of this age, when the kingdom of this world, the sovereignty of this world, becomes the kingdom of our Lord and of His Christ. In the days of the voice of the seventh trumpet (described in chapter eleven), the mystery of God is finished. There upon our Lord gives us a preview, a prophetic outline, of the final days of this present world. God's glorious plans have been revealed, and now Satan's schemes are unmasked.

(The mystery of anti-Semitism. Satan loathes and detests the nation of Israel because it is one nation over which he has no direct authority. All the other nations, he received, as a grant from Adam, in whom God had vested dominion of the earth, fell. Israel is an exception. Israel was created by direct decree of God. From the inception of Israel, Satan has tried to destroy by assimilation and war.) In a word, Satan's ruling passion is to exterminate the Jews.

The Woman

There have been many identifications of this radiant woman. There are many who say that she is the Virgin Mary. But the identification of this radiant woman as the human mother of Jesus is impossible, as we look at the whole passage. In verse 6 we read, "Then the woman fled into the wilderness, where she has a place prepared by God, that they should feed her there one thousand two hundred and sixty days" and verse 14, "But the woman was given two wings of a great eagle that she might fly into the wilderness to her place, where she is nourished for a time and times and half a time, from the presence of the serpent." Based on the above mentioned verses, the application of those scriptures to the Virgin Mary would be unspeakable. Interpretations that take the woman as the Church cannot be correct either, for the Church did not bring God's son into the world. He had come and gone before ever the Church was born. It is Christ who gave birth to the Church. The Church is taken out of the side of Christ. We are born out of His flesh and His blood and His bones. When Eve was taken out of the side of Adam, Adam said, "This is now bone of my bones and flesh of my flesh." The Apostle Paul, commenting on the passage in Gen. 2:21-24, said, "This is a great mystery, but I speak concerning Christ and the Church." (Eph. 5:25-32).

Who is This Radiant Woman?

This woman is identified in the Bible. Romans 9:4 states, "who are Israelites, to whom pertain the adoption, the glory, the covenants, the giving of the law, the service of God, and the promises, of whom are the fathers and from whom according to the flesh, Christ came, who is overall, the eternally blessed God. Amen."

The inspired apostle says that the one who gave birth to the Messiah is the nation and the family and the people of Israel. It is Israel who produced Christ.

When you thus interpret the passage, everything in the Bible will beautifully and marvelously fit together. Israel is called a married woman again and again (Isaiah 54:1; 47:7-9; 50:1). Israel in her rejection and in her captivity is referred to as a widow and as a divorced woman. But always the Church is referred to as a chaste virgin, a bride who is someday to be presented to Christ. (2 Cor. 11:2). In the scripture the Church is never referred to as a mother. She is always the bride. That identification can also be seen in her description. She is clothed with the sun and the moon is under her feet, and upon her head is a crown of twelve stars. This is a description that is taken from the 37th chapter of Genesis (verse 9). It refers to Israel and the family of Jacob. The twelfth star is Joseph, himself, the sun and moon and the eleven stars, and he is the 12th star. So this glorious, radiant woman is prefigured in the life of Joseph. The woman is Israel, the chosen family and people of God, and the child is the Messiah, our Lord Christ.

The text speaks of the prolonged sufferings of the woman. No nation on earth has suffered so severely and for so long as Israel. We are left with no doubt as to the cause of Israel's sufferings. John says, "and there appeared another wonder in heaven; and behold a great red dragon, having seven heads and ten horns, and seven crowns upon his heads." The word dragon occurs 13 times in revelation. A dragon is a flying serpent, a biblical symbol for Satan. (Rev. 20:2). The heads, horns, and the crowns of the dragon are symbols of earthly power that Satan claims. Eph. 2:2 states "he is the Prince of the power of the air, "and…. this world (John 12:31).

Satan and his minions are responsible for the sufferings of Israel. It might be appropriate here to consider the course of Israel's sufferings. Both sacred and secular histories tell the long tale.

The first large scale attempt to exterminate the Jews was made by Pharaoh. Significantly, the turning point came in Moses' life when he saw, in the desert, the mysterious burning bush. The bush clearly symbolized Israel, which cannot be consumed despite the ceaseless hatred of her foes, because God is in her midst. Israel cannot be assimilated into the nations, nor can she be exterminated by the nations. She is a burning bush in the wilderness.

The Mystery of Anti-Semitism

One of the grimmest recurrences of history has been the continuing irrational hatred and persecution of the Jewish people. Twice these people had their national homeland torn from them; twice they were led as captives in to other lands and nations; twice they miraculously survived incomparable persecutions in foreign lands; and twice they miraculously returned to the land of their fathers to reestablish their nation, each time against such opposition that the world stood and watched in amazement.

The Jews' second dispersion from the land of Israel lasted from A.D. 70 to 1948. During that time the Jewish people endured some of the most inhumane treatment ever inflicted in human history, and yet they survived as a distinct race. Virtually every country in which they took refuge ultimately turned against them. From the holocaust of Titus and the Roman legion's destruction of Jerusalem through the Inquisitions and Crusades, and on to the gas ovens of the

Hitler era, anti-Semitism has kept rekindling into insane flames of hatred and slaughter.

Chapter 12 of Revelation answers the puzzling mystery of anti-Semitism. It shows that anyone who hates and persecutes a Jew is actually doing so at the instigation of a mighty spirit being who hates all Jews.

Because of God's selection of this nation to be the physical race through which he would allow His Son to be born into this world, Satan has a special hatred for the "woman" and her "child." In fact, he has a special hatred for anyone who loves the woman (Israel) or her child (Jesus Christ). On several occasions in the history of Israel, Satan sought to annihilate the whole race of Jews in order to prevent the Messiah's birth. His final attempt was to inspire Herod to murder all the baby boys two years and under at the time of Jesus' birth.

It is at the time of the great Tribulation that the woman flees into the wilderness where she is cared for (Dan. 9:27) three and a half years, 1,260 days, 42 months. We have come to the great and final end time of this world – this is the day of Jacob's trouble.

In this prophecy, all of the vast period in which we now live is left out. No reference is made to it. In the gap between verse 5 and verse 6, all of this period of grace in which we now live intervenes. Look at the time here in the fifth verse "she bore a male child who was to rule all nations with a rod of iron. And her child was caught up to God and His throne." Verse 6, "Then the woman fled into the wilderness, where she has a place prepared by God that they should feed her there 1,260 days." Reading verse 5, one could think Christ had no life at all. One might think He never lived at all; that He was born as a child and was caught up to the throne immediately. His life and ministry is not referred to, His death and atoning sacrifice is not referred to. His entire life is skipped over, all in one breath.

God is talking about something else here. He was not chronologizing the life of Christ. The Lord has another intent and purpose, and He is speaking of those things that are pertinent to what He is talking about, which in this instance is the great prophetic preview now before us. He leaves out great gaps and great periods of time, centering on those things that are pertinent to the particular prophecy.

This method of prophecy is found throughout the word of God. Look, for example, at the way Jesus used a certain passage in the 61st chapter of Isaiah. All in one breath the prophet says, "To proclaim the acceptable year of the Lord, and the day of vengeance of our God." That is the way the passage reads in Isaiah. Now look at it in Luke, as Jesus reads the passage. Luke 4:18-19, "To proclaim the acceptable year of the Lord." Then He closed the book. Right in the middle of a phrase, right in the middle of a clause, right in the middle of a sentence, right in the middle of a great prophecy the Lord cuts it off. "To proclaim the acceptable year of the Lord and the day of vengeance of our God." Between those two statements, 2,000 years have already passed. The great day of the vengeance of our God and the judgment of the Lord God upon this earth is yet future, even at this late hour. Paul says in the third chapter of the Book of Ephesians that this age of grace and the body of Christ, the Church, are a Mystery ("musterion,") hidden in the heart of God and unknown until the Lord revealed it to His apostles. In the prophecies we find the outline of ages in one sentence, with millennia omitted between the clauses.

Let us take one another instance of the unusual method by which God outlines the future. In the eleventh chapter of the Book of Isaiah, 11:1-16, "There shall come forth a rod from the stem of Jesse, and a branch shall grow out of his roots. The spirit of the Lord shall rest upon Him" v.6, "The wolf also shall dwell with the lamb, the leopard shall lie down with the young goat." Here is that method again. The first verse – the branch shall grow out of Jesse – refers to the birth of the Lord Jesus, the Messiah, coming out of the loins of David. Though cut down, the branch sprouts up in Jesus. "And the wolf shall dwell with the lamb." This prophecy has not come to pass yet. The first part of it was fulfilled 2,000 years ago in the birth of Jesus. Yet, the last part of the prophecy does not come to pass until the millennial kingdom of Christ is established on this earth. But the prophets did not see the time separation as they looked at those two vast mountain peaks side by side – the coming of our Lord and the establishment of the millennial kingdom on earth. It was only as we drew near to the peaks that we saw that there was a distance in-between. One of them is in front of the other.

In chapter 12 we have seen the male child is born and is caught up to the throne of God in heaven. Between v.5 and v.6 there is no reference to the whole church period. Why? Because God is dealing with Israel here and Israel has no scriptural history in this day of grace. The clock stopped for Israel when she rejected her messiah and the 69 weeks were closed. In this present day, the Israelites, like any other people, are lost without Jesus. They have to repent. They have to be born into the kingdom of God. They have to be regenerated just as we are. There is no difference today between a Jew and a Greek or anyone else. All are lost without Jesus today. But God says there is coming a time when this age will be finished, and when the purposes of God for His Church shall be accomplished: there is coming a time when the Church is to be taken out of this earth. There is coming a time when the clock will start again with Israel. That will be the 70th week, the last week of Daniel. This revelation has to do with the climactic week. This is the day, here in Revelation, of Jacob's trouble. This is the day of his agony. This is the day of his great indescribable sorrow. This final week, God will purge His nation.

This is what Israel, cannot see today. This is what John the Baptist, in his day, could not see. For when John the Baptist came, he announced the coming of the kingdom, and he said the axe is laid at the root of the tree, and the Lord is going to winnow the chaff from the wheat with His winnowing fan. But there was no axe laid at the root of the tree, and there was no winnowing fan, and the kingdom did not come. John, in his despair and discouragement, sent word to Jesus and said, "Lord I do not understand. Are you the one that was to come or do we look for another?"

Ephesians 3:1-13

3:2 Paul was entrusted with the message of the grace of God as the apostle to the Gentiles (Gal. 2:7).

3:3 The mystery. A mystery was not something mysterious, but something unknown until revealed. (Rom. 16:25). The mystery spoken here is not that Gentiles would be blessed (for that was predicted in the OT), but that Jews and Gentiles would be equal heirs in the one body of Christ (v.6). This was unknown in OT prophecy, but was revealed by the NT apostles and prophets. (v.5)

The content of the mystery is that in the Body of Christ all are fellow heirs, fellow members and fellow partakers.

I can see the suffering servant and minister in you, but where is that messiah who is to rule with a rod of iron, who is to cut down the tree of iniquity and separate the chaff from the wheat? Where is the messiah that I announced when I preached the gospel of the kingdom? John the Baptist fell into that error. John never saw the great gap between the first and the second comings, the dying of our Lord and the reigning of our Lord. John never saw it.

Paul said the reason he did not see it was that it was not revealed until it was made known to the apostles. The prophets never saw it, and that is the veil that covers Israel's heart today.

The Expulsion of Satan

Rev.12:7-9. In this section we see the violence was between Michael and Lucifer and their cohorts: the angels of glory. The war precipitates the last Great Tribulation period, that last 3 ½ years, 42 months, 1,260 days, a time, times and half a time, the last half of the 70th week of Daniel. The violent conflict between good and evil, between God and Satan, rises to its final chapter in these concluding days. There is war in heaven and Satan knows that he has a short time. When this war is fought, it is the beginning of the end. It is remarkable that this Great Tribulation period begins with a war in heaven and at Armageddon, a war on earth in which God intervenes in human history and Christ comes in glory and power.

This violent conflict between these two celestial heavenly personalities has been a strife renewed and repeated throughout the millennia past. In Jude v. 9 we see these antagonists. These are the identical participants, antagonists, which are named here in this final war in heaven.

In the 14th chapter of Isaiah, Satan is called Lucifer, "son of the morning". In the 28th chapter of the Book of Ezekiel, he is described as "the anointed cherub that covers," that is, he was assigned as the highest created angel of God, the guardianship of the throne of glory itself. But arrogance filled his heart. Even Michael, the arch angel of God, could not stand in his own strength and in his own power before the tremendous might and glory of Lucifer. Michael said to Lucifer "The Lord rebuke thee."

In the 12th chapter of the Book of Daniel we read that God said, when Michael shall stand up, the time has come when those sleeping in the dust of the earth shall be resurrected. (Or as Paul would say it, when the last trump of the archangel sounds.) It is the time when those whose names are found written in the Book of Life shall be rewarded. It is the time God's saints shall shine as the brightness of the firmament and as the stars forever and forever. When Satan fails here, he fails everywhere, for this is the dissolution of his kingdom of darkness. This is the emptying of all graves. This is the destruction of the sovereignty of death. The end of death means the end of the kingdom of Satan. Paul said that the last enemy that shall be destroyed is death.

Notice where the war is fought. John says, "And there was war in heaven." That is about the very last place one would expect to find war. War in heaven! No wonder that at the end of the apocalypse God makes both a new heaven and a new earth, for Satan has defiled both places. Sin is much older than mankind. It did not originate on earth; it originated in heaven and began, not in a human heart, but in the soul of Lucifer. So this war is fought in heaven.

Now what is Satan like? He is like a dragon, a serpent, vicious, vile, ferocious, and terrible. He is fiery red, like fire. He is a murderer from the beginning. He has seven heads. The number seven refers to fullness; here, to the fullness of evil. On each one of his heads is a diadem. He is always presented as a crowned monarch. In Matt. 12, our Lord referred to Satan as a king with a kingdom. Three times in the book of John, our Lord referred to Satan as "the prince of this world." In 2 Cor. 4:4, Paul referred to Satan as the god of this world. In Eph. 2, Paul refers to him as "the Prince of the power of the air."

The kingdom of this world, the sovereignty of this world, does not become the sovereignty of our Lord and of His Christ until the sounding of the 7th trumpet, described in the eleventh chapter of the Book of the Revelation. The dragon's tail drew a third part of the stars of heaven and did cast them to the earth. Lucifer is a star, himself. The word "Lucifer" means "star of the morning." God's angel's hosts are called 'stars' when they sing together in the 38th chapter of Job.

Satan fell long ago, and with him, one-third of the angels. In Jude and in the second chapter of 2 Peter, evil angels are spoken of as being imprisoned and chained, until the great day of judgment. But Lucifer and one third of the angels are not thus imprisoned. In the Book of Job, he has access to the very presence of God Himself. Here he is in heaven warring against Michael and his angels.

Who are the fallen angels in 2 Peter and Jude?

(2 Peter 2:4-5) King James Version (KJV)

⁴ For if God spared not the angels that sinned, but cast them down to hell, and delivered them into chains of darkness, to be reserved unto judgment;

⁵ And spared not the old world, but saved Noah the eighth person, a preacher of righteousness, bringing in the flood upon the world of the ungodly.

(Jude 1:6-7) New King James Version (NKJV)

⁶ And the angels who did not keep their proper domain, but left their own abode, He has reserved in everlasting chains under darkness for the judgment of the great day; ⁷ as Sodom and Gomorrah, and the cities around them in a similar manner to these, having given themselves over to sexual immorality and gone after strange flesh, are set forth as an example, suffering the vengeance of eternal fire."

They are not Satan's angels, for his angels are free, and like Satan, roam around. But these angels are in prison, "in darkness", and reserved in chains for judgment. Clarence Larkin says that the place of their confinement is not Hell, but Tartarus. "What was their sin? It was "fornication" and fornication of an abnormal character, the unlawful sexual intercourse of angelic beings with "strange flesh", that is with beings of a different nature." Larkin continues "when was this sin committed? The text says in the "Days of Noah", and that it was the cause of the flood.

Why did God send the judgment of the flood in the days of Noah? Far more than simply a historical issue, or a Prophetic issue, the unique events leading to the flood are a prerequisite to understanding the Prophetic implications of our Lord's predictions regarding his Second Coming.

The strange events recorded in Genesis 6 were understood by the ancient rabbinical sources as well as the Septuagint translators as referring to fallen angels procreating weird hybrid offspring with human women known as the "Nephilim". So it was also understood by the early church fathers. These bizarre events are also echoed in the legends and myths of every ancient culture upon the earth: the ancient Greeks, the Egyptians, the Hindus, the South Sea Islanders, the American Indians, and virtually all the others.

In Hindu epics of Ramayana and Mahabharata, giants or Rakshasas were populous race. There were both good and evil Rakshasas. They were powerful warriors, expert magicians and illusionists.

(Genesis 6:1-6) New King James Version (NKJV)

The Wickedness and Judgment of Man

1 Now it came to pass, when men began to multiply on the face of the earth, and daughters were born to them, [2] that the sons of God saw the daughters of men, that they *were* beautiful; and they took wives for themselves of all whom they chose.

[3] And the Lord said, "My Spirit shall not strive [] with man forever, for he *is* indeed flesh; yet his days shall be one hundred and twenty years." [4] There were giants on the earth in those days, and also afterward, when the sons of God came in to the daughters of men and they bore *children* to them. Those *were* the mighty men who *were* of old, men of renown.[5] Then the Lord saw that the wickedness of man *was* great in the earth, and *that* every intent of the thoughts of

his heart *was* only evil continually. ⁶And the Lord was sorry that He had made man on the earth, and He was grieved in His heart.

Some Scholars have taken the view that this passage refers to the intermarriage of the Sethites with the Cainites. This theory has been espoused by Chrysostom Cyril of Alexandria, Theodoret, Keil, Lange, Jamieson, Fausset, Brown, Mathew Henry, C.I. Scofield and many others.

According to them the passage in Genesis 6 actually refers to a failure to keep the "faithful" line of Seth separates from the "worldly" line of Cain. The idea has been advanced that after Cain killed Abel, the line of Seth remained separate and faithful, but the line of Cain turned ungodly and rebellious. The sons of God are deemed to refer to leadership in the line of Seth; the "daughters of men" is deemed restricted to the line of Cain. That means the good sons of Seth married the bad daughters of Cain, and the result of these mixed marriages was a mongrel offspring. The resulting marriages blurred separation between them. Why the resulting offspring are called the "Nephilim" has only vague explanations and circular reasoning.

If the text was intended to contrast the "sons of Seth and the daughters of Cain," why didn't it say so? Seth was not God, and Cain was not Adam. Why not the "sons of Cain" and the "daughters of Seth? There is no basis for restricting the text to either subset of Adam's descendants. Further, there exists no mention of *daughters of Elohim*.

Since Jesus prophesied "As the days of Noah were so shall the coming of the Son of man be". It becomes essential to understand what these days included.

The idea that the sons of God were the descendants of Seth is based on the assumption that the descendants of Seth lived apart from the descendants of Cain up to the time shortly before the flood, and that they were a pure and a holy race, while the descendants of Cain were ungodly. And the women of Cain's descendants were carnal, evil and possessed of physical attractions and the women of the tribe of Seth lacked attraction and beauty. Such an assumption has no foundation in the scripture. Genesis 4:26 says after the birth of Enos, a son of Seth, that men began to call upon the Lord, but it does not follow that those men were limited to the descendants of Seth, nor that all the descendants of Seth from that time were righteous. As in the early days of the human race it was necessary that brothers and sisters and near relatives should marry, it was very unlikely that the descendants of Seth and Cain did not intermarry until sometime before the flood. Another strange thing is that when they did marry, their offspring would be a race of giants or mighty men and nothing is mentioned in the Bible about giantesses or mighty women".

As both the descendants of Seth (except 8 persons) and of Cain were destroyed in the flood, it is evident that they were not separate tribes at that time and were equally sinners in the sight of God.

The scriptures are supposed to mean what they say. When MEN, we are told, began to multiply on the face of the earth, and daughters were born unto them, the "Sons of God" saw the "daughters of men". The use of the word MEN means the whole

Adamic race and not simply the descendants of Cain, thus distinguishing the "Sons of God" from the descendants of Adam.

In the New Testament sons of God have a different meaning. In the New Testament it applies to those who have become the "Sons of God "of the New Birth. John 1:12; Romans 8:14-16; Galatians: 4:6; I John 3:1-2. In the Old Testament it applies exclusively to the angels, and is so used five times. Twice in Genesis (Gen.6:2-4) and three times in Job where Satan, an angelic being is classed with the sons of God. Job 1:6; 2:1; 38:7. A son of God denotes a being brought into existence by a creative act of God.

The idea that the Sons of God of Genesis 6:1-4 were Angels was maintained by the ancient Jewish Synagogue of Hellenistic Jews even before the time of Christ. The Christian Church had the same view until the Fourth Century, when the interpretation was changed to "Sons of Seth" for two reasons.

The angel interpretation of Genesis 6 was increasingly viewed as an embarrassment when attacked by critics. The worship of angels had begun within the Church also. Celibacy had also become an institution of the Church. The "angel" view of Genesis 6 was feared as impacting these views. Celsus and Julian the Apostate used the traditional "angel" belief to attack Christianity. Julius Africanus resorted to the Sethite interpretation as a more comfortable ground. Augustine and Cyril of Alexandria embraced the Sethite theory, thus it prevailed into the Middle Ages.

In the eighteenth century the "Angelic interpretation" was revived and is now largely held by majority of the Brethren and Baptist Bible expositors.

The objection to the "Angelic Interpretation" is based on the words of Jesus as to the Marriage relation of the redeemed in Heaven, when He said "They neither marry nor are given in marriage, but are as the angels of God in Heaven", Mat.22:30; Mark 12:25; Luke 20: 35-36. The legitimate conclusion from this statement is that the Angels do not marry, but it does not therefore follow that they are sexless". It says they do not marry in Heaven, not that they don't have the power of procreation, but that it is not the nature of "Holy Angels" to seek such a relationship. What these passages teach us is that angels do not multiply by procreation. Angels as far as we know were created "en masse," and as they are immortal and never die, there is no necessity for marriage among them.

Marriage is a human institution to prevent the extinction of the race by death. If the bodies of the dead are to be resurrected, as the scriptures teach, the inference is that those bodies will be male and female. To teach otherwise is to declare that such a relationship as husband and wife and sister and brother will be unknown in Heaven.

Another fact worthy of note is that the angels are always spoken of in the masculine gender. If this is true, the reason why they do not marry in Heaven is because there are no female angels to marry.

Let me quote Clarence Larkin.

"Angels and human beings are members of the great family of God and this kinship between them implies a relationship that under certain conditions might result in a fruitful marriage union. Angels are spirit beings clothed in celestial bodies. These bodies are not ethereal in the sense that they are mere 'ether' for they have a materialistic form and can fly Daniel 9:21; Rev. 14: 6-7) and assume the form of a man and could eat of Abraham's calf (Gen.18:1-8) and of Lot's unleavened bread (Gen.19:1-3). Man is also a 'Spirit Being' clothed in a material body of flesh and here after, as a redeemed man, is to have a spirit body like unto the angels. "As we have borne the image of the earthly, we shall also bear the image of the Heavenly" (1 Cor.15:49).

Let me quote Merrill F. Unger from (Biblical Demonology Page 48).

"If the sons of God are simply pious Sethites who mixed with the Cainites, the prominent question is left unexplained as to why their progeny should have been "giants", mighty heroes who were of old "men of renown". The Reviser's obvious dissatisfaction with the Authorized Version's rendering of Nephilim by "giants", and the mere transliteration of the term by "Nephilim" obviously leaves the difficulty unanswered. The Septuagint translator's rendering of the expression by 'giant' seems clearly an indication that they thought of the Nephilim in this passage and its only other occurrence in Numbers 13:13 as the offspring of the sons of God (angels) and the daughters of men (mortal women); for the basic idea of the Greek term is not monstrous size, which is a secondary and developed meaning, but gegenes "earth born", and employed of the Titans who were partly of celestial and partly of terrestrial origin. These monstrous beings of mixed birth rebelled against their father Uranus (Heaven), and after a prolonged contest were defeated by Zeus and thrown into Tartarus.

There is no doubt that the authorized version misunderstood the Septuagint in translating Nephilim by "giants", for the form the Hebrew word denotes a plural verbal adjective or noun of passive signification, certainly from naphal "to fall", so that the connotation is Nephilim "the fallen ones", clearly meaning the unnatural offspring which were in the earth in the years before the flood "and also after that" (Numbers 13:33)

Another interesting event took place in Sodom. Two angels came there. This incident is connected with the account of the "Fallen Angels" in 2 Peter 2:4-6; and Jude 6-7. From the account in Genesis 19:1-11, it is clear that the men of Sodom sought to seize the two angels that came to Lot that they might commit the unnatural vice of Sodomy with them, as described in Romans 1:26-27, thus revealing that the angels had the generative organs of men.

When Moses sent the twelve spies into Canaan (Numbers 13:1-12) they reported on their return "And there we saw the 'giants' (Nephilim), the sons of Anak, which came of the Giants (Nephilim) and we were in our own sight as grasshoppers, and so we were in their sight". Where did these giants, called "Nephilim", the same as the 'Giants' of Genesis 6:1-4, come from? They did not come from the other side of the Flood, unless there was such blood in Noah and his sons and their wives, which we must believe that God prevented, for the purpose of the Flood was to destroy such contamination of the race. It looks like even after the Flood, there were some sporadic cases of angelic intercourse with the daughters of men and was not this the reason why God called for the extermination of the Canaanites, that He might blot out the descendants of the Nephilims.

Genesis 6:4 says "The Nephilim were on the earth in these days, **and also after that**". That is after the Flood. This author believes that close to the time of the tribulation, some activities similar to this may take place by some fallen angels. Modern day evils in the world point toward that direction. There are the fallen angels that still exist in heaven and seem to have all the freedom and abilities of the elect angels. These will remain in that environment until the middle of the Tribulation period when they make war with the angel Michael (Revelation 12.7-9).

The Original Rebellion

In Satan's primal rebellion he drew with him a great multitude of lesser celestial beings. (Mat. 25:41; Rev.: 12:4). These fallen angels are divided into two classes: (1) Those that are free and (2) Those that are bound. Those that are free are abroad in the heavenlies under their leader, Satan, who alone is given particular mention in the scriptures. He is called Beelzebub, Prince of the demons. (Mat. 12:24), "Satan and his angels" (Mat.25:41) and "the dragon and his angels (Rev.12:7). These free wicked spirits under Satan's kingdom and dominion who are his emissaries and subjects (Mat.12:26) and who are numerous as to make his power practically ubiquitous, seem to be identical with demons.

Satan's methods of activity and his highly organized empire of roving spirits in the heavenlies are set forth in (Ephesians 6: 11-12). His methods are suggested by the expression "wiles of the devil" while his organization is graduated as "principalities", "powers", "world rulers of this darkness", and spiritual host of wickedness in the heavenly places". The Serried spirits can be none other than his angels or demons with different stations of rank and responsibility who are the unseen though real agents behind the visible human actors in the great world drama enacted in his wicked world system.

It is thus in the heavenlies that Satan has his abode and base of operation. But his base is not in the third heaven or heaven of heavens (2 Cor.12:2), where the ascended Christ is seated" far above all rule, and authority, and power and dominion" (Eph. 1:21). From it Satan and his demons are barred. From the glorious place Satan was cast out, evidently not at the time of his primeval fall, but consequent upon Christ's finished redemptive work and glorious ascension (Job 1:6). Satan and his demons are confined to the first and second heavens and as the "prince of the power of the air" (Eph.2:2). Satan and his demons will be cast down to the earth (Rev.12:7-12) for their tragic role in the closing days of this age. (Rev.19:20; 20:2-3)

But the fallen angels that are bound must not be confused with the fallen angels that are free. The fallen angels that are bound are those described by Peter and Jude, who are guilty of such enormous wickedness as to no longer be allowed them to roam the heavenlies with their leader Satan, and the other evil angels. This angel's incarceration cannot be connected with the original rebellion of Satan and the fall of angels is obvious.

Today most of the Brethren and Baptist expositors support the fallen angel theory. Martin Luther espoused the angel theory. The major supporters of the fallen angel theory that connect with Genesis chapter 6 are John MacArthur, William MacDonald, John Philips, Harry Ironside, Arnold C. Gaebelein, F. F Bruce, Clarence Larkin, Merrill F. Unger, Walter Scott, G.H. Pember William Kelly, John Nelson Darby, F.W. Grant, Delitzsch, and J.B. Mayor, Alfred Plummer, C. H. McIntosh, Chuck *Missler,* and many others. Most Baptist expositors considered John Darby, William Kelly and F.W Grant as the greatest Bible teachers after Apostle Paul.

F.W Grant says in his numerical Bible "These angels who are bound must be kept distinct from the more general class of Satan and his angels". Dr. Arnold Gaebelein "They are being described in

Genesis 6:1-4 as the "sons of God" (a term which in the Old Testament means angels) who came down and mingled with the daughters of men and by their disobedience became the means of corrupting the race in such a manner that the judgment of God had to get in the deluge. John Nelson Darby "Notes and comments", Vol.1 Page 23 "Jude and Peter seem to make the B'ney ha – Elohim (sons of God) the angels: but God effaced all this in the Deluge and so may we; but the Titans and mighty men, heroes, find the origin of their traditions here".

Notes by Charles Ryrie on 2 Peter 2:4: Ryrie Study Bible - Angels when they sinned. These are the fallen angels who sinned grievously by cohabiting with women, as described in Genesis 6:1-4 (see Jude 6) Jude 6 "Angels who did not keep their positions of authority. A reference to that group of fallen angels whom Satan persuaded to cohabit with women (Genesis 6:1-4) and who were confined immediately because of the gross nature of that sin. The apocryphal book of Enoch describes their dramatic end".

According to F.F. Bruce, "My own judgment is that the "sons of God" in Genesis 6 are angels being just as they are in Job – that they are in fact, the angels of Jude 6, who "did not keep their own position but left their proper dwelling."

The MacArthur Study Bible – Study notes on 2 Peter 2:4

These angels according to Jude 6 "did not keep their proper domain" i.e. they entered men who promiscuously cohabited with women. Apparently this is a reference to the fallen angels of Genesis 6 (sons of God).

1) Before the flood (v .5; Gen. 6:1-3) who left their normal state and lusted after women and,

2) Before the destruction of Sodom and Gomorrah (v. 6 Gen.19) were cast into hell. Peter borrows a word from Greek mythology for hell "Tartarus" The Greeks taught that Tartarus was a place lower than Hades reserved for the wicked or human beings, gods and demons. The Jews eventually came to use the term to describe the place where fallen angels were sent. It defined for them the lowest hell, the deepest pit, the most terrible place of torture and eternal suffering. Jesus in spirit entered that place when his body was in the grave, and proclaimed triumph over the demons during the time between His death and resurrection (1 Peter 3:18-19) Chains of darkness. The demons feared going there and begged Jesus during His life on earth not to send them there. (Mat. 8:29; Luke 8: 31) Not all demons are bound. Many roam the heavens and earth (Rev. 12:7-9). Some are temporarily bound. These were, permanently bound in darkness because of their sin described in Genesis 6.

The following section is quoted from the book "The Omega Conspiracy by I.D.E. Thomas.

I don't have a doctrinal opinion on this subject. I am here just providing another opinion.

"NEPHILIM -- NO RESURRECTION
The Book of Isaiah says that the Nephilim and their descendants will not participate in a resurrection as is the portion of ordinary mortals. Isaiah 26:14 reads: "They are dead, they shall not live; they are deceased, they shall not rise." The original Hebrew word translated "deceased" here is the word "Rephaim." It would have saved a lot of misinterpretation if the translators had left the word as it was

in the original. The verse actually reads: "Dead, they shall not live; Rephaim, they shall not rise." The Rephaim are generally understood to be one of the branches of the Nephilim, and God's Word makes it clear that they are to partake in no resurrection. But with humans it is different: all humans will be resurrected either to life or to damnation (John 5:28-29). (Note: The Nephilim had human mothers, but no human fathers, so they were not considered members of Adam's race. Only the members of Adam's race are offered redemption--the angels are not. Thus when they died the Nephilim spirits could have become disembodied and free to roam, seeking other bodies of men or animals to possess and dwell in. It has been suggested that this group of fallen spirits is responsible for the phenomenon of demon possession in the world today--ed.)

We have already seen that the Greek Version of the Old Testament (The Septuagint) translated "Nephilim" as "gegenes;" we shall now inquire how it translates "sons of God." In some of the manuscripts it is left as "sons of God," but in the others-- including the Alexandrian text--it is rendered by the word "angelos." This text was in existence in the time of Christ, but there is no indication that He ever corrected or queried it. Can we not assume from His silence that He agreed with the translation!

These beasts are not now nor ever will be saved. Salvation is not for them. Yes, Christ died for all, but only his children are allowed to except eternal life. Many are called and few are chosen. The death of Christ calls us for salvation, but to these beasts, are called out for judgement. We are called for eternal life while they are called to damnation. We are called to repentance while they are called to rebellion. They are the Nephilim, the children of the damned that have mingled with the seed of men. As at the time of the flood, the modern Nephilim are beasts that are excluded from salvation. So how can we know this from scripture?

In 1 Cor 15:31-32, Paul's says that he fought with beasts, then states that the beasts desire to eat and drink knowing that their time will pass. "I protest by your rejoicing which I have in Christ Jesus our Lord, I die daily. If after the manner of men, I have fought with beasts at Ephesus, what advantages it me, if the dead rise not? Let us eat and drink; for tomorrow we die." Notice how Paul adds the eating and drinking here. It reminds me of the words found in Isa 26:14 where it says "They are dead, they shall not live; they are deceased, they shall not rise: therefore, hast thou visited and destroyed them, and made all their memory to perish."

The word "deceased" is the word Rapha, which some scholars believe is a reference to the Nephilim. Rephaim is word related to Rephaim who were primitive giants who lived in Canaan, Edom, Moab, and Ammon. They were also known as Emims (Deut. 2:11), and Zamzummims (Deut. 2:20). feet). So if you render Isaiah 26:14 with the proper translation, it should read, "They are dead, they shall not live; they are the Nephilim, they shall not rise" Now this begs the question, rise to what? The answer is found in Ps. 88:10 where it says, "Wilt thou shew wonders to the dead? Shall the dead arise and praise thee? Selah." So Isaiah makes it very clear that the Nephilim will never rise to salvation. They are totally without hope. So it is very logical to assume that the religion of the Nephilim is to "eat, drink, and be merry, for tomorrow we die." Now let's look at this in context of scripture. What the Nephilim did was to drink blood, eat the flesh of man, and chose any wife they wanted for sex.

All humans are children of God and all are pre-destined for salvation. All the Nephilim hybrids are pre-destined for hell then the Lake of Fire
.The fact that the Rephaim have no resurrection (Isaiah 26:14) proves the reality of giants and that they were not ordinary men. All ordinary men are to be resurrected (John 5:28-29); therefore, giants must be a different class from pure Adamites.

The Rephaim were the other lords of Isaiah 26:13; they shall not rise because God visited and destroyed them (Isaiah 26:14). This plainly teaches that the giants or Rephaim have no resurrection like the dead of Israel referred to in Isaiah 26:19. They were the offspring of fallen angels, not ordinary men who do have a resurrection. See Giants and the Sons of God.

1. Rephaim under waters (see The Dead Under the Waters). 2.Shall the Rephaim arise and praise You? (Psalm 88:10-11) 3. Her paths unto the Rephaim (Proverbs 2:1- 4. The Rephaim are there (Proverbs 9:1-. 5.Congregation to the Rephaim

(Proverbs 21:16) 6. It stirred up the Rephaim for you (Isaiah 14:9). 7.They are Rephaim (Isaiah 26:14). 8.The earth shall cast out the Rephaim (Isaiah 26:19, notes).

We have already seen that the Greek Version of the Old Testament (The Septuagint) translated "Nephilim" as "gegenes;" we shall now inquire how it translates "sons of God." In some of the manuscripts it is left as "sons of God," but in the others-- including the Alexandrian text--it is rendered by the word "angelos." This text was in existence in the time of Christ, but there is no indication that He ever corrected or queried it. Can we not assume from His silence that He agreed with the translation!

we find no hope for these Nephilim, since they were not of Adamic stock. We call your attention to the fact that our Lord Jesus, not being of Adamic stock, was not a sharer in its condemnation and curse, and hence, similarly, would not have been a sharer in its blessings. We are to remember that the way in which he profits our race is not by being one of us in sin and imperfection, but because he was not one of us he was able to give his separate and uncontaminated existence as our ransom-price. The blessing upon Adam and his family, coming, as it will, through Jesus, as its purchaser, who gave himself instead of Adam, thus redeemed him and all who were in him at the time of his transgression and condemnation. This clear-cut distinction most positively shows us that the fallen angels and their progeny were in no sense of the word Adamic stock, and, hence, were in no sense of the word covered by the ransom." (Z.W.T. March 15,

1904).

Fallen angels are not eligible for redemption like fallen humans are. The reason is that because of the status of angels from which they chose to rebel. It was in the presence of God, in their inherited body and from their inheritance that some angels chose to rebel from and became fallen angels. There is not another inheritance or body for the fallen angels; nor can they remain forever in the visible presence of God because of their sin".

The Purpose of Satan to Destroy the Promised Seed

The passage continues "and the dragon stood before the woman which was ready to be delivered, for to devour her child as soon as it was born." In the beginning, Satan was present, listening when God said, "And the seed of the woman shall crush thy head." From that faraway hour in the unknown ages of the past in the Garden of Eden, Satan has been seeking to destroy the Promised seed. He moved Cain to slay Abel. He sewed wickedness in the earth so that the antediluvians were destroyed in the terrible flood. At last when the child was born and the dragon stood before the woman who was ready to be delivered for to devour her child. Satan moved Herod to slay all of the babes in Bethlehem, hoping to destroy the life of the infant, the Promised Child.

Rev.12: 10-12 We can note also the effect of the operation which was twofold. There was a double proclamation, one having to do with heaven and the other having to do with the earth. The great proclamation in heaven has to do with the Savior, with Satan, and with the saints. For countless ages, Satan has had access to the presence of God. We read of his accusations in connection with Job and in connection with

Joshua the high priest. He came even with a smirk and a sneer to tell the spiteful tales about the faults and failings of the people of God. Satan has enjoyed himself to the full, relishing the tales he has been able to tell. But over and over again he has been defeated by the high priestly work of our advocate. Now the door is shut. Satan's way into the presence of God is bolted and barred forever.

The great proclamation in heaven is followed by a grim proclamation on earth. The voice continues. "Woe to the inhabitants of the earth and of the sea..." Soon after this woe is pronounced, the woe trumpets begin. Satan is now like a caged lion, enraged beyond words by the limitations now placed upon his freedom.

The Woe (Rev. 12:13-17)

Now Satan's fury is directed against Israel and the saints of God. He cannot touch the man-child, so he attacks the woman who brought Him in to the world. How symmetrical is the unfolding of divine truth? The Bible begins with the story of the woman, the serpent, and the seed; and here it comes full circle and traces that Edenic struggle to its final end.

Three factors come into view in connection with the woe. First, there is the time factor. John says, "And when the dragon saw that he was cast unto the earth..." Satan has always detested Israel. Now his animosity and antagonism was epitomized beyond description. The devil himself will personally supervise the last blood bath of anti-Semitic persecution.

The second factor is the Tribulation factor. The Lord Jesus spoke of this flight of Israel in His Olivet discourse (Matt. 24:15-25).

Israel's plight will be desperate, but even so, God will raise up among the Gentiles those who will render help. They will shield and shelter the Jews at great personal risk and will be numbered among the sheep at the judgment of the living nations when the Lord returns.

(Matt. 25:31-46). But Israel's chief hiding place will be in what is called here "the wilderness." The greatest flight will be from Jerusalem and the land of Israel, the focal point of the Beast's hatred, and God will repeat His former miracles, and furnish for His beloved refugees, a table in the wilderness.

What a time of terror lays ahead for Israel. The world has seen dress rehearsals for the coming onslaught already – the knock on the door at dead of night; the dreaded secret police; the swift ride through the darkened streets to the sidings where the boxcars wait; the dreadful ordeal of days a nights without food, drink, or sanitation, with men and women and children herded like cattle in the dark, and with little babies flung on top of the struggling heap of humanity like so many sacks of four; the barbed wire, the concentration camps; the callous treatment and cruel tortures; and then the gas ovens and the firing squads. It has been rehearsed already in preparation for the full stage production of terror. No wonder God himself intervenes to provide a place of hiding for those who exercise saving faith in His word and flee.

Last of all our attention is drawn to the triumph factor. Satan cannot win. Just as the blood of the martyrs has proved to be the seed of the Church, so it will be during the

Tribulation. Persecution will drive many Jewish people into the arms of the Lord Jesus Christ. The godly Jews will not retreat. They will only scatter far and wide, preaching the gospel of the kingdom. What can Satan do with the likes of these? Lock them up in prison, and they convert their jailors; torture them, and they become partakers of Christ's sufferings and heirs to a great reward.

REVELATION CHAPTER 13

The Antichrist

"The streets of our country are in turmoil; the universities are filled with students rebelling and rioting; Communists are seeking to destroy our country, and the Republic is in danger – yes, danger from within and without. We need law and order! Without law and order our nation cannot survive!"

Who do you think uttered these words? An irate congressman, a senator, or a mayor? It was none of these. The words were spoken in 1932 by Adolf Hitler. Dictators rarely take over nations by brute force. Almost always political or economic problems pave the way for tyranny. Even the notorious Roman Empire did not exercise dictatorial authority in its early years. The nations it conquered were customarily ruled by local dignitaries. Only the later Caesars played God over the people. How did the Roman Empire get started? What led to the ultimate outrage of Caesar worship?

How Caesars Became "gods"

When the Roman Empire first started taking over countries, the conquered people felt indebted to Rome for the law and order which it provided. The smaller countries in particular were grateful for the newfound stability which replaced their once-shaky political structures. In a number of cases, obnoxious little tyrants were replaced by temperate Roman rulers – so the people were happy.

In Asia Minor especially, the people became so enthusiastic about the Roman Empire that they came to regard it as an object of veneration. As historian Arnold Toynbee wisely pointed out, it's hard to worship an impersonal system! Eventually, therefore, the Roman subjects conceived the idea of emperor-worship. The first actual case of emperor-worship on record took place in Pergamum in 29 B.C. Here the local citizens erected the first known statue of a Roman Caesar.

But full-blown Caesar-worship took a number of years to develop. The first Caesars to be worshipped were actually somewhat embarrassed by all the public attention. Later Caesars, however, came to realize the important advantage of accepting public veneration. The first Roman Empire extended into the entire known world of the time, embracing dozens of cultures, languages, and religions. What the Roman senate was looking for was some strong unifying principle – something that would bind the entire empire together. The mandating of Caesar worship seemed to be the answer.

So late in the first century A.D. the worshipping of Caesar became an official government requirement. At first the edict wasn't taken very seriously, but later, under Emperor Domitian, every Roman subject was expected to comply with the order. Once a year, each person had to appear before an official "priest" and swear allegiance to Caesar. The oath would be witnessed by a signed certificate and would also often be accompanied by an animal sacrifice.

Caesar-Worship Got out of Hand

The Caesar worship that was once kind of an inside joke among the government leaders, was now turning into a Frankenstein monster. Nero came to believe that he actually was God in the flesh. Other Caesars had self-delusions almost as strong as Nero's. The whole episode turned out to be a nightmare for the Christians and the Jews. The Romans added another 'god' to their list of deities. But for the Christians, the picture was entirely different. Christians refused to swear allegiance to Caesar, and instead quoted a little chant: "Jesus Christ is the Lord, and none other."

In no time at all, the believers were labeled as traitors: feed them to the lions. And so the coliseum games began to feature half-time shows of lion feeding, with whole families of devoted believers as "one-time guest stars."

The Lesson Learned from the Caesars

Now remember how all this got started: Nations in political or economic turmoil succumbed to the seemingly benevolent tentacles of Rome. For a while there was unprecedented peace, justice, and order.

Nazi Germany replayed the drama of dictatorship in the 30's and 40's. In 1930, Germany was in desperate financial straits. Inflation was so severe that thousands of people were virtually starving. The Communists stirred up riots in the streets and created pandemonium in the universities. No one seemed able to create order out of the confusion. Germany was on the verge of collapse. Then Adolf Hitler appeared. With impassioned fury, he proclaimed the glory of the nation of destiny.

He wept as he rehearsed the past glories of the nation, and shouted as he promised its glories to come. Once again Germany would rule the world! The Roman Empire would live again, and Hitler would be its king. Eighty percent of the evangelicals voted for Hitler. Mankind never learns.

What a tragic way to relearn world history. The sad truth is, as Hegel said, "History teaches us that man learns nothing from history." Adolf Hitler was but a "choir boy" when compared with the dictator that will take over the world during the Tribulation.

He is called by various names throughout the Bible. King of Babylon, Isaiah 14:4; Little Horn, Daniel 7:8, 8:9; Man of Sin, Son of Perdition, 2 Thess. 2:3; Antichrist, 1 John 2:18; Beast, Rev. 13:1.

He will be a supreme humanist, believing passionately that man can solve his own dilemmas. He will not accept the Bible's evaluation that man is on the verge of chaos because of sin. In fact, he'll no doubt react violently to groups and individuals who analyze man's problem as sin. Modern day American liberals are also violently reacting to their opponents. Modern day liberals are neo-Nazi and neo fascists. He will feel that he is doing a good thing by bringing repressive measures against believers, whom he will consider "Non- progressives." This antichrist will be against every solution the Bible presents for the world's problems, and because he will be so persuasive, he will turn the whole world against Christ and the believers.

The antichrist is called a "beast" because that's what he is in the sight of God – a ruthless, unfeeling dictator.

Now why does the Beast emerge from the sea? Hone explains the figure in Revelation 17:15. "The waters which you saw are peoples and multitudes and nations and tongues." In Biblical usage the ocean pictures the restless strivings of the nations of the world. As Isaiah put it, "The wicked are like the troubled sea when it cannot rest, whose waters cast up mire and dirt" (Isaiah 57:20). It is from this chaos of the nations that the Antichrist will rise.

Personal Attractiveness of the Ultimate Antichrist

The Antichrist, this last world-ruler is superlatively fascinating, intriguing and bewitching in his personal power and prowess. When the Lord, here in the Revelation, describes Satan as a dragon, fiery red, with seven heads and ten horns and seven diadems upon his head, the language is symbolical of Satan's character. Actually Satan is like an angel of light, Lucifer, the morning star, the summation of God's glorious creation.

What do the ten horns with crowns represent? In Biblical symbology, horns almost always represent political power. In this case the Beast's ten horns picture these nations that will form a confederacy which the beast will rule during the tribulation. Daniel elaborates on this in Daniel 7 and 8.

When you see the Antichrist, you will not see a creature like a panther, like a leopard, his feet like a bear, with a mouth like a lion. When he appears, you will see the most fascinating, the most scintillating, the most magnetic mortal man that has ever walked across the stage of human history. In all time and tide and history, there will never have appeared a human being with the glory, the personality, the intriguing bewitching, and ingratiating manner of this man; a veritable god of wisdom, insight, accomplishment and achievement.

Satan gave him power and his throne and his authority. This man accepts the gift that our Lord Jesus spurred when Satan offered him all of the glories of the kingdom of this world; and the whole earth acclaims the man as the very incarnation of glory and wisdom and might and power and honor.

This final Antichrist will be received in gladness, and the kings of the earth will peaceable yield their power to him, "for there is none like him." John says he stood upon the sand of a raging sea. The raging sea, pictured also in Daniel, is a symbol of the violent, chaotic masses of humanity in a day of crisis and revolution. Out of these horrible, chaotic revolutions, arise these tyrannical leaders. Out of the chaos of the blood and mass of the French revolution, Napoleon was born. Out of the vast chaotic revolution of the labor movement, Lenin was born. Out of the chaos and mass of revolution, Hitler was born. Always out of the raging turmoil of social chaos, these antichrists come.

It is also with this one. In a day of revolution, in a day of chaos, in a day of storm and fury, comes this great and final ruler. That is the meaning of the opening of the first seal in Revelation 6. In keeping with the opening of the first seal, chapter 17 of Revelation says that those ten kings willingly, with one mind, gave to him their power, their strength and their authority. When the first seal is opened, this final Antichrist appears. He comes riding a white horse with a bow and no arrow. He comes conquering and to conquer, but he is a bloodless conqueror. There is no war, there is no battle, and there is no resistance. In the midst of their chaos and despair, these kings of the earth, the rulers of the earth, gladly yield to him the authority and dominion of the governments of the entire world.

In another place (Rev. 17:8) John beholds the beast arise out of the abyss. When John sees him rise out of a raging sea, he is describing his political origin. He arises out of social turmoil and trouble. When John sees him arise out of the abyss, he is describing his actual origin. The monster is diabolical, a son of damnation and perdition. He is like a leopard; he is like a bear, he is like a lion; he is a terrible beast.

The Lord Jesus said, "I have come in my Father's name, and you do not receive me; if another comes in his own name, him you will receive." (John 5:43). He was referring to the coming of Satan's messiah, (Daniel 7:4-6) where the lion, the bear, and the leopard have already been seen in an apocalyptic vision. The lion symbolized the empire of Babylon, the bear stood for the Mede-Persian Empire, and the leopard signified Greece. This beast will have the characteristics of all three empires. He is the heir of the ages, the last and worst of all Caesars. He will be a combination of Hitler, Stalin, Mao Te sung, Mussolini, Polpot, Saddam Hussein and Ayatollah Khomeini, Genghis Khan. He is the last Gentile claimant to the throne of the world, heir and successor of Nebuchadnezzar, to whom the first Gentile throne was given. The body of a leopard is covered with spots. "Can the Ethiopian change his skin or the leopard his spots?" cried the prophet in describing the ingrained, immutable character of Judah's sins (Jer. 13:23). The beast has the body of a leopard, full of spots. This is a picturesque way of describing how ferocious, wild, harmful, and immutable is his nature. Now look at the Lord Jesus. He is no leopard. He is the lamb "without blemish and without spot" (1 Peter 1:19). Satan has his spotted leopard; God has is spotless Lamb.

The beast, however, is not only a real person, he is a representative person. Totalitarian status has frequently arisen in which the state and the head of the state have been closely identified. The Beast, as head of a state and he is the state. The Beast of Revelation 13 is both an emperor and an empire.

Machiavelli published his book *The Prince* in 1513. Mussolini acknowledged his debt to *The Prince*. "The State is God," he said. Hitler is reported to have kept a copy of *The Prince*. Another philosopher whose writings have played a major part in the development of the modern totalitarian state is Hegel. Nearly every principle guiding Soviet Russia was proposed by this German philosopher. Hegel taught that the state is, in its final expression, the complete embodiment of social and ethical ideals, the nearest approach to divinity. He believed the state to be final and absolute and the highest court of appeal. He taught that all the worth an individual possesses and all his spiritual reality, was only through the state.

All modern totalitarian governments, fascist Italy, Nazi Germany, Communist Russia and China, have been molded upon these ideas. In a complete dictatorship, the head of state is the state. This will be consummated in the Beast, who will be a truly representative person. He will not only head the revived Roman Empire; he will be the empire.

When God ordained that political system over the nations be taken away from Israel and given to the Gentiles, He said to Nebuchadnezzar, "You, O king, are a king of kings. For the God of heaven has given you a kingdom, power, strength, and glory; and wherever the children of men dwell, or the beasts of the field and the birds of the heaven, He has given them into your hand, and has made you ruler over them all – you are this head of gold." (Daniel 2:37-38). Nebuchadnezzar, the first Gentile world ruler, possessed only a tithe of his inheritance. Babylon was the smallest of all the world empires. But in principle, world dominion was given to him. What Nebuchadnezzar did not take, the Beast, the last world ruler, will take. Ultimately his authority will be universal.

There have been daring blasphemers on earth before, but none like the Beast. He will have a vocabulary for invective and vituperation never equaled on earth. His next purpose is to destroy the saints of God. He cannot harm the glorified saints in heaven, but he can harm the believers on earth, at least those who were not specially sealed against him.

The False Prophet

(Revelation 13:11-18)

The first part of the chapter deals with the coming of Satan's false prince; the remainder of the chapter has to do with a second mysterious person stirred up by Satan to act as the propaganda chief for the Beast.

This person is called the false prophet. The great function of the second beast is to glorify the first beast. Thus, Satan, the Beast, and the false prophet form a satanic trinity.

The first beast has ten horns; the second one has two horns. Territory is symbolized by the ten horns of the first beast (Rev. 17:12); testimony is symbolized by the two horns of the second beast and, of course, it is a false testimony. The second beast looks like a lamb, and is thus most deceptive in appearance. Nobody is afraid of a lamb. A lamb is gentle, harmless, innocent, and, in scripture, ceremonially clean. When the false prophet appears, he will, at first, seem to be all these things. But that is part of Satan's plan.

If the second beast has the horns of a lamb, he speaks like a dragon. The very voice of Satan is heard when he speaks. The idiom of Satan's language is the lie; he is the father of lies (John 8:44). The time has come when men must believe the lie, what Paul calls the "strong delusion" (2 Thes. 2:11)?

German Nazi party member Joseph Goebbels became Adolf Hitler's propaganda minister in 1933, which gave him power over all German radio, press, cinema and theater. He blamed Jews for all the calamities of Germany and convinced the population to exterminate Jews.

Attracted by the dynamic of the beast, and assured by the seeming docility of the false prophet, men will take at its face value the monstrous lie they are now told. The false prophet becomes the chief executive officer of the new regime under the Beast. He is the head vicar of the new false religion.

The role of the false prophet will be to make the new religion appealing and palatable to men. No doubt it will combine all the features of the religious systems of men, will appeal to man's total personality, and will take full advantage of his carnal appetite. The dynamic appeal of the false prophet will lie in his skill in combining political expediency with religious passion, self-interest with the benevolent philanthropy, lofty sentiment with blatant sophistry, moral platitude with unbridled self-indulgence. His arguments will be subtle, convincing, and appealing. His oratory will be hypnotic, for he will be able to move the masses to tears or whip them into a frenzy. He will control the communication media of the world and will skillfully organize mass publicity to promote his ends. He will manage the truth with guile beyond words, bending it, twisting, and distorting it. He will mold world thought and shape human opinion like a potter's clay. His deadly appeal will lie in the fact that what he says will sound so right, so sensible, so exactly what unregenerate men have always wanted to hear.

The false prophet has a deadly approach. He will do great miracles. The beast, having turned against the Jews, will march his troops into the temple, set up his image in the holy place, and command that it be worshipped. This is the "abomination of desolation" referred to by the Lord Jesus in His great prophetic discourse. (Matt.24:22; Dan. 12:1) To worship this image will be the crowning act of blasphemy for mankind. For this sin there will be no forgiveness, either in this life or the next. Yet to refuse to worship will be to incur the wrath of the Beast and to court imminent death. The bringing to life of the image is an unexplained miracle of Satan.

The Amazing Number 666

666 is a riddle wrapped in a mystery inside an enigma. John now writes a verse, closing chapter 13, which in itself is enigmatical. He says, "Here is wisdom." This number 666 is the most famous of all the apocalyptic figures in history and in literature. What does it mean? The righteous will understand what that means when the time comes. God's saints will understand what that refers to when the hour arrives. We do not know.

There is only one thing about it that we know and that is this the number six. Six is the number of a man, six – falling short of the perfect seven. Man was created on the sixth day. He is to work six of the seven days. The beast in his number represents the ultimate of all human ingenuity and competence.

The Counterfeit Church

There are several things that characterize the counterfeit Church. The first is that it says what the world wants to hear. It pleases the itching ears of the people. The false prophet believes what the world wants to believe. The religion of the false prophet and of the counterfeit church is one that looks upon scriptural doctrine as being outdated. He will declare that we have out-lived the usefulness of the old-time faith. It asserts that we have so progressed in this enlightened, scientific era that we need a new theology, a new enlightenment. The exponents of the new faith say that no man in his enlightened age can believe in the miracles of the Bible.

REVELATION CHAPTER 14

Revelation 12 delineates the malice of Satan and the rage of the evil one who is cast down onto the Earth. Revelation 13 describes the terrific and sickening horror of the beast.

This beautiful chapter 14 immediately follows the horror of those darkening days. It reminds us that, after the storm and rage of the tempest is over, then, in the quiet beauty of the calm, God over-arches the heavens with a rainbow of promise. In those terrible trying times the Lord says "For the elects' sake those days are going to be shortened."

144,000

We have met this company before, only last time they were on earth. This is the illustrious company of the 144,000 who are sealed from the twelve of Israel's tribes. (Revelation

7). These sealed ones have been preserved unharmed throughout the Great Tribulation, despite the rage of the dragon and the Beast.

In chapter 7 this company was seen in anticipation of the Great Tribulation, which then lay ahead. They are seen now in anticipation of the glorious triumph that lies ahead. There were 144,000 before the tribulation began; all are safe now in heaven. The heavenly Zion is evidently in view, because the Lord has not yet descended to earth. We are not told how or when these Jewish believers were caught up to heaven. But there they are, the first fruits of the tribulation harvest (14:5), standing now in the very location described by John in chapter 4 and 5; standing before God, before the living creatures, and before the 24 elders.

There are different groups in the same vision. Elders, the 144,000, and great throngs of Gentiles, who stand before God and the lamb clothed with white robes, out of every kindred and nation and people and tongue and tribe under the sun. they are all here together.

The 24 elders represent the resurrected, glorified saints of God in the Old Testament and the New Testament. The twelve patriarchs, the twelve apostles, stand before God. The same symbolism is in the beautiful city of Jerusalem: there are 12 gates, and each one of those gates represents one of the twelve patriarchs. The city has 12 foundations, and each one of those foundations, the Apocalypse says, represents the name of an apostle. The city represents the name of an apostle. The city represents the old and the new, all the saints of God, the old dispensation and the new dispensation. It includes the old era, those who were saved by looking to the cross. It includes the new dispensation, the new era, the age of grace in which we live, those who are saved by looking back to the cross. The elders represent all of the saved of God, 12 for the old and 12 for the new, 24 of them, in the presence of the Lord.

The great multitude coming out of every nation and language and tribe are those who have been won to Christ by these 144,000 sealed messengers of God. There never has been, nor will there ever be again, any revival meeting comparable to that which is coming to pass in those dark days when men will lay down their lives as martyrs with their confession of Christ. The blood of the martyrs is the seed of the Church. In those days of terrible and indescribable martyrdom, in those days of blood and sickening horror, the earth will witness its greatest revival. It will be led by these messengers of God sealed by the Holy Spirit of God, the 144,000. They are an elect, separate, unique group who pour out, in those dark and terrible days, their testimony to the saving grace of the blessed Lord Jesus.

The text presents these as the first fruits unto God and to the Lamb - "the first fruits." We must delineate her because the elders, after Christ, also represent the first fruits. But they are already in heaven. They have already been translated. The Lord has already come for them. They have been resurrected and glorified, and they sit in the presence of God on their thrones, gold crowned, victorious. Christ the first fruits, and afterwards, they that are Christ's at his coming. These are represented by the elders, yet the 144,000 also are called the first fruits unto God and to the Lamb. This 144,000 must be the first fruits unto God to this new era, of this new time, after the translation of the Church, after the rapture.

When our present history has run its course; when the church service is done, and the age of grace has passed;

when God has taken His people out of the earth and we are raptured and translated; then comes this final day described here in the Apocalypse.

The text says, "I looked and, lo a lamb stood on Mount Zion, and with him 144,000." In Isaiah 2, which describes the millennial earth with its capital in Mount Zion, Mount Zion was the capital city of David. It was the home of the royal palace and king. This passage in Revelation describes a scene in that heavenly, millennial day when the Lord Christ shall reign on Mount Zion; and to be with Him is the reward of the 144,000, when their task is finished and their assignment is done. In chapter 7, therefore, we see the 144,000 in their ministry upon earth. They are preaching the Gospel. They are calling men to repentance and faith; and men, by the myriads and millions are coming out of those heavy, dark days of the tribulation, having washed their robes and made them white in the blood of the lamb. There, 144,000 are seen in their work upon the earth. Here in chapter 14 of the Revelation, the 144,000 are seen on Mount Zion. Their task is finished, their work is done, and they are being rewarded by the Lord God for their faithfulness.

Let us notice the attributes of these unusual preachers of Christ, the 144,000.

In chapter 7 we saw 144,000 and in chapter 14 we see the same number. Of the 144,000 whom God sealed at the beginning of this terrible tribulation, when the roll is called in heaven and they are assembled on Mount Zion to receive the reward of their faithfulness, there are 144,000 in the presence of the Lord. Not a single one has been lost.

Another uniqueness is that they sing a new song no one else on earth can sing. That is, they have a separate ministry, they are unique. It is foolish for all of us to try to be alike in our separate ministries. God does not want us to be alike. God is a God of diversity. God likes differences. He does not make any two leaves alike. He does not make any two snowflakes alike. And so in His churches, God called one to be a preacher; He calls another, to be a singer, another to be a shepherd of the sheep, etc. For believers to be jealous or envious of one another and not to be happy where God has placed us, is unchristian.

Then, the text also says that the 144,000 are virgins, and that they follow the lamb. Marriage has nothing to do with it here. For example, 2 Corinthians 11:12, where Paul says to the church at Corinth, "for I espoused you to Christ, that I may present you as a chaste virgin to our Lord." Now, does that mean that all those believers in the church at Corinth were unmarried, that all the men were bachelors? Paul says to the Corinthians that the church is going to be presented to Christ as a chaste virgin. Likewise, when the text describes these men in Revelation as virgins, it refers to the fact that they separated themselves from the pollutions and the corruptions of the earth. They were virgins unto God. They had given themselves in pure devotion to the Lord, and they were without fault.

The Special Commission in Heaven

Rev. 14:6-13 Three angels now appear, commissioned with messages, announcements, and warnings for the earth.

The first angel-messenger is a preacher. He stands with his pulpit in the firmament of the sky, and his voice reaches to the extremities of the earth. He announces the great judgment of God and calls men to reverential fear and worship of the Lord. God raises up His witnesses when human lips are silent. At the triumphant entry of our Savior into Jerusalem, when the Pharisees and the scribes objected to the praise of the people, our Lord replied, "verily if these were silent the very stones would cry out." So in the days of the Apocalypse, when the witness of God's servants is drowned in blood, there is an angel messenger that stands in the sky, who thunders to the ends of the earth the almighty and eternal gospel message of the Son of God. Chains and blood, martyrdom and death, prisons and bars, cannot stop the testimony of the word of God. As the apostle Paul wrote from the Mamertine dungeon in his last letter to Timothy, his son in the ministry, "I may be in chains, I may be bound, but the word of God is not bound" (2 Tim.2:9). And I saw another angel fly in the midst of heaven, having the everlasting gospel to preach unto them that dwell on the earth."

The second angel-messenger announces the fall of Babylon. In one vast intervention of God, the whole vile system that debauches this earth is taken away in order that God may create a new world in which righteousness shall prevail.

The third angel-messenger announces the torment of those who give themselves to the worship of the beast and his image. This torment is to last forever.

The position of the saints who die in the Lord. (Rev.14:12-13). This is a decree by God the Father from heaven. The saints who die are blessed of the Lord. The words are written, of course, for those who were martyred and perished in that day of awful trial and tribulation. But the comfort and assurance, and the strength of it is for all God's saints in all generations.

God says death is an enemy. God calls death the king of terrors. Death is an interloper; it is an intruder. It was never planned in the purposive, elective, goodness and grace of God. It wastes, it destroys God's creation. The aspirations of a man, the dreams of his heart, the tender ties that bind to those whom he loves, are severed by the cruel and merciless hand of this pale horseman. But God in Christ has taken the sting out of death and has taken away the victory from the grave. "Blessed are the dead which die in the Lord." The Bible, without exception, confirms the confronting truth that upon death, immediately we are blessed; but in the moment of death, the child of God is blessed in being received into the presence of the Lord.

The Harvest of the Earth

Rev.14:14-20. In the Old Testament, the harvest and vintage time preceded the Feast of Tabernacles, that great annual feast of jubilation and joy.

It is the same here. The golden age is soon to come, the long-awaited millennial reign of Christ; but first the ripened harvest must be reaped, and the reddened vintage must be trod.

The first vision of a harvest (verses 14-16) uses terminology that would be applicable to the reaping of wheat. It is personally superintended by the "son of man," who, as predicted in a parable by Jesus, is careful to gather in all the wheat and keep it separate from the tares. The parable reads as follows: "The harvest is the end of the age; and the reapers are the angels. Therefore, just as the tares are gathered and burned in the fire, so shall it be at the end of the age. The Son of man will send forth His angels, and they will gather out of His kingdom things that cause stumbling, and those who practice lawlessness, and shall cast them into the furnace of fire; there shall be wailing and gnashing of teeth. Then the righteous will shine forth as the sun in the kingdom of their father." (Matthew 13:39-43). this parable explains the first vision. Jesus does not do the dividing Himself but instead carefully supervises the separation of wheat and tares so that not one believer (wheat) is judged with the tares (unbelievers). This separating work is done by angels, and happens just prior to the Lord's triumphant reappearance back to the earth at the end of the tribulation. The day of grace is ended at this point.

This same truth is repeated in another parable of the mysteries of the kingdom. (Matthew 13:47-50).

The Children of the Lord Likened unto Wheat

Wheat is a beautiful, magnificently meaningful representation and symbol of God's children. When it ripens, the full, rich heads are bowed to the earth. When the tares ripen, they standup erect, but when the wheat ripens, it bends its face to the ground. As God's children grow in grace, as they are made heavy with the knowledge, presence, and goodness of God, they bow lower toward the ground. A church member who is proud of himself, proud of his goodness, proud of his personal excellence, walking in his self-sufficiency and adequacy, is, in God's sight, a tare. But a Church member who is lowly and humble, in honor preferring others before himself, and whose life is given to intercession and to prayer on behalf of those who do not know God, belongs, you may be sure, in the garner of heaven. The more we grow in grace and in the knowledge of the Lord, the more our faces will bow to the earth, weighted down with the presence and the grace of God.

Another fact about wheat, the harvest of God, is that as the wheat ripens upward, it dies downward. As we grow God ward and heavenward, and as we draw near the end of our pilgrimage, more and more there will be the relaxing of our head upon this earth and this life, until finally when we near the gates of heaven, the things of this present earth fade away.

The Grapes of Wrath

Rev. 14:18-20 The second vision is one of carnage. This vision has reference to a very definite and horrible holocaust that is prophesied through all of the word of God. From the alter there came an angel who had power over fire. Notice where this fire-angel came from. In Revelation 6:9-11 we read, "When He opened the fifth seal, I saw under the altar the souls of those who had been slain for the word of God and for the testimony which they held. And they cried with a loud voice, saying, 'How long, O Lord, holy and true, until You judge and avenge our blood on those who dwell on the earth?'". That is the altar from which comes this angel of fire with wrathful indignation and burning fury because of the evil in this earth, the wickedness of men, the injustice of mankind. He comes to answer that cry of Abel's blood unto God; like the cry of the wickedness of Sodom and Gomorrah unto heaven; like the cry of that sinful Babylon described here, in Revelation, a cry that reached the very throne of God: the cry of judgment and of wrath and of indignation. This fire-angel comes in fury from that altar, and he says to the angel with the sharp sickle, "gather the clusters of the vine of the earth; for her grapes are fully ripe."

This vision describes the last day of God's permissive will for wickedness and rejection. The last hour of evil has finally come. "And the angel thrust in his sickle unto the earth, and gathered the vine of the earth." the vine of the earth is a reference used in contradistinction to the vine of heaven, which is our blessed Lord, with us the branches. "The vine of the earth" is the vine of rejection, of unbelief, of blasphemy and of non-repentance. For two hundred miles, (and four feet high) there was a river of blood in this final holocaust of the great day of the Almighty.

That is the first reference in the Apocalypse to the indescribably awesome, terrible and final battle of the great day of the Lord, called the battle of Armageddon. It is the judgment of God upon unbelieving and blasphemous men.

REVELATION CHAPTER 15

The Seven Last Plagues

Chapters 15 and 16 of the Revelation go together. They are part of the same vision, describing the seven last plagues, in what is called in the last part of chapter 8 of the Revelation "the last woe," the third of the three terrible woes. This section, chapters 15 and 16, is also the judgment of the last trumpet, the seventh trumpet that is sounded in the last part of chapter 11. In chapter eleven a temple of God was opened in heaven, and that temple appears now in chapters 15 and 16. In chapter 11 the elders announce that the great day of the judgment of Almighty God is come "and the nations are angry and the time is come that they who would destroy the world should be destroyed." That delineation is found in chapter 15 and 16. In chapter 11, with the sounding of the seventh trumpet, the kingdom of this world is become the kingdom of our Lord and of His Christ. The final preparation for the establishment of that kingdom is found in this vision of the seven last plagues.

Rev.15:1. "And I saw another sign in heaven, great and marvelous, the seven angels having the seven last plagues."

The emphasis is upon the word "last "or "eschatas." The word "eschatology," the doctrine of last things, comes from that word "eschatas." Having the seven last plagues; "for in them the wrath of God is complete." After the seals, were the trumpets; after the trumpets, are these bowls of wrath; and after the bowls of wrath, there is finished the judgment of God in the earth, and the kingdom has come.

The Song of Moses and of the Lamb

In chapter 4 of the Revelation, when God has taken His saints up into heaven, John saw before the great throne of the Almighty, a crystal sea, a sea of glass, calm and beautiful. Those elders enthroned by the side of that quiet, beautiful, crystal sea are we, God's sainted children of this day and age, or the New Testament believers. But when John sees this sea before the throne of God and these saints standing by its shore, he says this sea is a sea of glass, mingled with fire. The added words "mingled with fire" refer to the fact that these saints have come out of great trial and tribulation. "And they sing the song of Moses, the servant of God, and the song of the Lamb."

In Exodus 15, on the farther shore of the Red Sea, delivered from the enemies that oppressed them, the children of Israel sang the song of Moses. And on that final shore beyond the fiery sea, there shall gather in immortality, and glory, in heavenly salvation, God's tribulation saints. They are singing the songs of infinite and glorious redemption, the song of Moses and the song of the Lamb. The song of the Lamb is the song of the victory He won for us over sin, death and the grave, like the triumphant song that Moses sang over the destruction of the enemies of Jehovah. It is a strange coincidence that the first recorded song in the word of God is in chapter 15 of Exodus, the song of Moses, and that the last recorded song in the Bible is in chapter 15 of the Revelation, the song of Moses, the servant of God, and the song of the Lamb.

The vision further states that "to these were given the harps of God." There are three groups in glory to whom God gives the harps of heaven. In chapter 5 of the Revelation, those who were raptured and taken up to glory have harps from God. In chapter 14 of the Revelation, the 144,000 gathered to the Lamb on Mount Zion possess the harps of God. This third company is standing on the shores of the fiery sea, having the harps of God and singing the song of Moses and of the Lamb, a song of triumph and heavenly deliverance.

Rev. 15:5-8 From looking at the wonder of the victorious tribulation saints, John's attention is drawn to another breathtaking sight. The heavenly tabernacle, of which the earthly tabernacle and temple were patterned, was thrown open, and John was permitted to look into the Holy of Holies. This concept of a tabernacle in heaven has been a hard thing for many people to understand. Remember that God gave Moses specific instructions on how to build the tabernacle in the wilderness, and He told him it was to be made from the same pattern as the one in heaven.

Now and then in the Bible we are given glimpses of what has gone on in the tabernacle in heaven. The book of Hebrews in the New Testament draws many parallels between the function of the priests in the earthly tabernacle and Christ, our High Priest, in the heavenly tabernacle. It makes clear that the rituals and symbols of the earthly tabernacle worship were all designed to portray things that would have an ultimate fulfillment in heaven's temple.

Earthly Tabernacle

In order to better understand the scene which John is describing for us in Revelation 15, let's get a better picture of the earthly tabernacle and its function.

The tabernacle itself was a portable building made of cloth and skins and carried from place to place by the Jews during their forty years in the wilderness and their first few years in the Promised Land. Later they built their temple in Jerusalem, using the exact floor plan of the tabernacle. The main difference was the opulence of the materials used in the temple in Jerusalem.

There was only one gate in the fence that surrounded the tabernacle. Squarely in front of the gate, inside the fence, was the brazen altar of sacrifice. This showed man that there was only one way to God, and that it was through an innocent sacrifice, which would bear the guilt and death-penalty of the person making the sacrifice.

There was only one light inside the building; it was by this light that all the divine services of the priests were performed. This single light taught that only God could provide illumination for the understanding of divine truths and divine worship.

There was also the altar of incense, on which the priests were to continually burn incense. The incense was symbolic of the people's prayers. The fragment aroma drifting into the rear third of the tabernacle, called the Holy of Holies, was a picture of our prayers continually coming into the presence of God.

Day of Atonement

One of the greatest witnesses to man was the Day of Atonement. Once a year, the high priest would select a spotless lamb and offer it on the altar for the sins of the people. He would then take some of its blood and go into the tabernacle.

Before entering the Holy of Holies the high priest would take a censer of incense and thrust it through the heavy veil that separated it from the Holy place, which was the main room of the tabernacle. This symbolized his preparing the way into the holy presence of God by the people's prayers.

Then he would go into the Holy of Holies. In front of Him he would see the ark of the covenant, a small gold-overlaid wooden chest with angelic figures of gold standing upon its lid, facing each other and looking down at the box.

Between the two cherubim there was a radiant, dazzling multicolored light called the Shekinah glory. This was the manifestation of God's presence on earth. No other spot in the world could boast of this special presence of God; only the high priest enjoyed this privilege, and only in the Holy of Holies of their tabernacle.

Atop the lid of the ark and beneath the blazing glory of light was a golden throne called the mercy seat. It bore this name because it was here that the high priest obtained mercy for the people each year as he sprinkled the blood of a sacrifice on it.

The Ark Condemns

What was really significant about this golden box was that under the throne inside the ark, were three unusual objects which God instructed the people to put there. First were the second tablets of stone on which the Ten Commandments were rewritten. (Remember that Moses angrily broke the original tablets when he came down from Sinai and found the people steeped in gross sin.) These second tablets were put into the ark as a witness to man's rejection of God's perfect law.

Second, there was a pot of manna in the ark. This was placed there after the people complained about this heavenly food that God had provided in the wilderness. They were tired of manna for breakfast, lunch, and dinner.

God had them place a pot of manna in the ark to show man's rejection of God's provisions for their daily needs.

Thirdly, there was Aaron's staff, which had miraculously sprouted leaves. This had occurred when a rebel group tried to take over the leadership of the nation from Moses and Aaron. God told the two groups of leaders to stand before the tabernacle and hold out wooden staffs or rods – the symbols of their leadership. God proclaimed that whoever's rod sprouted leaves was the one He had chosen to be the leader. The rod of Aaron sprouted. God then instructed the people to put this rod into the ark as a witness of man's rejection of God's chosen leadership.

Utter Rejection of God

These three articles taken together were a symbol of man's utter rejection of God. So these symbols were placed in the ark as a continual witness to the fact that man was sinful and rightfully deserving of God's judgment.

Once a year the high priest would sprinkle blood seven times on the Mercy Seat. This blood of an innocent substitute symbolically covered the symbols of man's sin from the sight of God. As God looked at this blood His justice would be satisfied, for the penalty of man's sin, which was death, had been paid. He could then change His throne from one of judgment to one of mercy, since the blood of the innocent sacrificial substitute was the loving provision which He, Himself had ordained to provide a way of escape for sinful men.

The name given to the lid of the ark was "The Mercy Seat" because this is where God's mercy was displayed toward man. All who came by faith in the atonement (sin covering) provided by God were forgiven and accepted by God. All of this was intended to prefigure Jesus Christ, the "Lamb of God," whose blood would not merely cover but actually take away the sin of the world, thereby turning the throne of God in heaven's tabernacle to one of mercy for all who come by faith in Jesus.

Back to the Heavenly Tabernacle

This is now a different tabernacle from the earthly tabernacle. The Heavenly tabernacle has become a place from which the seven final plagues were sent forth. No longer was it a place where men were reconciled to God. The throne of mercy had now become a throne of judgment against those who rejected God's Lamb.

REVELATION CHAPTER 16

In chapter 15 we saw God's final decision near the end of the Tribulation to close the gates of heaven to any further entrants. A world ruined by man and a world ruled by Satan has been described. Now the time has come for the world to be rescued by God. Down into the arena of human affairs He comes, shortening the days and making a swift, sudden end of the Beast and his hideous strength. The vials, and shallow bowls used in the temple worship, are filled with wrath and are swiftly poured out. Notice that these golden censers or vials are given to the angels of judgment by one of the cherubim. Remember that in chapter 6 of the Revelation, the cherubim are instruments of judgment. When the seven angels received those censers, the temple was filled with smoke from the glorious power of God, and no man was able to enter into the temple until the seven plagues of the seven angels were fulfilled. As God has set a boundary to the restless sea that thus far can those tides arise and no further, thus can those waves beat and no more, so God has set a boundary to the evil days of the nations of the earth.

When that time comes, all mediation ceases. The door is shut and the temple has become a house of indignation of wrath until these seven plagues have been poured out onto the earth.

The Seven Visitations

Rev.16:1 Even though we live in the age of miracle drugs, there are many diseases for which we still have no cure. Many doctors have expressed concern that the indiscriminate use of antibiotics has made many people immunes to their effectiveness. If a truly serious epidemic breakout occurs due to chemical or biological warfare, or for any other reasons, people will not be able to resist infection – much like AIDS affects its victims. There is a concern over the development of a super bug, or super- bacteria, which cannot be stopped by any of the drugs presently being used.

Several strains of flu have fallen into this category. The bubonic plague has had a remarkable resurgence in recent years. Leprosy has increased in many parts of the world at an alarming rate. One of the most dreaded diseases of our age is cancer. Nothing can so strike terror to a person's heart like the words, "I am sorry, but the biopsy showed malignancy." However, the malady which the first angel pours out onto the earth will produce such intense suffering, that cancer would seem like a welcome relief by comparison. There will be no cure for this malignancy, and it will afflict all unbelievers who have sworn allegiance to the antichrist.

Whatever the sore is, God will supernaturally protect the believers from this horrible plague, as He did when a similar plague was inflicted on Egypt in the days of Moses. (Exodus 9:8-11).

Rev. 16:3 In Moses' day, it was the Nile that was turned to blood; now it is the sea itself. What a sight! The Sea becomes useless for man!

Rev. 16:4-7 The description of this next judgment is somewhat longer. An ecological disaster in the sea is bad enough, but what will it be like when rivers and lakes, fountains and streams are likewise corrupted. When all sources of fresh water turn to blood, as they did in Egypt in the days of Moses, men's horror and despair will know no bounds. The Lord's first miracle was to turn water into wine; now He turns water into blood. This section here proves that the angels have authority over nature. In chapter 7:1 we saw that the angels were standing at the four corners of the earth holding the winds. The angel, whose sphere it is to guard the water supplies of earth, instantly recognizes the poetic justice of God in turning the rivers and fountains into blood. The beast and his followers have shed the blood of the martyrs in rivers, and now they are given blood to drink.

Our attention is then drawn to the response to this judgment. John says, "And I heard another angel out of the altar say, 'Even so, Lord God Almighty, true and righteous are thy judgments.'"

As we have seen in previous chapters, the most vicious and bloody time of slaughter of believers which the world has ever seen is going to take place during these seven years of Tribulation.

The Real Global Warming

Rev. 16:8-9 The surface of the earth is shielded from deadly solar ultraviolet radiation by a layer of ozone. Partial destruction of this ozone layer can have serious consequences for the biology of the entire planet. As the clouds from the nuclear exchange begin to dissipate, holes in the ozone layer will let in deadly radiation, heating up the planet's surface until it becomes unbearably hot. This will be one of the worst judgments that man will experience, since there will be no water to drink to gain any relief.

But the most startling thing about the whole chapter is that men will go through all of this and still not repent. When men reject Jesus Christ, even a foretaste of hell doesn't make them change their minds.

Rev.16:10-11 So far the Beast has been immune, but now his throne is shaken, and, like pharaoh of old, he is powerless to defend himself. Darkness sweeps in as Joel long ago foretold. (Joel 2:1-2). "For the day of the Lord is coming, for it is at hand: A day of darkness and gloominess, a day of clouds and thick darkness." In His Olivet discourse, the Lord warned that the sun would be darkened and the moon would withhold her light (Matthew 24:29). Since men have chosen the powers of darkness as their spiritual guides and have scorned the Light of the world, God gives them what they want – darkness, their darkness, like that of Egypt.

{Armageddon}

Tel Megiddo, the ancient site of the final battle between God and Evil is situated high above the Jezebel Valley in Israel, the apocalyptic Armageddon. The Via Maris, so called by the Romans as it linked Egypt with Mesopotamia, was the main road that both armies and trade caravans could pass through from the coast to the Jordan. Nazareth lies between the Valley and the Sea of Galilee not far from Mount Tabor in the east. On a modern map, it is called Tel Megiddo.

A "tel" is a geographic feature, a hill often rising out of a flat plain. Megiddo is a site that has seen more battles than any other location on earth. It will be the staging ground for the final battle at the time of Christ's return. The Jezreel Valley, the Esdraelon Valley, the Kishon Valley, and Armageddon, are all one and the same place.

In Revelation 16:16 we see the armies of the kings of the east being gathered together to the place called in Hebrew, "Armageddon". This is the only place in scripture where the term Armageddon is mentioned. The word Armageddon comes from the Greek rendering of the Hebrew name Har Megiddo (the Hebrew prefix 'Har' means "hill" or "mountain").

Today this site of Megiddo is one of the crown jewels of Israeli archeology. Remains of more than 25 cities, representing every period of ancient history in the land of Israel, have been uncovered.

Megiddo controlled a narrow strategic stretch of road called the Via Maris, "the way of the sea", a major international highway in the ancient world. This road stretched from Egypt in the south to Babylon in Mesopotamia, linking the major empires and trade routes of that day.

Valley of Megiddo

Megiddo's position on this highway made it a prime mercantile city. Whoever controlled Megiddo, controlled access to trade all along this road. Megiddo was a choke point; therefore, for the empires of the ancient world. Control of Megiddo was crucial to controlling any regional empire. Many battles took place at Megiddo over the course of history. In 1479 B.C., Egyptian Pharaoh Thutmose III launched a campaign near Megiddo to assert dominion over territories in and north of Canaan.

In Joshua 12:21 we find the first reference to Megiddo in scripture in a list of Canaanite kings defeated during the

Israelite conquest. In Joshua 17:11 we see that Megiddo fell within the inheritance of the tribe of Manasseh. In 1 Kings 9:5 we see reference to the largest period of building at Megiddo during the reign of King Solomon of Israel. Solomon made Megiddo one of his district capitals, as well as one of his three main fortress cities.

Deborah and Barak sang a song of praise to God extolling Him for helping Israel defeat the Canaanite army and Sisera near Megiddo. (Judges 5:19-21).

Gideon, a later hero of Israel, defeated the Midianites in the Valley of Jezreel, also known as the Plain of Esdraelon, or Megiddo. (Judges 7 and Judges 6:33).

Two great Israelite disasters took place near Megiddo: the deaths of King Saul (1 Samuel 31:8) and King Josiah (2 Kings 23:29-30; 2 Chronicles 35:22-24). Pharaoh-Necho, leading his army from Egypt to Carchemish to battle the Babylonians, was confronted by Josiah, who was killed in the ensuing battle.

(When Jesus Christ comes back again, the Jews will cry just like the cried and wept when good King Josiah died. Jews mourned his death for centuries. Zechariah 12:12.)

Under Tiglath-Pilesar III (745 – 727 B.C.), Megiddo became the capital of a province in the Assyrian empire.

Later the Romans stationed a legion at or near Megiddo, giving the name of Legio to the general area. Napoleon fought here in 1799. He said "All the armies of the world could maneuver their forces on this vast plain."

General Edmund Allenby defeated the Turkish Ottoman Empire in the First World War here in the same location (1918).

The living word of God in the Book of Revelation conveys to those who will understand, that the greatest gathering of armed forces in history is yet to occur here. (Revelation 16). It is the sixth bowl that deals with the gathering of forces at Megiddo. (Revelation 16:12-16).

Powerful demons influence the political and religious leaders of the world to send armies into this region of the modern state of Israel. Prior to this, there will have been war, possibly involving nuclear, chemical and biological wars between nations leading to a movement of troops into this region (Revelation 9; Daniel 11:40-45). This struggle for global dominion involves the armies of the Beast and the armies from beyond the Euphrates River, all moving toward a final confrontation. It is the final battle that Jesus Christ prophesied when he said all life would be destroyed if not for divine intervention. (Matthew 24:22). The Old Testament prophets Zechariah and Joel also detail this final conflagration. (Zechariah 14:1-3; Joel 2:1; Joel 3:2, verse 12.)

The Battle of Armageddon

Rev.16:12-16 The time has come for the fighting of that final war of the world; the name of which has become a byword among men since John first wrote it down – Armageddon. The Holy land has been chosen by God as the stage upon which two crucial events take place, one on a mountain and one on a plain. Mount Calvary and the plain of Megiddo are the two altars of sacrifice that dominate the history of the world. On Mount Calvary, grace redeemed the world by the sacrifice of God's Son; on the plain of Megiddo vengeance offers up the armies of the world in a sacrifice of doom. Both are blood baths; both are the descent of wrath upon sin; both are brought about by God's bitterest foes who work out, despite themselves, God's perfect and sovereign will. Across both can be written the words of Peter, "The Gentiles, and the peoples of Israel, were gathered together, for to do whatsoever thy hand and thy counsel determined before to be done." (Acts 4: 27-28). From each proceeds a supper, a feast of remembrance for the people of God, and the other a feast of retribution for the carrion. At Calvary there rang up to the gates of heaven a victorious cry, "It is finished." And at Armageddon there rings down to earth an answering cry from the temple gates in glory, "It is done"!

The sixth vial judgment is a horrible extension of the judgment of the sixth trumpet recorded in chapter 9. You will recall that the sixth trumpet revealed the vast hordes of the orient mustered to prepare to march into the Middle East undercover of what appeared to be a limited nuclear strike. In this present situation of the sixth bowl, the terrifying army of the 200 million Orientals has reached the banks of the Euphrates, the ancient boundary between the empires of the east and west.

The great army is designated as the "Kings of the East." This tells us that there will likely be a coalition of powers from the Eastern countries and it will be led by China. India, Pakistan, Afghanistan, Japan, and other eastern countries may form a coalition under the leadership of China.

The West Mobilizes for War

Satan (the dragon), the Roman Antichrist, and the False Prophet will be the unholy trinity of the Tribulation. These three personalities act virtually as one, setting into action demons who perform miraculous signs in front of the leaders of the whole earth. Since the eastern leaders are already massed at the Euphrates in readiness for war, these miraculous signs must be performed for the benefit of those world leaders from the west, which the unholy trinity is trying to mobilize to fight against the Eastern army.

Sequence of World War III

The battle of Armageddon covers three and one-half years, the last half of the Tribulation. This period is usually referred to as the "Great Tribulation." The battle of Armageddon consists of many stages.

Islamic Alliance

The first stage of this war begins when the Arab-African-Iranian alliance (called "the King of the South" in Daniel 11:40) launches a massive attack against Israel. The second stage is an immediate full-scale invasion against Israel by Russia (called "the King of the North" (Daniel 11:40-45); see also (Ezekiel 38:14-17 and Joel 2:1-10, 20.)

The first two stages of the war of Armageddon commence with the opening of the second seal (Revelation 6:3-4) when the red horseman goes forth and takes peace from the earth. According to the prophet Daniel, the King of the South and King of the North will attempt a pincer movement against the Antichrist. (Daniel 11:40). With Palestine as his base (v41), he will first defeat Egypt, and then Libya and Nubia (Sudan). Reports from the east and the north, may relate to the armies of Revelation 9:13-21; 16:12. The threat of these armies will cause the Antichrist to return to Palestine, making his headquarters between Jerusalem and the Mediterranean (v45). However, he will come to his end at the hands of the victorious, returning Christ (Revelation 19:11)

The third stage of the campaign finds the Russian army completely annihilated in Israel by the European forces of the Roman Antichrist. (Daniel 11:45; Ezekiel 38:18 – 39:5). Zechariah 14:12 predicts the plague that will inflict the soldiers who attack Jerusalem. He predicts that "their flesh will be consumed from their bones, their eyes burned out of their sockets, and their tongues consumed out of their mouths while they stand upon their feet."

For hundreds of years' students of Bible prophecy have wondered what kind of plague could produce such instant ravaging of humans while still on their feet. Until the advent of the atomic bomb, such a thing was not humanly possible. But now everything Zechariah predicted could come true instantly in a thermonuclear exchange.

Nuclear weapons will surely be used in any warfare in the future. The major powers of the world aren't stockpiling nuclear weapons for nothing, and even an effective arms control agreement between nations wouldn't do away with the existing weapons. Ezekiel, the prophet, adds a further descriptive note to this martial exchange between Russia and the Revived Roman Empire in his prediction of "a torrential rain of hailstones, fire and brimstone." (Ezekiel 38:32).

Part of the consequences of this confrontation will be the devastation of Russia and her satellite nations. Israel will also suffer greatly from the bombings. Ezekiel 39:5-8 predicts this and adds that "fire" will fall upon many of the great population centers of the world, described as "those who inhabit the coastlands in safety." China now has missiles capable of hitting Russia, Europe and even the American continent.

China may unleash some of her nuclear weapons on Russia at this time. The Roman Antichrist will also use tactical weapons against this great Northern confederacy.

Red China and Her Allies

The fourth stage of the war is when the 200 million-man army from the orient reaches the Euphrates and prepares to attack the Antichrist, who will be in Israel at that time. (Revelation 16:12).

The fifth stage is the mobilization of all the rest of the world's armies to fight under the command of the Antichrist against the Kings of the East. (Revelation 16:12). At this point all the armies move into the middle east and spread out along the entire length and breadth of Israel, with the greatest concentration poised for the fiercest and final battle on the plains of Armageddon. (Revelation 16:13-14).

The Final Destruction

It is almost impossible for us to imagine the magnitude of what is predicted here. Just imagine– at least 300 million soldiers, about the current size of the U.S. Population, positioned across the entire Middle East and poised for the final mad act in man's most finely-developed art – war! The human waves of the east are pitted against the superior weaponry of the west for the horrible carnage of the valley of Armageddon. Revelation 16:16 – The indescribable clashes around Jerusalem and Judea (Zechariah 14:1-15) take place. No wonder John predicts that blood will stand to the horse's bridles for two hundred miles in the Jordan Valley. (See Revelation 14:20).

Rev.16:17-21 The temple is seen at the close of each of the three series of judgments. It will be seen no more in the apocalypse after this, because in the new heaven there will be no temple. Ezekiel's millennial temple is not a subject of mention in Revelation, for the closing book of the Bible looks upon that golden age from heaven's perspective, not earth's. "It is done!" cries the voice, and one can almost hear the great sigh of relief that must surely go up from every lover of God in the universe.

While this great battle is raging, every city in the world is going to be leveled. This will take place by what is called an earthquake. The word itself simply means "a great shaking of the earth." The earth could be shaken either by a literal earthquake or by a full scale nuclear exchange. Just think of the great cities of the world – London, Rome, Paris, Berlin, New York, San Francisco, Los Angeles, Mexico City, Tokyo – all of these great cities are going to be judged at that time.

(Rev: 16.19.) "Now the great city was divided into three parts".

Jerusalem will be split into three parts (Zech, 14:4), not as a judgment but as an improvement. The additional water supply (Zech 14:8) and topographical changes will prepare the city for its central place in the millennial Kingdom. Jerusalem is the only city to be spared the judgment (1 Chro.23:25; Ps125:1-2; Micah 4:7) and will be made more beautiful (Psalm 48:2), because of her repentance.

There is a thunderstorm, and earthquake, and a hailstorm. John says here "And there were voices, and thunders and lightnings." Similar phenomena accompanied the breaking of the seventh seal (Revelation 7:5) and the blowing of the seventh trumpet (Revelation 11:19), as though dumb nature found herself a voice with which to tell deluded men that the heavens do rule. The earth is now besieged by an unprecedented thunderstorm. Blinding flashes of lightning burn and blaze across the sky, deafening peals thunder crash and roll like some celestial cannonade, thunder balls of fire skip and roll around the earth, and terrible voices rumble through the skies. How men must tremble!

These portent herald the approaching demise of the last Roman Caesar. The time has come for the second death to swallow up the last Caesar of Rome. Fierce, fiery warrior clouds in ranks and squadrons marshal in the blazing of heaven's dread artillery which deadens every sound on earth. The fiery darts of the living God flame across the sky, striking earthward in sheets and forks of lurid flame.

The Role of the United States of America

Many people have wondered what the United States will be doing during this conflict. The United States is destined to lose its role as the leader of the West. This leadership will instead fall to the European confederacy which the Antichrist will rule. There is no scriptural indication that the United States will have been wiped out before this time, so we can only deduce that she will be part of the Western Confederacy which unifies nations against the great Asian power. However, in this last outpouring of judgment, no nation will escape — every city in the world is going to be leveled.

Apparently the devastation will be so tremendous that not only will all the cities be destroyed, but the land itself will be ripped apart. The coastlines and continents will be changed and all the mountains will be shifted in elevation.

The earth will be bombarded by hailstones weighing 100 pounds. Imagine the destruction caused by hailstones weighing a hundred pounds, each coming down from the sky in solid missiles of ice! And for the third time we are told that men, demented by their torments, will blaspheme God.

REVELATION CHAPTER 17

The Modern Babylon

In chapters 17 and 18 John deviates from his chronological unfolding of future history and pulls back the curtain to give a flashback to the development of the two great dynamics behind the Revived Roman Empire's meteoric rise to world dominion. Many symbols used in the book of Daniel and Revelation are explained throughout this chapter. So this section in Revelation, chapters 17 and 18, is an interlude.

The passage begins: "And there came one of the seven angels which had the seven vials of the wrath and the final judgment of Almighty God."[1] Those seven angels were introduced to us in chapters 15 and 16. At the end of chapter 16, the seventh angel poured out his vial of the wrath and judgment of God upon this Christ-rejecting and sinful world. Immediately thereafter, we would have expected the personal appearance of Christ upon this earth. But the Lord does not come from heaven until chapter 19. Before the final coming of Jesus, there is this interlude, this intermission. In this parenthesis one of those seven-vialed angels of the judgment and wrath of God comes to the scene and says, "God would reveal to you, God would make known to you, the future of religion in the earth." So this intermission between chapters 16 and 19 reveals to us the mystery Babylon, the course of religion in this world, (chapter 18) and the city Babylon, the course of culture and commerce in this world. The vial angel says to John, "Come hither, I will show thee the judgment of the great whore that sits upon many waters with whom the kings of the earth have committed fornication and the inhabitants of the earth have been made drunk with the wine of her adultery." He then carries John away in the spirit into the wilderness. When the Lord showed the Apostle John the bride of Christ, the New Jerusalem, the city and the people of the Lord, He took him to a mountain, great and high. But when the Lord shows to John the course and development of religion in this world, He carries him into the wilderness. Wherever there is spiritual harlotry, there is desolation and a desert of dreary, weary waste.

So he carries John into a wilderness, and there John says, "I saw a woman sit upon a scarlet beast, full of names of blasphemy...And the woman was arrayed in purple and scarlet color, and decked with gold and precious stones and pearls, having in her hand a golden cup full of abominations and filthiness of her fornication."

The Great Amazement of the Apostle John

In the first part of the vision, John sees this woman with her name on her forehead, "Mystery, Babylon the Great, the Mother of Harlots and of the Abominations of the Earth." In the interpretation which follows in the remainder of the chapter, John writes his own personal reaction in language that is extremely strong. Verse 6: "I was amazed with a great amazement, I was filled with the wonder of a great wonder, and I was astonished with a great astonishment." He did not write these words of amazement when he saw the beast, the course of the political empire and governments of this world. He did not write of that astonishment when he saw any other thing that God revealed to him concerning the future. But when John saw this scarlet woman, and came to understand what she represented, as he saw the development of the course of religion in this earth, he wondered with a great wonder.

The background of the development of this religious idolatry, this scarlet woman (whore), is seen in the very name written on her forehead. Idolatry began in the city of Babel, or Babylon.

The Babylonian system is both religious and political. The religious system paves the way for the political system. In the beginning, the religious system supports the political system, but in the end the political system supplants the religious one.

The historical drama of Babylon began on the plains of Shinar, where the first world dictator established the world's first religious center. The dictator's name was Nimrod, which means "we will revolt." He is described literally as "a mighty hunter of men in defiance of the Lord." The beginning of his kingdom was Babel, or Babylon (Genesis 10:8-10). Under this leader the first united religious act was performed – the building of a tower "whose top would reach into the heavens." (Genesis 11:4). This tower was to aid them in a better observation of the stars. It was in essence an astrological observatory. Many centuries later, when God pronounced future judgment on Babylon, He said that, she had labored with sorceries and astrology from her youth," indicating that these were practiced in Babylon from her very beginning in history. (Isaiah 47: 12-13).

The Prophet Daniel in Babylon

In the 7th century B.C. the prophet Daniel, while captive in Babylon, was made a member of the king's special advisors. They were all steeped in the religion of Babylon, except Daniel. When the king had a nightmare one night, he called for his advisors to interpret what it meant. "Then the kind commanded to summon the magicians, the astrologers, the sorcerers, and the Chaldean, to reveal to the king his dreams." (Daniel 2:2).

These magicians practiced black magic and performed various supernatural feats through contact with demon spirits. By calling on the spirits of the dead, they made contact with demons, who then impersonated the dead person being summoned. The sorcerer specialized in witchcraft. The Chaldean was the highest of all the advisors. He was a part of a special priestly caste which was perpetuated by inheritance. A Chaldean was a master of astrology!

Babylon and the Harlot

When the angel told John that he would tell him the mystery of the woman, he meant that this harlot, the false religious system, would have as its main teachings the same occultic practices as ancient Babylon. It would include black magic, demon contact, séance, miraculous materializations, witchcraft, astrology, and sorcery. Her luxurious external appearance of jewels and royal clothes meant that she would have a great appeal to the sensual nature of men, but her gold cup filled with abominations represented her corrupt and perverse teachings.

The ancient city of Babylon was ruled by this occultic influence, but not many people are aware that the religion of Babylon passed from empire to empire until the days of ancient Rome. The mystery that John was seeking to unveil for his readers was that religious Babylon would be revived to control the last great world power in the last days of history. This religion will be an occultic amalgamation of all the world's religious. For the first three and one-half years of the Tribulation, it will enjoy a position of great power and influence over the Revived Roman Empire and its leader, the Antichrist.

Babylon Becomes Prominent

Babylon became prominent under Hammurabi (1728-1686 B.C.) who was the guiding light to the empire during the old Babylonian period. Babylon's greatest glory was achieved under Nebuchadnezzar, who lived during the Neo-Babylonian period about 600 years before Christ.

Of primary importance in the study of Babylon is its relation to religion as unfolded in Revelation 17. In addition to the historical records given in the Bible itself, ancient accounts indicate that the wife of Nimrod, who founded the city of Babylon, became the head of the so-called Babylonian mysteries, which consisted of secret religious rites which were developed as a part of the worship of idols in Babylon. She was known by the name of Semiramis. In Assyria and Nineveh, she was called Ishtar. In the Phoenician pantheon she was called Ashtoreth or Astarte. In Egypt she was called

Isis. Among the Latins, the Romans, she was called Venus. She became the first high priestess of an idolatrous system. In answer to the promise made to Eve that the seed of the woman would deliver Semiramis, when she gave birth to a son, she said he was miraculously conceived by a sunbeam, and she offered her son as the promised deliverer of the earth. His name was Tammuz. When he was grown, a wild boar slew him; but after forty days of the mother's weeping, he was raised from the dead. In this fabricated story of Semiramis and Tammuz began the cult of worship of the mother and child that spread throughout the whole world. In Assyria she is called Ishtar and her son, still Tammuz. In Phoenicia she was called Astarte or Ashtoreth, and her son, Baal or Tammuz. In Egypt she was called Isis, and her son was called Osiris or Horus. In Greece she was called Aphrodite, and her son was Eros. Among the Romans she was called Venus, and her son was called Cupid.

The cult of the worship of mother and child spread throughout the whole earth. She was worshiped by the offering of a wafer (a little cake) to her as the queen of heaven. And there were always forty days of Lent, of weeping of the destruction of Tammuz, before the feast of Ishtar, at which time his resurrection was celebrated.

The sign of Tammuz was an Ishtar egg, a symbol of his resurrection to life. The secret of the Babylonian mystery was to be found in priestly ablutions, in sacramental rites and rituals, in the dedication of virgins to the gods, in purgatorial fires, and in a thousand other rituals that are familiar to us today. The prophet Jeremiah bitterly rebuked against the mother and child cult. In chapter 44 of Jeremiah, Jeremiah described the idol worshipers among the children of Israel, who burned incense to the queen of heaven and who offered cakes in her name. In chapter 8 of Ezekiel, God takes the prophet and shows him the inner life of the people of God who are idolatrous: Ezekiel 8:13 "And He said to me, 'Turn again, and you will see greater abominations that they are doing.' So He brought me to the door of the north gate of the Lord's house: and to my dismay, women were sitting there weeping for Tammuz." Ezekiel was beholding the forty days of Lent in which they afflicted themselves and wept for Tammuz, the child that was slain by the wild boar. But after those forty days, in commemoration of the story of his being raised from the dead, the end of weeping was celebrated with the feast of Ishtar, in which the people exchanged Ishtar eggs.

As we have observed, that cult of the worship of mother and child spread throughout the whole world, from Babylon to Assyria, to Phoenicia, to Pergamos, and finally to Rome itself. There the Roman Emperor was elected Pontifex Maximums, the high priest of all of the idolatrous systems of the Roman Empire. And when the Roman Emperor passed away, that title of high priest of the rites and mysteries of the cult of mother and child, the Babylonian mystery of idolatry, was assumed by the Bishop of Rome.

There is no such thing in the Bible as the exaltation of a female deity, and least of all is there any hint or suggestion that Mary was other than what she is presented to be in the New Testament. The last time she is seen, she is a humble fellow, suppliant in the prayer meeting described in the first chapter of the Book of Acts. After that, she is never mentioned or seen again. This cult of the idolatrous worship of the mother and child is, purely and simply, Babylonian idolatry.

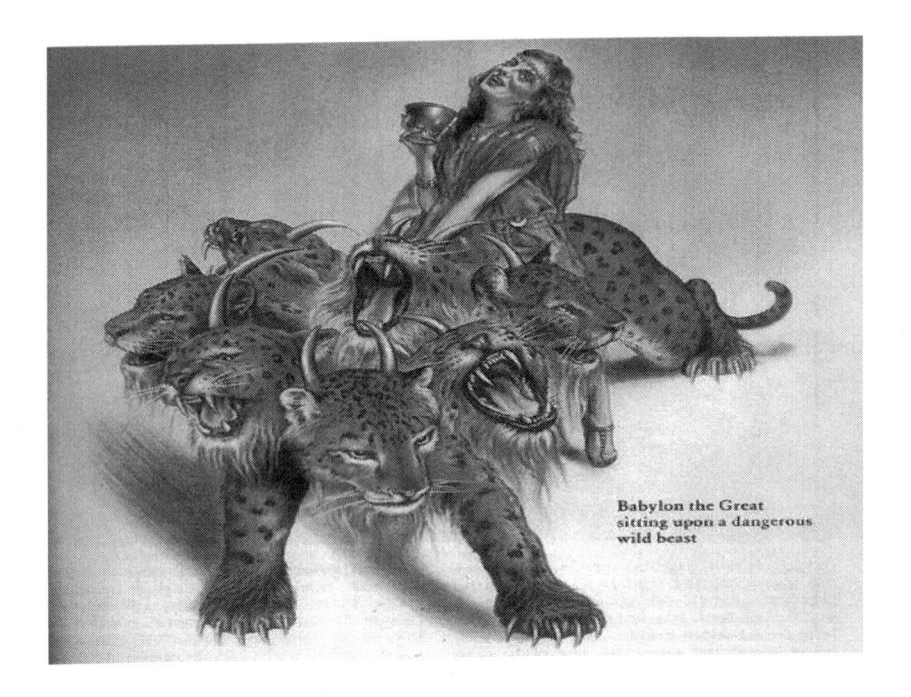

Babylon the Great sitting upon a dangerous wild beast

However further on, as the angel interprets this scarlet whore to the sacred seer, he writes: "And I saw the woman drunken", a present active linear principle, meaning continuously drunk; not that just one time she made a mistake and slew God's servants, but continuously drunken. "I saw the scarlet whore drunken with the blood of the saints, and with the blood of the martyrs of Jesus." John could not believe his eyes, for in his day it was pagan Rome that was persecuting the Christians. But in this vision that God gave to John, the blood of the saints and the blood of the martyrs of Jesus is shed by that rich and scarlet idolatrous church. John wondered with a great wonder.

Who invented the Inquisition? Who invented the torture chamber and the rack? Who burned at the stake uncounted thousands and millions of God's servants in the earth? It has been estimated that she has slain more than fifty million of the servants of Jesus Christ.

There is a remarkable thing here. In chapter 18 of Revelation, it is God who destroys the city of Babylon; it is God who destroys the Beast and the false prophet. But do you notice here that it is not God who destroys the scarlet whore? It is man who destroys her. That is an astonishing thing.

The Destruction of the Idolatrous System of the World

When we read history and watch the course of this world, that is exactly what God has said and what God has done. We are not to think that God is peculiarly different here in the Revelation. The great eternal, spiritual principles and destiny are not different in the Revelation from what they were yesterday, or will be tomorrow, or are today. We can follow these things in history books; we can read these things in daily newspapers. God is ever true to the great principles by which He governs the world. We can herein follow the work of God as it is projected out to the end of time. The apocalypse says it is not the intervention of Christ; it is no appearing from God that destroys this scarlet whore.

Men Do It

Let us see if this prophecy which was made two thousand years ago is demonstrated in history. God has said in the text that men shall destroy this whore, this idolatrous system. Do you remember reading in history of the ferocious onslaught of the terrible Islamic conquest? That terrible, bloody conquest began in the seventh century and still continues today as worldwide Jihad and terrorism. The Islamic conquest was against idolatry. In the fierce conquest of the Caliphs of Islam who overran the world, they destroyed idolatry. Whether the idol is named Krishna or Christ, whether that idol is named Minerva or Mary, whether that idol is named Jove or Joseph, it is an idol; and when the Mohammedan Caliph came with his sword in hand, he destroyed the idol temples, the Churches of Africa, of all Palestine, of all Asia Minor and Turkey and Istanbul, and thrust himself to the Philippine islands on the east. It was against idolatry that the Mohammedan religion arose as a fierce and terrible antagonist. The sweep of Islam was the sweep of the fierceness of the wrath and the judgment of Almighty God. Men destroyed the idolatrous whore in Africa and Asia.

And the prophecy is that the kingdom of the world, someday, is going to get weary of the same idolatrous church. The prophecy is that the kingdoms of the world shall hate the whore, make her desolate, rob her of all of her riches and make her naked, stripping her of her beautiful scarlet robe and her purple gowns and her bedecking pearls and precious stones. The world, these kingdoms, shall "eat her flesh" that is, they shall appropriate all of her riches.

Revelation 17:8

The angel first gives a detailed description of the beast in his general character. The beast is explained chronologically as that which was, is not, and is about to ascend from the abyss and go into perdition. The bottomless pit in Greek, abyssos, meaning, "Bottomless" or the "abyss" is the home of Satan and the demons, and indicates that the power of the political is satanic in its origin, as is plainly stated in 13:4.

There is a confusing similarity between the descriptions afforded Satan who was apparently described as the king over the demons in the abyss (9:11, 11:7, and 13:3), and the beast of 17:8. The solution to this intricate problem is that there is an identification of the world ruler with his world government.

Each of the three entities is described as a beast. Only Satan himself actually comes from the abyss. The world government which he promotes is entirely satanic in its power and to this extent is identified with Satan. It is the beast, as the world government, which is revived. The man who is the world ruler, however, has power and great authority given to him by Satan. The fact that Satan and the world ruler are referred to in such similar terms indicates their close relationship one to the another.

While many have attempted to demonstrate from this verse that the final world ruler is some resurrected being such as Judas Iscariot, Nero, or one of the more recent world rulers, it would seem preferable to regard the "eighth" beast as the political power of the world government rather than its human ruler. What is revived is an imperial government, not an imperial ruler (Rev. 13:3). That which seemingly went out of existence in history never to be revived is thus miraculously resuscitated at the end of the age.

The Seven Heads of the Beast

(Rev.17:9-11) The explanation of the beast introduced by the unusual phrase "Here is the mind which has wisdom:" anticipates the difficulty and complexity of the

Revelation to follow. The reader is warned that spiritual wisdom is required to understand that which is unfolded. The first key to the revelation is in the statement "The seven heads are seven mountains on which the woman sits."

Many expositions refer this to Rome. Seven Hills formed the nucleus of the ancient city of the left bank of the Tiber. These hills received the names of Palatine, Aventine, Caelian, Esquiline, Viminal, Quirinal, and Capitoline. As Rome grew, however, the hill Janiculum on the other side of the river Tiber was often included among the seven. Later the hill Pincian to the north of the ancient city was also included in the hills of Rome, as the city developed and moved north. This passage in Revelation is taken, therefore, to indicate that the seat of the ecclesiastical power will be in Rome, geographically, rather than in Babylon. Throughout its history Rome has been described as the city of seven hills, as indicated in coins which refer to it in this way and in countless allusions in Roman literature.

The seven heads of the beast, however, are said to be symbolic of seven kings described in verse 10. Five of these are said to have fallen, one is in contemporary existence, that is, in John's lifetime, the seventh is yet to come and will be followed by another described as the eighth, which is the beast itself. In the Greek there is no word for "there," thus translated literally, the phrase is "and are seven kings." The seven heads are best explained as referring to seven kings who represent seven successive forms of the kingdom. Because the seven heads are identified with kings in verse 10, some prefer to divorce the meaning from the city of Rome entirely and center the ultimate fulfillment in a rebuilt Babylon on the site of ancient Babylon.

John tells us that the seven heads also represent seven kingdoms; five have fallen, one is, and the other is still to come. Here he is referring to those great world empires from the time of the original Babylon of Nimrod's day, which have been dominated by the false occultic religion of Babylon.

"Babylonish" Influence Over Empires

The first kingdom was Assyria, with its occult-made capital city of Nineveh (Nahum 3:4). The second was Egypt, which devoted much of its total wealth to the construction of the pyramids, all built according to astrological specifications. Egypt was also given to black magic (see Exodus 7:11, 22, 8:7, 18; 2 Timothy 3:9). The third was the neo-Babylonian empire of Daniel's day, which really perfected the black arts. The fourth was Medo-Persia, which conquered Babylon but was in turn enslaved by the Babylonian religion. The fifth was the Greek empire. One visit to Greece and her ancient temple sites will convince you of the sway which idolatrous religions held there!

Running through the culture of all these great past empires was an underlying belief in astrology. This was the cohesive force which found together all the witchcraft, sorcery, and magic. Kings would seldom make a move without consulting advisors steeped in the ancient art of Babylonian religion. The ancient priests enjoyed royal stature and power, especially in Egypt. When John speaks of the "five kingdoms that have fallen," he means the five above mentioned empires. But then he says, "one is." This has to refer to the great empire of his day, Rome, which was filled with the same occultic beliefs that had originated on the plains of Shinar in ancient Babylon. This was the sixth kingdom of John's vision.

John looks to the future when he says of the seventh head (kingdom) that "the other is not yet come, and when it comes, it must continue a short while." (Revelation 17:10). This refers to the future revival of the Roman Empire.

The seventh head is different from all the other six because it has ten horns on it. This indicates that this seventh kingdom will be made up of ten nations from the old Roman Empire (the sixth head) which will have confederated. This entity may be the current European Union. The revived Roman Empire will become dominated by the same Babylonian religious system.

After having given John a panoramic view of all the past world powers and their seduction by the Harlot of Babylon, the angel now narrows his focus to the 'beast' in its final form. Looking from this perspective, he says the beast was and is not, and then will exist again and be destroyed. He must be referring to the fact that Rome existed in his day, but that a day was coming, when it would no longer exist. Then it would rise again and be destroyed.

If you review the history of Rome, you will see that it was never conquered by anyone; it fell from within because of its own decadence. For nearly fifteen centuries Rome has not existed as a viable world political power. But the European Union has become a resurrected Roman Empire in its rudimentary form. All the nation, who are banding together in the European Union have roots in the old Roman culture and civilization. This is the 'beast' that will rise up and then be destroyed.

Although the beast has only seven heads, John says that it briefly sprouts another, an eighth head, but this head is only an outgrowth of the seventh (Revived Roman empire) and is quickly destroyed.

REVELATION CHAPTER 18

The End of the European Union

When the heavens open as a rolled back scroll and when the Lord is revealed in personal triumph, how shall these things be? What is the sign of Christ's coming and the end of the world"? The Apocalypse, the unveiling of Christ, is the presentation of our Lord when God intervenes in human history. Chapter 19 of the Revelation records the second coming of Christ. Chapter 20 is the binding of Satan and their introduction of the long-prayed-for millennium. Chapter 21 and 22 describe the new heaven, the new earth, and the New Jerusalem; the new home of the soul. As the Revelation develops, as these events fall into consecutive, chronological order, chapter 19, (describing the coming of Christ) should have immediately followed chapter 16, which depicts the pouring out of the seven bowls of wrath in which are filled up the judgment of God. But, between chapter 16 and chapter 19 there is an interlude, a parenthesis, an intermission. In these two intervening chapters of 17 and 18, one of the seven angels in whose hands are the bowls of the wrath of God, took John and said "come, I will show you the judgment of the great harlot who sits on many waters."

The angel would also show John the judgment of the city of Babylon, which epitomizes the life of a godless and Christ- rejecting world. So, in this interlude, there is uncovered to John in chapter 17 the judgment of God upon mystery Babylon, the ecclesiastical system that is described as a great whore. Then in chapter 18 the angel reveals to the seer the judgment of the Lord upon the city Babylon, upon the great center of the social, political, cultural, and commercial life of this globe.

Babylon in Prophecy

We have already twice been introduced to the ultimate destruction of Babylon. In Revelation 14:8 there came a great announcement from heaven, carried by the voice of an angel messenger, crying "Babylon is fallen, is fallen." In Revelation 16:19, when the seventh bowl of the judgment and the wrath of God is poured out upon the earth, are written these words, "And great Babylon was remembered before God, to give her the cup of the wine of the fierceness of His wrath." And in chapter 18 the announcement is made about the sudden destruction of Babylon. When God destroys this great city, it will not be over a period of time, it will not be by continuous assault that lasts through weeks or months or years. Rather, its destruction will come suddenly, as lightning cleaves to the bosom of the livid sky. It will come instantaneously, "mia hora," in one hour. In mia hora, and the thing is done. The judgment is poured out.

The city of Babylon is mentioned more times in the Bible than any other city except Jerusalem. Babylon is referred to more than 260 times in the Holy Scriptures. For example, in chapter 50 and 51 of Jeremiah, Babylon is called by name thirty-seven times.

It was the city of the first great monarch of the earth, the capital of the golden kingdom of Nebuchadnezzar. It was the cry of the king who destroyed Judea, and the Solomonic temple of God. It was the city of the great Babylonian captivity, located among the rivers (canals) of Babylon. "By the rivers of Babylon, there we sat down, yea, we wept, when we remembered Zion. We hung our harps upon the willows in the midst of it." (Psalm 137:1-2).

The city has a great part in prophecy. For example, in chapter 5 of the Book of Zechariah, beginning with verse 5 and reading to the end of the chapter, there is the vision of the ephah, and in the ephah (when a talent of lead covering it was lifted up by the angel) he saw a woman. The angel said this woman is wickedness. In the vision the prophet also saw two women who had wings like a stork and the wind was in their wings and they lifted up that ephah between the earth and the sky. The prophet then said to the angel, "Where are the baskets? And he said to me, "To build a house for it in the land of Shinar; when it is ready the basket will be set there on its base.'" (Zechariah 5:10-11). An ephah (basket) was smaller than a bushel, holding about 5 gallons. Like the flying scroll (chapt. 5:1) this was obviously enlarged for the purpose of the vision. The people of Israel are seen as pieces of grain, perhaps indicating that the wickedness is particularly materialistic. This was a sin that Israel picked up in Babylon and it has influenced them through the centuries until it is removed by the Messiah in the last days. This secular commercialism is central to the final world system. (Revelation 18)]

Did you notice the reference in Revelation 18 that Babylon is to be judged by God Himself? It is the hand of man that destroys the whore in chapter 17. It is the political power and governments of the world, who hate her, destroy her flesh, burn her with fire, make her naked and confiscate all of her wealth and property. That is done by man. Read chapter 17: when her destruction comes to pass, everyone is glad. They are tired of the system. They are weary of it, burdened by it.

But the destruction of the city of Babylon is an altogether different category. It is God who destroys Babylon. The beast is not mentioned, the ten kings are not mentioned, the governments of the earth are not mentioned. This is an intervention of God. When Babylon is destroyed, there is lamentation all over the world. The kings of the earth lament, the virgins of the earth lament, the seamen of the merchant marines lament.

There would be rejoicing. But, the great mass of this world would lament and wail because their hearts and their lives, their visions, their hopes are all in this world. What about my stocks, what about my bonds, what about my treasures? What about my wealth, and possessions?

Remembrance

Rev.<u>18:5</u> The first Babel confederacy tried to build a tower to heaven. (Genesis 11:4): The last piles up her sins to heaven, and God remembers. Although He acts in such long-suffering that men may think He does not notice what is happening, God remembers; and because of this the judgment of Babylon is inevitable and just.

What Does Babylon Represent?

Many answers are offered. There are scholars who believe that this Babylon is to be an actual, rebuilt city on the banks of the Euphrates River, on the great plain of Shinar, at the heart of the Persian Gulf. We see the great economic Power of China, India and other Asian countries. There is a possibility that a great city in the Middle East rivaling, New York, Los Angeles, Tokyo and Rome can be built. In 2010 Dubai inaugurated the tallest building in the world. Dubai has become a hub for the travel and commerce in Asia. There are many scholars who believe that this Babylon refers to a rebuilt city in the heart of the earth. To build a gigantic city in the original place of the Babylonian system is unattainable based on today's Islamic religious system.

Under Saddam Hussein, a semblance of secularism was provided. All Muslim nations have strict sharia law in force. To build a new Babylon city, they have to reject Islam and become an extreme secular culture similar to California. All the wickedness, vile, evil, pornographic systems are embraced by a liberal culture. So we have to wait and see the future changes in those countries. Even in 2016, women couldn't drive in Saudi Arabia. Malaysian court sentenced 10 lashes for a woman who had been drinking beer. The Mangalorean reported on April 4, 2010 the following report: Kuala Lumpur, April 1 "A Muslim woman who was sentenced to be caned for drinking beer has instead been ordered to perform community service after a state Sultan decided to commute the sentence, her father said Thursday. Kartika Sari Dewi Shukarno, 33, was found guilty of drinking beer at a club." Thus the term stands both for a city and for a system (religious and commercial) related to the city (much like Wall Street) which is both a place and a system.

Then, there are other scholars who believe that this Babylon represents a system of life and culture whose basic, essential principle is alienated from God. They are persuaded that this secular system is epitomized and symbolized by this great world-city. Again, there are those who believe that this Babylon represents the social, cultural, political and commercial life of the end times and that this entire system is summarized in one great world city called Babylon. Al these three interpretations can be true. But I lean toward the third opinion expressed above.

The Reasons for the Destruction of Babylon

Let us now consider another pertinent question. Why is it that God's judgment so terribly falls upon this city? Whether it is a city in America or abroad, whether it is a particular city built on the plain of Shinar or the commercial capital of another land, why is God's judgment so severely to fall upon it? Since the time of Nimrod, the sin of Babylon has been incorporated into every culture, and its influence is still growing. Materialism, secularism and denial of Christ are common in our modern society. Babylon's sins have reached unto heaven like the tower of Babel. The second reason for the judgment of God is described in Revelation 18:7-8. "In the measure that she glorified herself and lived luxuriously, in the same measure give her torment and sorrow; for she says in her heart, I sit as queen, and am no widow, and will not see sorrow."

There is a third reason for the destruction of this great city. Look closely at verses 12 and 13. In them are listed twenty-eight articles of merchandise. The enumeration starts off with gold and after the list is completed it closes with the "sounds of men." The slave trade, long banned by the civilized nations of the world, will reappear in the Antichrist's debauched commercial system. As we advance in our culture, as we go further into scientific achievements, as civilization and culture becomes more merciless, cruel, and ruthless, we become more blasphemous and God-dishonoring. These facts are corroborated in the newspapers, internet and the magazines of our day.

In Roe V. Wade, 1973, a landmark case divided by the United States Supreme Court on the issue of abortion is one of the most controversial and politically significant cases in US Supreme Court history. More than 50 million unborn babies have been murdered after the Supreme Court verdict of 1973. This is a conservative estimate and the actual numbers may be more.

Remember what Lenin said, "What would it matter if two-thirds of this earth were destroyed, if the one third that remains be communist?" Did you ever think what that saying might mean? There are more than six billion people on the earth today. Trafficking in the souls of men! To them it is nothing for a man to be slain.

When a people lose the concept of God, no longer is a man anything, but an animal. Where do we get the idea that a man is worth something anyway? We receive it not from Hitler or from Karl Mark who was a communist philosopher. We learned that idea from our Lord, who told the story of the one lost sheep and the one lost coin and the one lost boy. From our Lord we learned that the life of man is very precious. When we depart from God, we say 'no' to those things. Woe to a nation that can slay a man and think no more about it than the destruction of an animal. God brings upon this arrogance, His terrible judgment. God says the evil is here and will continue to grow.

The fourth reason for God's judgment upon Babylon is stated in verse 24. "And in her was found the blood of the prophets and saints, and of all who were slain on the earth." In this one city of Babylon! That is an amazing indictment. Personal accountability for sin is one of those great principles by which God governs our destiny, and yet we hardly realize it at all. Do you remember in chapter 23 of Matthew where the Lord is condemning the scribes and the Pharisees? He says that "upon the city of Jerusalem will come all the blood of Abel to the blood of Zacharias, the son of Barachias, whom you slew between the altar and the holy place." Upon that generation, upon that city, will come all the blood of the prophets and all the saints that was ever shed from the days of Abe to the death of Zacharias, the prophet of God, whom they slew by the side of the altar. How could this be? How could that one generation be guilty of murders they never actually committed? The answer is found in one of God's principles illustrated here, "for in Babylon was found the blood of the prophets, and of saints, and of all that were slain upon this earth." The truth is simple and it applies to us as it applies to them. You do not need to murder all of the prophets to be guilty of all the prophets' blood. You do not have to kill all the saints in order to be guilty of all of the blood of the saints. You do not have to commit every sin in the Decalogue (Ten commandments) in order to be judged by God. You do not have to commit every sin – just one – for it is the tendency and propensity toward sin that God judges.

In the courts of earth, a man is judged for his wrong acts. One man is judged because he slew another man. There are murders and culpable homicides. Judgment is given based on the intent and actions. But, in heaven, God judges that man for the sin of murder that was in his heart. God looks at the tendency of his sin. God looks at the spirit of his act of murder. It may be just one overt act of murder in the earth that human courts will judge, but in heaven, it is the tendency of the man to destroy, which God's court will judge. James says, "He that breaks the law in one part is guilty of all." It is like a chain; you do not have to break every link in order for the chandelier to fall. Break one link and the whole thing falls. So it is with our sins. When a man sins in one transgression, God sees the tendency of that sin. God knows that the man will do it again and if he will live a thousand years he still be doing it. So the Lord calls this city in judgment for all the blood of the prophets, that were slain upon the earth, though they slew only some of them. When a city slays a prophet of God, though they may not have slain but that one prophet, God judges that city as though they had slain every prophet, because the tendency of that sin is to destroy all God's messengers. It is the evil in a man's heart that condemns him. It is the evil in the city that would destroy the prophet of God that God judges. Just think of the judgment of some of the nations and cities of this world who have slain God's people and who have exiled God's witnesses! Just think of the sins in our own lives.

The Call for Separation

The judgment of God upon Babylon is seen in verse 1 of chapter 18: "And after these things I saw another angel come down from heaven, having great power; and the earth was lightened with his glory." And Babylon in the light of that glory looked like a habitation of demons, a prison of every foul spirit and a cage of every unclean and hateful bird. In the light of the glory of heaven the city looked cheap. What seemed to be so glorious was nothing but the depths of iniquity, scum, and corruption; the sewer of every vile and unclean thing. In the cities that we think are so glorious today, when the light of the judgment of God falls upon them, how ugly and how bestial they are going to appear! That is the judgment of God upon Babylon.

Verse 21 is a recapitulation of the prophecy of Jeremiah 51. "And a mighty angel took up a stone like a great millstone, and cast it into the sea, saying, "thus with violence shall that great city Babylon be thrown down." The phrase "no more "and "not" is used more than six times in verses 21, 22 and 23.

The final cry is in verse 4: "And I heard another voice from heaven, saying, come out of her, my people, that ye be not partakers of her sins, and that ye receive not of her plagues." God wants believers to be separate from the world. This is the appeal of the Apostle Paul in 2 Corinthians 6: 14-18: If we refuse the salvation offered in Christ, we are not going to escape the judgment of God. We have an appointment to make before God someday.

REVELATION CHAPTER 19

The Marriage of the Lamb Revelation 19

This chapter resumes the chronological picture of the future point where it left off at the end of chapter 16. In this chapter we see the final acts of a godless world coming to a roaring crescendo: millions of troops deployed along the battle line from Turkey to the Arabian and Sinai Peninsula are attacking each other with an insane frenzy. Cities are leveled, hundred-pound hailstones pulverize the earth, and the planet itself reels under the force of the greatest earthquake in the history of mankind. These are the days in which Jesus had warned them, (Matt 24: 21-22).

The earth will be on a precipice of self-annihilation, but in heaven it will be "the beginning of the end for all human suffering".

Notice the four "Hallelujahs" (Alleluias). The first Hallelujah is over the destruction of the great whore, mystery Babylon, the scarlet woman with a golden cup in her hand. When she is destroyed, all heaven says, Hallelujah!"

The second Hallelujah is over the destruction of the city Babylon. The iniquity of Babylon lies heavy on the heart of God's holy universe, and when she is annihilated, when the final apostasy of evil, depraved and Christ rejecting men is destroyed, all heaven feels the triumph of the glory and grace of God. "And again they said, Alleluia. And her smoke rose up forever and ever".

The next Hallelujah is uttered by the exalted and glorified creation of our Lord in heaven. "And the four and twenty elders and the four beasts fell down and worshipped God that sat on the throne, saying, "Amen; alleluia."

Notice the word "Amen". We first come to the word "Amen" in Numbers 5:22. It is the special word of sacred ratification, of holy acquiescence. It continues as the sealing word of the gospels and the epistles. It is the heavenly word of avowal, of committal to truth. It seals, it affirms, it binds. It is the highest word of praise that human speech can utter. In Psalm 72 we read "He (Jesus) shall have dominion also from sea, to sea, and from the river to the ends of the earth (v8). Ps 72:17, 19, 20 also. (v19) "And blessed be his glorious name forever! And let the whole earth be filled with His glory. Amen and Amen. The Amen is the highest word of sealing affirmation. Human utterance could go no higher. It is thus with the twenty-four elders and the four Cherubims, who are most intimately connected with the throne of God. They express their utmost consent to the razing of the wicked Babylon.

The fourth Hallelujah is uttered in answer to a call from the throne itself. (v5).

Rev.19:4-8. The fine linen is the righteous nesses (plural) of the saints. What a day! What a prospect! What a consummation! What a victory! What a triumph! "For the marriage of the Lamb has come, and His wife has made herself ready" And to her it was granted to be arrayed in fine linen", lustrous, iridescent, white, like the light of the glory of God. That fine linen is the righteous acts and deeds of the saints.

The Bridegroom and the Bride

We are first introduced to the bridegroom at the marriage of the Lamb. The bridegroom is Christ, referred to as "the Lamb", a description of His blood-bought, redemptive relationship with us who have been saved by His grace. Many times we read from His own words the reference to Christ as the bridegroom. For example, in Matt 9:15, when the Pharisees and others were finding fault with His disciples because they did not fast, the Lord replied, "How could the disciples fast when the bridegroom is with them". In Matt 22:1-13, He tells the story of the marriage of the king's son and of the wedding garment. He is the son who is being married. In (Matt 25:1-10), our Lord tells the parable of the ten maidens, and of their going out to meet the bridegroom when he comes. John the Baptist referred to Jesus as the bridegroom. (John 3:29-30). The apostle Paul, in 2 Corinthians 11:2 and in Eph 5:23-32, refers to Jesus as the bridegroom, the husband of the bride that God is preparing for Him.

Who is the bride? The bride is the church is our Christ. The bride is not the OT Israel. OT Israel in Isaiah, in Ezekiel, and in Hosea is described as the wife of Jehovah who is now a put-away wife. Israel is a forsaken wife; she is a repudiated wife. Because of her idolatries and her adulteries and because of her rejection of her great maker to whom God married her, she is a divorced wife. The prophets say that someday she will be restored. But when she is restored, when she comes back, even then she will not be a bride. No restored wife is ever referred to as a virgin. But this bride in Revelation is a virgin. For example, in 2 Corinthians 11:2, Paul says, "I have espoused you to one husband that I may present you as a chase virgin to Christ". And in Eph 5:30-32. Paul says "For we are members of his body, of his flesh, and of his bones. For this cause shall a man leave his father and mother, and shall be joined unto his wife, and they two shall be one flesh." This is a great mystery (musterion): but I speak concerning Christ and the Church". The bride married to our Lord is the church, the household of the Christian faith. Out of all the languages, tribes, peoples, and families of the earth, among the Jews, Gentiles, barbarians, and the Scythians, and the provincials over this earth, God is now calling out a people for His name, that He might present them unto the Lord at the great marriage day of the Lamb.

There are two robes that the bride of Christ, the Christian, will wear. As was the custom of the Roman world, our Lord wore an inner garment called a tunic. He also wore an outer garment that the Romans called a toga. Both of those garments, the inner garment that Christ gives us, and the outer garment, the weaving of our own works, we shall wear in that beautiful, consummating day of our Lord. There is an inner garment of justification by faith which is the gift of God. There is also an outer garment of our own obedience to the mandates and commandments of our Lord. There is an inner garment of imputation, the righteousness that comes to a child of faith. There is also an outer garment, the deeds by which we have sought to adorn the doctrine and to glorify the name of our Savior. There is a positional righteousness that a Christian has that is given him by our Lord. There is also a practical righteousness that we have in doing good deeds of our Lord. So the inner garment is something that Christ bestows upon us when he washes our sins away, when we wash our robes, our souls, and make them white in the blood of the Lamb. But there is also an outer garment that we shall wear which is woven by our own hands and is made up of all of these deeds we have sought to do for our blessed Jesus.

The text says: "And His wife has made herself ready." She has her garments beautiful and white, ready to go to her marriage with her Lord. When did she make herself ready? When were all of those rewards given to her? How was that beautiful robe so arrayed and adorned? We are told that very plainly. Paul says in 2 Corinthians 5:10 "For we must all appear before the judgment seat of Christ". This is the judgment seat, the Bema, of our Lord, before which all of His people shall stand, that we may receive the things done in the body, whether they be good or bad. That is the great reward judgment. So Paul writes again in 1 Corinthians 3:11-16 that we shall stand before our Christ when we are taken up into heaven and there shall our works be tried as if by fire. If our works are wood, hay and stubble, they are burned, they are destroyed. If our works are gold, silver and precious stones, they abide as an adornment for the beautiful wedding garment we shall wear when we are presented to the Lamb- "for his wife has made himself ready".

Some of our people will have beautiful garments. All the good things they have done and the works by which they have dedicated a holy life to the Savior will make up their garments that sparkle like the jewels of heaven, their rewards at the precious hand of Jesus. Some of our people are going to be practically naked, "saved as if by fire". All their works burned up, all of them. Some of the things our people do issue in nothing but loss. Their deeds are going to be burned up by fire. Their souls are going to be saved as if by fire, as if they ran out of a house naked. What a day! What a day!

O Lord, may we be found worthy in that awesome hour when God shall give us the fruit of our hands, and the reward of our deeds! Therefore, "my beloved brethren," (how often did Paul this plead with us) "therefore, my beloved brethren, be you steadfast, unmovable, always abounding in the work of the Lord, for as much as you know that your labor is not in vain in the Lord". (1 Corinthians 15:58). The garment will belong to you forever and forever, God's eternal reward. The beautiful robe is of our own weaving- "when the wife has made herself ready".

The Marriage Ceremony

Concerning the marriage itself, is it not a strange narrative that God should omit to describe it? Nothing is said about this, no word is used to describe it. "The marriage of the Lamb has come" and that is all. Just the fact of it. John just hears the Hallelujah chorus announcing it. He has a word to say about the wife, the bride of Christ, who has made herself ready. He describes the robe of our righteousness that shall be our reward at the Bema of Christ, but he never recounts the actual wedding itself. The event just happens, and all heaven bursts into Hallelujahs concerning it, but there is no word about the ceremony itself.

The Banquet Described 19: 9-10

"Then he said to me, "Write: Blessed are those who are called to the marriage supper of the Lamb". The wedding is something, but the supper is something altogether different. The bride is wed, the guests sup, and the angels are the spectators-three different groups. You will find the difference in the following example in Matthew (25:1-13).

We read about the ten virgins; five were wise and five were foolish. The ten virgins go out to meet the bridegroom. Where is the bride? She is in the father's house. These friends of the bridegroom and of the bride are there to meet them and to rejoice with them and to enter with them into the festivities, the gladness of the nuptials. They are there to share in the feast, the marriage supper of the Lamb. They are the friends, they are the guests, and they are waiting until the couple comes out and they can enter in with them to the feast, to the supper, to the bridal refreshments. It is thus in (Rev 21:9-10). The city includes the bride and all her friends. In that city we will find all of God's children. But there is a bride there as well as her attendants, her companions and her friends. The whole city is called the bride because they do honor and glory to her. But the bride in the city is one thing and all of the friends, companions and attendants are another. The city is made up of the bride and the guests.

The blessedness in the beatitude of Revelation 19:9 covers a greater, broader group than is represented by the bride. "Blessed are they which are called unto the marriage supper of the Lamb." Let us take, for example, one of those honored guests, John the Baptist. John the Baptist died before the time of the cross. He was never a part of the visible Church of Jesus Christ. He belonged to and he died in the old dispensation. That is why the great Baptist says in the third chapter of the fourth gospel: John 3:29. "He who has the bride is the bridegroom; but the friend of the bridegroom, who stands and hears him, rejoices greatly because of the bridegroom's voice." John the Baptist is not a part of the bride. He is not a part of the Church. John is a guest. John is a friend who stands and rejoices in the favor of God upon the couple who are married. Connect this with Matt 11:11, speaking of John the Baptist: but he that is least in the Kingdom of Heaven (in the dispensation and age of our Lord's Church) is greater than he. Why? Because the least of us who have been saved, the humblest, belongs to the bride of our Lord. We belong to His Church. These others are the guests, who are invited to the marriage supper of the Lamb, but they do not belong to the body that God is now calling out in this age of grace. The guests are specially blessed. This is a special blessing for the saved of the old covenant. (The Tribulation saints also will be guests.)

John the Baptist will be the most honored of all. He comes in and is seated at the great banquet of our Lord. Then, may be Abraham, is next, who saw the day of our Lord and rejoiced in seeing it. All the great prophets, Noah, Moses, Daniel, all will have prominent places. (Rev 19:10. Watch out whom you kneel to)

A most educating incident occurred after John witnessed the breathtaking wedding scene of the Son and the joyous praise session. He was so awestruck by what the angel had showed him that he fell down at the angel's feet and worshipped him. Now this was no ordinary angel. He is described in Rev 18:1 as having great authority and illuminating the earth with his glory. Yet look what he told John about worshipping him: "Don't do that! I am your fellow servant, and one of your brothers who declare the testimony about Jesus. Worship God". Since this mighty angel refused to accept worship, how much less should any other created being be worshipped or prayed to! Yet a common denominator of many of the religions of the world is that the person who founded the religious system eventually ends up being adulated or worshipped by his followers.

The angel also reminded John that every aspect of prophecy is ultimately a testimony about Jesus. His spirit permeates it.

The Battle of Armageddon Rev 19:11-21

What an unimaginable catastrophe! What death and carnage! This vast holocaust closes human history. The Battle of Armageddon, the war of Megiddo, is the scene in which the great God and Savior Jesus Christ appears, intervening in human history. Immediately after the marriage of the Lamb and after the nuptial supper, the gates of heaven burst open in the triumph of the hosts of glory. As Jude said in verses 14 and 15, "Behold, the Lord comes with ten thousand of His saints, to execute judgment on all, to convict all who are ungodly among them of all their ungodly deeds". Notice that history does not quietly and gradually merge into the kingdom of our Messiah. The end comes violently; it comes in fury. The whole earth is bathed in blood, in the judgment of the great day of God Almighty.

The final Battle Described throughout the Bible

The mighty conflict described here in chapter 19 of the Revelation is one that has been foretold all through the Bible. Prophecy, in the OT and in the NT, without exception, says that the end of the world comes in a vast, mighty, indescribable conflict. World history ends in war and destruction.

This great battle called Armageddon has been described several times previously in the Book of the

Revelation. For example, in Revelation 11:15 we read, at the sounding of the seventh trumpet: "And the seventh angel sounded; and there were great voices in heaven, saying, the kingdoms of this world are become the kingdoms of our Lord, and of his Christ, and he shall reign forever and ever." Read verses up to 18: The conflict is mentioned again in Revelation 14:17-20: Imagine blood up to the bridles of the horses for two hundred miles! It is unimaginable. The world has never read of, it has never conceived, it has never seen anything comparable to this last, great battle that will destroy apostate humanity. There is another reference to this last conflict in Revelation 16:12-16. Revelation 9:16 describes the army of one of the kings. Two hundred million. It is unbelievable, it is unimaginable. These passages in the revelation add vivid details to the account of the battle described in the text here in chapter 19.

The Battle of Armageddon, the final conflict that dissolves human history and at which time Christ comes from heaven in glory and in great power, is referred to time and again in OT prophecies. For example, Isaiah 63:1, Ezekiel 38, 39, Daniel chapters 2, 7, 9, and 11, Zachariah 14:1, 2, 4, and 5 are references to the same great holocaust.

The prophets with one accord say that the armies of the earth will be assembled in Palestine. They will gather from one end of the globe to the other. The great rendezvous, the great assembly of those hosts will be at Megiddo. This is the battlefield of the world- Megiddo. There Barak and Deborah fought against Sisera. There Gideon fought against the Midianites. There Saul was slain at the hand of the Philistines. There Ahaziah was slain by the arrows of Jehu. There Pharaoh Necho slew good king Josiah. There Jeremiah lamented the slain of the armies of Josiah. And through the ages since, each battle fought there, whether by the Druses or the Turks or the armies of Napoleon, is a harbinger of the great day of the battle of God Almighty. The whole earth is plunged into a vast militarism. There is the spirit and march of the slaughter; murder, bloodshed and violence among all mankind. This is the war of the great day of God Almighty. It has many phases and many parts and the whole earth is involved in it. That is why a man who reads the Bible and looks out over the world today and sees the immeasurable preparation for war is not taken by surprise. It is the development of history according to the prophets. Always remember, there is no such thing as having instruments of war and not using them. When the scientists were trying to split the atom and thus discover nuclear power, the prophecy was made that if it was ever achieved it would first be used in an atomic bomb. Was atomic fission first used in order to manufacture electricity? Was atomic power first used for peaceful purposes? No. It was used in war. Thus, the whole earth is getting ready for a final holocaust.

When we read the Word of God, then look at the newspapers, television and internet; we tremble in the presence of the prophets who describe this coming day.

The Victorious Warrior Christ

Now, let us look at the text more closely. First, in the midst of that terrible and indescribable conflict, there is the bursting open of heaven and the appearing of the Son of God. He is thus described "His eyes were like a flame of fire [burning fire, probing into the darkest recesses of the human soul], and on his head were many crowns".

Next we read, "and he has a name written, that no man knows, but he himself". That refers to His essential deity, the incommunicable, unpronounceable, unknowable name of God. No man can know God. Finite as we are, restricted as we are, the essential deity of God is something a man cannot enter into.

It is the very Lord God who is coming; for Christ Jesus is God of the universe. There is one God, and this is the great God, called in the OT, Jehovah, the incarnate, in the New Testament He is called Jesus, the Prince of Heaven, who is coming.

We read again "and his name is called The Word of God". This is his pronounceable name; this is His communicable name; this is the name by which we who are mortal know Him. "In the beginning was the Word and the Word was with God and the Word was God. (John 1:1). He became incarnate and we saw His glory as the glory of the only begotten of the Father, full of grace and truth. This is the Word of God "the Lord Jesus Christ".

And out of His mouth goes a sharp sword. He does not need to strike. He speaks and the thing is done. There is illimitable power even in His voice. For example, in the days of His humility, in the days when He was condemned and rejected of men, evil men came to arrest Him. The Lord asked, "whom do you seek". And they said "Jesus of Nazareth". He said, "I am he". And they all fell to the ground. Even in the days of his humility, the armed guards of the Romans and of the Sanhedrin and of the temple could not stand in His presence. If it was thus in the days of his sorrow, think what it will be when He comes in glory with the hosts of heaven! What power! What strength. The sense is indescribable.

The Revelation also describes the saints that come with Him: "And the armies which are in heaven followed him upon white horses clothed in fine linen, white and clean".

The seer now describes the armies that are warring against the Lord Christ. By the side of the beast is the false prophet. All their followers stand with them. They are the product of godless government and godless religion. There they stand, all together. You just put this down as an axiom in human history: when a people, when a nation turns aside from the truth and from obedience to the mandates of God, they turn to the most unimaginable oppressions that mind can think of. They turn to slavery, to oppression, and to all things evil, sordid, damning and terrible. There is no exception to that axiom in history. Look at it today. Anywhere you find a government that repudiates God, and a people who say "No to our Lord, they are in the morass and the miasma of misery. That is where revelation and war come from. We are not going to have any trouble with a great Christian nation or a godly people. These terrible things come out of the evil spirits that find lodgment in the hearts of men who repudiate God. This is the beast and the false prophet.

Gathering of armies in Palestine.

It is astonishing that all of these vast multitudes of armies are in Palestine. How were they brought together? The answer is found in (Rev 16:13-16). When men give themselves to vile rejection, blasphemy, and atheism, then they open their hearts to the spirits of evil and to malicious lies of demons. This is the illustration of truth in 2 Thessalonians 2:11: "God shall send them strong delusion that they should believe a lie". To them a lie is mere truth than truth itself and atheism is more real than God Himself.

These evil spirits gather at this great judgment day of Almighty God.

Now let us look upon the invincible warrior, Christ, and His triumphant victory. The war is over instantly. Is not that a strange thing? You would think, "What power these men have, and these great nations, what power they have? Against God, they have no might at all. One angel from the Lord, just one, brought to the vast camp of the Assyrians destruction and death, when Sennacherib came against the people of Jehovah. Before the terrible power of the Assyrians, Hezekiah the king went down on his face, crying to God for help. The Lord listened and said, "I see your tears falling on the pavement of the temple and I hear your prayers". Then God sent just one angel, one. When Sennacherib woke up the next morning, as far as his eyes could see there were thousands and thousands of corpses that once comprised his proud army.

"He who sits in the heavens shall laugh; the Lord shall hold them in derision". (Psalm 2:4). Look how the battle is fought. The beast was taken. God just went down there and snatched him; he just grabbed him. The Almighty, like a big cat with a mouse, just shook the living daylights out of him! "And the beast was taken, with him the false prophet". Notice that a thousand years later, in Revelation 20, they are still in the lake of fire and brimstone. That is the way the Lord does. He works quickly, instantly, suddenly with blasphemers and unbelievers. He has always done that. In the Garden of Eden when the woman fell, God talked to her. He turned to the man and talked to him. But notice that He never asked the Serpent anything. He never said anything to him. There are no extenuating circumstances and there are no mitigating details. It is always thus with God-haters and Christ-rejecters. When an apostate who rejects God, stands in the presence of the Lord, there is nothing to be said. The judgment is over just like that. It is decisive and final.

John does not see the battle. As he did not see the marriage of the Lamb, so he does not see the battle here. He just sees the angel who stands in the sun, stationed in glory, calling for the fowls and the birds of the air to come. That is all John sees. This is the end of those who refuse our great God.

We close with Psalm 2, which is the picture of what we have been speaking about today: Verse 1. "Why do the nations rage and the people imagine a vain thing?" The word is in Hebrew for "anointed" is "Messiah". When translated into Greek, it is Christ. These apostates gather themselves against the Lord and against His Christ, saying "Let us do away with them". The kings of the earth and the rulers take counsel against his anointed saying, let us cast them out. "He who sits in the heavens shall laugh; the Lord shall hold them in derision." (Ps.2:4)

Oh the humor of God, the laughter of God! Psalms 2:6. "Yet I have set my king on my holy hill of Zion." An irrefutable, invincible, immovable, unchangeable decree of God is this: "Christ shall reign over this whole earth and over all the hosts of heaven. "You shall break them with a rod of iron; you shall dash them to pieces like a potter's vessel".

It is no light thing when a man says "No" to God. Blessed are all they that commit their soul's destiny to the Lord Christ.

REVELATION CHAPTER 20

The Binding of Satan

This chapter is one of the greatest and yet one of the most controversial in the Bible. It continues the chronological history of Jesus Christ's final judgment immediately after His return to earth.

In Revelation 19 the Antichrist and the False Prophet were cast alive into the Lake of Fire. Then all the armies that followed them were destroyed. And now at the beginning of chapter 20 Satan, the arch-fiend of the universe is finally judged.

There is a certain amount of theological dispute about this chapter, and it centers around a theme mentioned six times in the chapter, namely whether there will be a literal thousand-year period of history during which mortal and immortal men will live in an earthly kingdom ruled by Jesus the Messiah, after his return to earth. This is usually referred to as the Millennium, from the Latin words milli (one thousand) and annum (year).

The real issue at stake is whether God ever promised such an earthly kingdom, and if He did, will He keep His promise literally.

There are more prophecies in the Bible about this kingdom and its significance to the believing Jew than any other theme of prophecy. The heart of the OT prophetic message is the coming of the Messiah to set up an earthly kingdom over which He would rule from the throne of David. The only important detail which the Book of Revelation adds concerning this promised Messianic kingdom is its duration- one thousand years.

Different Views on the Millennium

Eschatology is the theological term for the study of the end times. Is comes from the Greek word eschatos, meaning "last or last things". Thus, it is for biblical prophecy.

One of the unique features of biblical prophecy is that it has been interpreted by different hermeneutical methods. There are four general views of eschatology that have been proposed within Christian theology.

Futuristic View

The futuristic view holds that prophetic events will be fulfilled in the future at the time of the end. Christ is viewed as coming in the future to establish His kingdom.

Preterist View

The Preterist view holds that prophetic events were actually fulfilled at the time they were written and are now in the past. Christ is viewed as already having come to destroy Jerusalem (AD 70) and establish His kingdom.

Historical View

The historicist view holds that prophetic events have been continually fulfilled throughout church history. Some may still come to pass in the future as Christ is viewed as continually coming.

Idealist View

The idealist view holds that prophetic events have no specific fulfillment in the past or the future, but are being fulfilled in the present experience of the individual. Christ is viewed as coming within the individual's own experience.

Within evangelical circles, several schools have thought to have developed around the theme of the millennium or the millennial reign of Christ. The issue at stake among evangelicals has generally involved how one interprets prophecy. Three main schools of thought have been proposed: while most evangelicals are premillennialists in their view of eschatology, a millennial and postmillennial options also exist.

Postmillennial

This school of thought believes that the Millennium (the thousand years of Revelation 20:1-13) is to be interpreted symbolically as synonymous with the church age. Satan's power is viewed as being bound by the power of the gospel. Postmillennialists believe that during this

"Millennium" (Church age) the Church is called upon to conquer unbelief, convert the masses, and govern society by the mandate of biblical law. Only after Christianity succeeds on earth will Christ return and announce that His kingdom has been realized. Post-millennial advocates have included Catholics, puritans, charismatic's, and Dominionists, who urge believers to take dominion over the earth. Postmillennialists believe that the world will get better and better through the spread of the gospel, and this will be the millennial age. Then, after the millennium, Christ will take the believers to heaven and condemn those who reject Him. However, this teaching suffered a severe reversal in the past 100 years because of two world wars and numerous regional wars. The world is obviously not getting better and better, even though the gospel has had its widest hearing of any era.

A millennial

A-millennium teaches that there will be no thousand-year reign of Christ on earth and no earthly kingdom of God. According to this view, when Christ returns to earth He will take all the believers out, condemn all the unbelievers, and eternity will begin right then. This is what they believe is meant by the dividing of the sheep (believers) from the goats (unbelievers).

This view tends to allegorize all the prophecies about the promised kingdom. It also teaches that Israel forfeited all that God promised to her because of unbelief, and that the Church will inherit all the promises originally intended for Israel. A-millennialists teach that the Church is the fulfillment of the millennial kingdom, and that Christ presently reigns through the Church in peace and righteousness. This interpretation allegorizes the chaining of Satan in this chapter and teaches that he was instead bound by Christ at His first coming, so that each time Christ gives a believer victory over temptation, it is a kind of reaffirmation of that binding of Satan. A-millennialism optimistically sees the church moving triumphantly to victory.

Pre-millennialism

The oldest interpretation is called pre-millennialism. This view holds that Christ will literally and bodily return to the earth before the thousand-year kingdom begins. He will set up this kingdom and reign from the throne of David out of a rebuilt city of Jerusalem. At the end of that thousand years He will turn the kingdom over to His Father, at which point it will merge with God's eternal kingdom.

Premillennialists also believe that God made unconditional promises and covenants with Israel, and that regardless of Israel's past history of spiritual failures, God will literally fulfill all His promises during this thousand-year kingdom period.

Church-age believers and tribulation believers will also be the recipients of these promises as the adopted sons of Abraham. The apostles and early Christians unanimously expected Jesus to set up the literal, earthly kingdom of God. In Acts 1:6, just before ascending into heaven, the disciples asked Him, "Lord, will you at this time restore the kingdom of Israel". In His answer, Christ didn't try to set them straight by telling them there wouldn't be an earthly kingdom for Israel. He simply told His disciples that it wasn't for them to know when it would come to pass, for this was something which only the God the Father knew.

In the Lord's Prayer, Jesus emphasized this anticipated earthly kingdom when He told His followers to pray, "Thy kingdom come". "Thy will be done on earth as it is in heaven". His will can't be done on earth in the same way it is in heaven until all of Christ's enemies have been put down and Satan hindered from tempting men! One of the major tenets of pre-millennialism is that the earth is getting worse rather than better, and that the kingdom age can't begin until Christ returns to destroy those who have led the world in its downward spiral.

The premillennial view of eschatology looks forward to the rapture (translation of believers to heaven) as the major prophetic event. The Rapture will end the church age and prepare the way for the tribulation period and the return of Christ. Biblical reference to rapture is given in (1 Thessalonians 4:16-17).

Rev.20:1-3. The angel came down with the key of the "abyss". Abyss is the actual Greek word; we took the word bodily in to the English language. In Revelation 9, a fallen angel appears with a key to open the abyss and out of it came the terrible plague of locusts that waged war on the earth. This angel came down from heaven with a key to lock up Satan. The angel had in his hand a great chain. In verse 6 of the book of Jude, he writes, "And the angels who did not keep their proper domain, but left their own abode, He has reserved in everlasting chains under darkness for the judgment of the great day". Whatever kind of a chain it is that God welds by which He holds these evil, black, foul demons in the abyss, it is that kind of a chain that the angel comes to lay upon Satan.

The meaning of Satan's four names

Satan is described here by four names, the same identical names in the same order by which he is described in chapter 12 of Revelation. The first two names reflect his personality, and the second two are his actual, personal names. As most of us have two names, so Satan has two personal names. The first two of the four employed here describe his character, his personality: "And he laid hold on that 'dragon'. The designation 'dragon' refers to his bestial leadership of the beast governments of the world. The second designation "that old serpent" refers to his subtle nature. In the beginning, in the Garden of Eden, it was as a serpent that he insinuated himself into the confidence of our first parents and defeated them away from God. The next two designations comprise his personal names. That ancient serpent is "the devil". There is only one devil. There are many demons. Demons are the agents of Satan. Diabolos, devil, refers to his character as a liar and a murderer. Jesus said he was a liar and a murderer from the beginning. He is Diabolos, an archfiend.

His first name is the same in Hebrew as it is in Greek and also in English. The Hebrew name is transliterated into Greek which in turn is transliterated into English, "Satan". 'Satan' means accuser. He is the one who deceived our first parents. He is the one who brought death into our world. God sent a mighty angel from heaven with a key and a great chain in his hand. The angel shut him up in the bottomless pit.

The difference between "The Abyss and Hell".

Now, where is the abyss? In answering that question we come to a discussion of the whole nether world, the world beyond this present life. The devil is cast into the abyss where he is bound for a thousand years. But after the thousand years, he is loosed for a season, after which he is cast into the lake of fire and brimstone, where the beast and the false prophet are. There he is tormented day and night, world without end and forever. What is the difference between the 'abyss' and the 'lake of fire'? The difference is plainly stated in the revealed word of God. The lake of fire is hell. The abyss is something else. The word "abyss" is used nine times in the NT. It is a Greek word meaning "bottomless pit". Seven of the nine times it is used in Revelation. One time it is used in Luke 8:31 and one time it is used in Romans 10:7. We get a good idea of what it refers to in Luke 8:31. The passage recounts the story of the Gadarene demoniac who had in him a legion of demons (not devils). He was filled with every vile and unclean thing, as men today are filled with all manner of concupiscence, iniquity, vile, lust, and immoral filth. There was a legion of them that lived in that man and drove him into violence. When the Lord came, those demons recognizing Jesus said, "Lord, don't send us into the abyss before the time". There is that word "abyss". It is a horrible place. It is an imprisonment; it is a place where demons, foul and wicked, are chained by the Lord God. Another time the word is used is in Romans 10:7. We are there warned not to say that the Lord Jesus is to come up from the abyss as if He were one of those demons. All seven times the word is used in the Book of Revelation it has the same meaning; it always refers to a place where fallen angels and where foul and evil spirits are imprisoned by God. That is where Satan is going to be cast, chained, locked and sealed for a thousand years.

But there are other places beyond this life and grave beside the abyss. We read in Revelation 19:20 "Both beast and false prophet were cast alive into the lake of fire. That is the ultimate place where the devil is cast Rev 20:10. That is also the place where the wicked dead are cast (Rev 20:13-14). Then in the next chapter, Revelation 21:8 "But the fearful, and unbelieving, and the abominable, and murderers, and whoremongers, and sorcerers, and idolaters, and all liars shall have their part in the lake which burns with fire and brimstone". Our continuous confusion lies in the translation. It lies in the King James Version, the Authorized Version. They take the word "sheol" and translate it "hell". They take the word "Hades" and translate it "hell". In these mistranslations we come to the position where we have no idea of what God has revealed to us of that other world.

The word, "abyss", the bottomless pit, is a place where God has imprisoned, against the day of judgment, evil, vile, fallen angels and demons, spirits of evil. That is the abyss. Now the word "sheol" is used in OT sixty-five times. Thirty-one times in the Authorized Version it is translated "hell". Thirty-one times it is translated "the grave"/ Three times it is translated "the pit". The Greek word "Hades" in the NT is the exact equivalent to "sheol" in the OT. They are identical words. One is the same as the other. The word "Hades" in the NT is used eleven times. Ten times it is translated "hell". One time it is translated "the grave". But there is nothing in the words "sheol" or "Hades" that refers to hell, nothing. All that sheol means and all that hades means is the departed, unseen worlds beyond this life. When we die, we enter into Sheol, we enter into hades.

But "hell" is something altogether different. In the OT the word "hell" is "Tophet"; in the NT it is "gehenna". "Gehenna" is used twelve times in the NT and each time it is properly translated "hell" in the Authorized Version. Gehenna is the valley of Hinnom, outside Jerusalem. In that valley idolaters once burned their children to Moloch, a thing that God despised. God cursed the place. The Jewish people used the valley of Hinnom for the refuse of the city. For centuries, filth, garbage, even the carcasses of animals were thrown into the valley. The fire never died and the worm was never killed and the jackals fought and gnashed one another with their teeth as they ate the refuse cast into the horrible pave. From this background the word Gehenna was used to describe the everlasting damnation of hell where there is weeping and wailing and gnashing of teeth, where the worm never dies, and the fire is never quenched". That is hell.

Up to this present moment no soul has ever entered hell. The first ones to be cast into hell are the beast and the false prophet. They are first. The second to be cast into the hell is the devil. The third to be cast into hell are those whose names are not written in the Lamb's book of life. That is why we have the urgency of preaching the Gospel of the cross. This is the imperative that brought our Lord down into this world. He never came just to preach us better ethics or a finer way to pronounce holy words. He came to die because we are in danger of hell fire.

Satan is loosened after the millennium

After Satan is bound for a thousand years, he must be loosed for a little season. When thousand years are expired, Satan shall be loosed out of his prison. Satan is loosed in order that those who grow up during the millennium, under the perfect and righteous reign of Christ, may have the chance to choose between good and evil, between God and Satan. They have never been tempted. They have never been tried. Everyone who is born during the millennium is going to have an opportunity to choose between God and Satan, between righteousness and unrighteousness. Satan is to be loosed to try them and to tempt them.

But this is the last confederation against God. This is the last deception. This is the last sin. Jesus comes down and takes that Diabolos, the Satan, and He cast him into hell, into the lake of fire, where the beast and the false prophet are, and there God will judge him. Hell was not made for man, but for the fallen angels. The lost man goes there by choice.

Rev.20:4-5. The vision begins "And I saw thrones and them that sat upon them, and judgment was given unto them". This is the occasion for the ultimate, final reward God has in store for His saints. "I saw all of them in glory" says John. When Satan is cast into the abyss and when God inaugurates the millennial age, the first vision that John sees is the glorious panorama of all of God's people rewarded and enthroned. A Christian does not get his crown of reward until the end time. The reason for this is simple. A man does not die when he dies. His influence lives on and on. Therefore, it is only at the end of the age that a reward can be given to him. Thus at the consummation of the ages, John sees all of these gloriously resurrected saints enthroned and rewarded. This is the fulfillment of the promise the Lord gave to His disciples in Matthew 19:28, that they would sit upon thrones judging the twelve tribes of Israel. This is the word of Apostle Paul in 1 Corinthians 6:2, that God's saints will judge the world. But the apostle goes even further in the next verse to say that God's saints will judge the angels. This is the promise of our Lord in Revelation 3:21, that we who overcome shall share His throne in heaven. This is the millennial, triumphant age of the enthronement, the exaltation, the glorification, the rewarding of God's resurrected people.

Here John sees a special and particular group. "And I saw the souls of them that were beheaded for the witness of Jesus and they lived and reigned with Christ a thousand years". The souls are seen under the altar at the time of the breaking of the fifth seal-the first fruits of those martyred by the beast (Rev 6:9-10).

The third class to be crowned are the tribulation saint themselves. John mentions a great company; "which has not worshipped the beast, neither his image, neither has received his mark upon their foreheads, or in their hands". These too are crowned. John says they lived and reigned with Christ a thousand years. "But the rest of the dead lived not again until the thousand years were finished. This is the first resurrection".

It is a strange thing that there is no place in the word of God where the entire vision of the resurrection from the dead is presented. The truth is always revealed in parts, in pieces. First, God says there is such a thing as the resurrection. In Matt 22:23-31 our Lord discussed the doctrine with the Sadducees, who avowed that there is no such thing as a resurrection. Our Lord, in answering a question the Sadducees brought to Him, began with the words, "But as touching the resurrection of the dead ..." Speaking of the resurrection, He avowed that in that perfected state we do not marry nor are given in marriage. We are as the angels in heaven. But the point of discussion centered around the fact that there is a resurrection. Again, in John 11:23, Jesus tells Martha that her brother, Lazarus, shall live again. Martha replied, "I know Lord, that he shall live again in the resurrection, at the last day". Jesus agreed with that statement. Again, in Act 26:8 the apostle Paul, in the defense of his life before King Agrippa, said to that Jewish monarch: "why should it be thought a thing incredible with you, that God should raise the dead".

From the scripture, we learn yet another thing about the raising of the body. There is also to be a resurrection of the lost, of the damned. Daniel 12:2 says, "And many of them that sleep in the dust of the earth shall awake, some to everlasting life, and some to shame and everlasting contempt". Also read (John 5:28-29) and Acts 24:15.

We learn from the scripture that the resurrection of God' people is not all at the same time, but comprises in itself a series. The raising of God's elect is in a succession. In (1 Corinthians 15:20-24) Paul outlines the succession, the series, the companies, the troops, that appear before God in resurrection glory. There are four groups in that tagma order. Tagma is a Greek word for "a series", or "a succession", or "a troop", or "a company". Paul says that everyone is to be raised in his own succession, in his own order, in his own time. Paul names those companies. One, Christ; two, the first fruits; three, they that are Christ's at His coming; four, those at the end. Paul is following here a pictorial typology found in the feast of the first fruits.

In Leviticus 23, God names the great convocations of Israel. All of them have a profound spiritual meaning. They are tremendous prophecies. They harbinger sublime events in the life of our Lord. For example, the first feast is the Passover, which represents the death of our Lord. The second one is the feast of unleavened bread, which represents the burial of our Lord, the taking of unleavened bread and hiding it away. The third is the feast of the first fruits. That is the resurrection of our Lord. The next, the fourth one, is the feast of Pentecost. That is the coming of the Holy Spirit. The fifth one is the feast of blowing of the trumpet. That is the harbinger of the return of Christ, the triumphant descent of our Lord. The next feast (the Jews later turned it into a fast) is that of Atonement and that pictures the tribulation and the mourning of the Jewish people when they come back to the Lord and accept their Messiah. The last is the feast of

Tabernacles, which is a pictorial representation of the glory and happiness of God's ultimate and final millennial age.

In those seven feasts, the apostle takes the feast of first fruits to depict the resurrection of our Lord. The feast of First fruits began on Sunday, on the first day after the Sabbath. It began on the first of the week after the Passover. Our Lord was crucified during the Passover. After His death and burial, on the first day of the week He was raised from the grave. Every time we met on Sunday, we celebrate the feast of the first fruits. Every time we gather in God's house on the first day of the week, we are celebrating the resurrection of our Lord.

The feast of first fruits had three parts. First, on that day, the first day after the Sabbath, on the Sunday after the Passover, the faithful Israelite went out into the barley field and there plucked a handful of the first fruits of the coming harvest to the priest and dedicated it to the Lord. The priest took the offering into the tabernacle and waved it before the Lord. It was a sign; it was a harbinger, of the dedication of the whole harvest promised by the Lord. The first fruits offered unto God were just a handful of the ears of barley. The second part of the harvest came in summer time. It was then that the whole crop was gathered. Finally, at the end of the season, the harvesters gathered the gleanings. So in the dedication of the harvest unto God there was first, the handful of the first fruits, then there was the harvest itself, and finally the gleanings, the picking up of the heads that had been crushed and trampled down in the gathering. Paul uses that imagery and follows it precisely here in the resurrection of the just, in the resurrection of God's people, in the resurrection of those who are saved. The harvest has a tagma, it has a succession, it has a series. We come before the Lord by troops and in different companies.

The first is Christ, He was the first one raised from the dead. In the scriptures we read of several resuscitations. For example, the dead man who in his burial touched the bones of Elisha and came to life again, was resuscitated. Remember the story of Elisha raising from the dead the son of Shunamite. Remember the story of Lazarus. Remember the story of the daughter of Jairus. But in all of those instances the body was merely revived. The body later and ultimately went back into the dust of the ground. They died. They were not immortalized. They were not resurrected. The first to be resurrected from the dead was our Lord Jesus Christ.

Paul says next in order is the first fruits, the little handful, the little company who are brought before the Lord as an earnest of the great harvest that is yet to be dedicated, to be raised. Let us see the order of resurrection by Paul. We are to look for a little harvest, a little first fruits, the earnest of a few heads of grain to be waved before the Lord. Matt 27:51-53. Read from the NKJV. Paul said Christ was first, then the first fruits, the little handful. When the Lord entered into heaven, raised from the dead, He did not go by Himself. He had a little company with Him. They were the first fruits. They are a harbinger, they are an earnest, they are a guarantee, they are a promise of the great harvest that is yet to come. Paul speaks of that. He says "Every man in his tagma. Christ is first, the first one raised from the dead.

Then Paul names the third group. "Afterward they that are Christ's at his coming." That is the rapture, the taking out of God's people from the world when the Lord comes. (1 Thessalonians 4:16). That is the great harvest, when the Lord comes for His own. We shall comprise the great, main body of the harvest of the resurrection. Paul says "Then the end". So we have some 'end' ones just as it was after the harvest, then the gleanings. The resurrection of those saved during the time of the tribulation will be the gleanings.

Why is there no salvation for the fallen angels? There is an essential difference between the sin of a human being and the sin of Lucifer and the fallen angels. Each angel chose to sin; we were born in sin. There is no salvation for them, however there is for us.

Rev 20:4-6. Rev 20:4 reads, "And I saw thrones, and they sat on them, and judgment was committed to them". This refers to the glorified, resurrected host of God's sainted people. Then John continues in the verse as he describes another group of those who had been beheaded for their witness to Jesus and for the word of God, who had not worshipped the beast or his image, and had not received his mark on their foreheads of on their hands. And they lived and reigned with Christ for a thousand years. But the rest of the dead did not live again until the thousand years were finished. This is the first resurrection. The verses that immediately follow describes the deception by Satan with the announcement that, "when the thousand years have expired, Satan will be released from his prison". The result of this loosing is seen in the gathering together of Satan's dupes against the Lord God. But they are immediately destroyed by fire from heaven, and the devil that deceived them is cast into the lake of fire, where the beast and the false prophet are, to be tormented day and night for ever and ever. Then follows the revelation of the Great White throne judgment. This is followed by the ultimate and eternal kingdom of our Lord and the new city in which His people will dwell in blessedness, in holiness, in righteousness, forever.

The dream of the golden age

As long as the human race has lived, there has been the dream of a "golden age". It is found in the literature of all the cultures of the world. Ancient writers have fabricated a story about an age where a good king ruled their land and everyone was prosperous. They create a mythical story about a mythical ruler. The story narrates how paradise was lost, and celebrates the good old days. But none has a concept about the future paradise. We find it recurring again and again in the literature of the ancient Egyptians, Babylonians, Chaldeans, Persians, Medes, Greeks, Romans, and in ancient Hindu mythology and

the mythology of "Onam" celebration in Kerala. Prophet after prophet, apostle after apostle, book after book records of a golden age.

There is more said in the prophetic scriptures regarding this millennial age than of any other subject in the prophecies themselves. For example, in the book of Daniel, when Daniel saw the course of world history in the likeness of an image, he saw last of all a stone cut without hands that broke in pieces- that vast image and the stone grew to fill the whole earth. Then Daniel interprets it. (Dan 2:44-45). There is a kingdom coming that will be established by the intervention of the Lord God himself. Daniel 7:13-14 also describes the eternal kingdom of God. The preaching of the apostles is not different from the visions of the prophets. Simon Peter declared this age in Acts 3:14-21. Again in chapter 11 of the book of Revelation, the seventh angel sounded, and by anticipation he announces the coming of the kingdom (Rev 11:15). There has never been a time when God has not purposed this for us; namely, that we, with our Lord, shall reign in holiness, in glory and in triumph on this earth. In chapter 20 of the book of Revelation that glorious millennial has come to pass. This is its reality.

The millennium is a time period. Several of the time words in the English language come from the Latin. "Millennium" is just another one of those several time words. The Greek word for the "hour" is hora, and when it comes into English we pronounce it "hour". The Latin word for year is "annus". Our 'annual' is derived from that Latin word referring to a year. The Latin word for one hundred is centum; our word century comes from the word "hundred". The English word "millennium" comes from two Latin words mille, which is a thousand and annum, which is a year. So, the millennium is a thousand-year period. The Millennium begins when Satan is bound after the great Battle of Armageddon, and it ends after a thousand years when Satan is loosed for a little season. It is a new age; it is a new order. There are many things concerning it that we cannot understand and there is no need to try. We cannot conceive of a world without sin, where Satan is bound, where righteousness reigns. These things to us are beyond experience, because we have never known a world that was not overgrown with sin, our lives have never known a time when we did not battle against iniquity. Weeping, crying, bereavement, separation, despair, these are common lot of every life. But in the Golden Age these shall be taken away.

Who enter the millennium?

No one will enter the millennium as a sinner. All who enter that holy and heavenly era will be saved, washed by the blood of the Lamb. The saints alone inherit the kingdom. For example, Daniel 7:18 says "But the saints of the most High shall take the kingdom, and possess the kingdom forever and ever". Daniel says again in verse 22 "The time came that the saints possessed the kingdom". And he repeats in verse 27 the same fact.

The judgment preceding the millennium

In preparation for the Golden Age, there are two great judgments the people on this earth will go through. First, Israel will go through a judgment. God's chosen people who now live in unbelief and who gather in their services in rejection of Christ will go through a judgment. No Israelite who refused the Lord Christ will ever enter the millennium. In chapter 20 of the Book of Ezekiel, there is described the judgment that Israel will go through. Ezekiel 20:33-38. As a shepherd places his rod, his staff, over the door of the sheepfold and as the sheep go through, one by one, he calls their names so the Lord says that He will bring all of Israel into the wilderness and plead with them there in the wilderness, causing them to pass under the rod, judging them one by one. There will be no rebel spared and there will be none left that transgress against the Lord. There will be no rejecter or unbeliever who will enter into the land. This is the great judgment of Israel before the days of the millennium.

There is also judgment of the Gentiles. No Gentile will enter the millennial kingdom of God who is not saved, born again, converted. The judgment of the Gentiles is described in Matthew 25:31-46. No one will enter that kingdom who is not saved, washed clean and white in the blood of the crucified one.

The millennial kingdom is not temporary. It is finally merged into the great, final kingdom of the Lord God Almighty in the eternities of the eternities. There is perpetuity of that kingdom that lasts forever and forever. Daniel even multiplies the forever. It is an everlasting kingdom and our Lord has in it an everlasting dominion. That is confirmed by the Apostle Paul in (1 Corinthians 15:14-28).

The Blessings of the millennial kingdom

First of all, let us consider the elect of God, the people of Israel. They are to be restored to their home and to their land. Amos 9:14-15 (Isa 43: 1-7; Jeremiah 24:6-7; Ezekiel 28:25-26; Zephaniah 3:20). God says His people are going to be given Palestine for an inheritance forever and no one shall ever take it from them. Not only is Israel to be restored to the land, but they are to be converted, they are to accept the Lord Christ as their Savior and their Messiah. Read (Jeremiah 23:3-8). The number of passages that could be read are many. Here are some more verses: Isaiah 4:3-6; Jeremiah 31:31-34; 32: 36-41; Ezekiel 11:18-20; 12:10-14; 13:1, 8, 9; 16: 60-63; 21:10-14; 13:1, 8, 9; 16:60-63; 21:40-44; 36:24-28; 37:26). Beside all these there is another tremendous passage from Paul in Romans 11:21-29.

After stating that, "Blindness in part has happened to Israel, until the fullness of the Gentiles becomes in", the apostle continues: But there is a time when "all Israel shall be saved. God made some great promises to Abraham, to Isaac, to Jacob, to David, through his holy prophets. He made an Abrahamic covenant with them; He made a Davidic covenant with them; He made a Palestinian covenant with them; He made a covenant of a "new heart" with them, and God does not change. Man may change. Man can forget what God has promised. Every promise that God has made to Israel God will faithfully keep. When Israel is converted, the Jews will mourn over their rejection of their Savior, and God will provide a healing fountain for their sins, in which they will be forgiven and will be saved. As there are blessings for Israel, so there are blessings for the Gentiles also. (Isaiah 2:2-4). Read Isaiah 19:23-25. Can you imagine things like that? Think of the hatred of Arabs and Muslims toward the Jews.

All creation will be blessed in the millennium

In that millennium kingdom there is to be a new creation. There are blessings for the whole universe. One of the most sublime and meaningful of all of the passages in the word of God is in Romans 8. Listen to Paul as he describes what God is going to do. (Rom 8:19-23). The prophecies of all OT confirm this passage from Paul. Isaiah 11:6-9 speaks of the change in the animal kingdom.

God never intended the balance of nature to be now as we have it in this world. God never intended for animals to eat one another, to lie in wait, to destroy, to drink blood. This is a mark of sin in the world. God never intended one man to kill another man, much less for one nation to go to war and slay millions of his fellow men. The Lord made His creation to be filled with light, goodness, glory, holiness, love and happiness. But all that we lost in Eden, God will give us back again in the new creation. Think of a day when the wolf and the lamb, the leopard and the kid, the lion and the fatling will lie down together? When that vicious, ferocious, carnivorous lion is a vegetarian! He will eat straw like an ox. Isaiah 35:5-6 says "Then the eyes of the blind shall be opened and the ears of the deaf shall be unstopped". The curse of Genesis 3:17-19 is removed. Compare Isaiah 35:1-2; 55:13). Sickness, sorrow, sighing and crying is no more.

As there are blessings in the millennium for God's chosen people, Israel, there are also blessings in the millennial kingdom for Gentiles, as well as for all God's creation. Zechariah 14:4-9: This is what God has promised for His Son. "He shall be King over all the earth". This is what God has promised for His Son. "He shall be King over all the earth". In Luke 1:32 the angel Gabriel said to Mary "And behold, you will conceive in your womb and bring forth a son, and shall call His name Jesus. He will be great, and will be called the Son of the Highest; and the Lord God will give Him the throne of His father David. And He will reign over the house of Jacob forever, and of His kingdom there will be no end." This is the ultimate and final glory that Paul describes for our Lord in Philippians 2:6-11. And that glorious consummation is seen in the Revelation, the unveiling of Jesus the Christ, the rightful Ruler of the universe. (Also Revelation 11:15.) In 2 Corinthians 4:4 Paul says that "Satan is the god of this world". Surely the Devil is a usurper God never intended it to be like that. But Satan shall be cast out and the rightful King- our living, Lord shall ascend the throne.

Throughout the millennium, righteousness has reigned. The golden age began with a population on earth of soundly saved people, filled with the Spirit, living according to the precepts of the Sermon on the Mount. But as the ages come and go, countless children are born, disease will be banished, and death will be exceedingly rare. Children born during this age will be born with sinful natures, needing to be saved, just as today. Children of believing parents today sometimes become gospel-hardened; so, during the millennium many will become glory- hardened. They will submit to Christ's rule and to the stern laws of the Kingdom because to rebel will mean instant punishment. During the millennium many will render only feigned obedience. Sin will reign in secret in their hearts, and they will long for a time when the strict rules will be relaxed. The Devil will find fertile soil in their souls.

Throughout millennium the nations will come up to Jerusalem to worship. During the golden age, the memory of Russia's disaster will linger on, and Gog and Magog will lend their names symbolically to the dissidents of earth. Satan will seek them out and will find them only too willing to listen to his lies.

During the millennial reign of Christ, Israel as a nation will fulfill the function for which they were originally set apart by God. They will become a kingdom of Priests (Exodus 19:6) who are intermediaries between those who need to be saved, and the king who provides salvation. They will become as they were originally appointed to be, God's lights to the world. Those born in the millennium who need salvation will approach the Savior through Israel. (Zechariah 8:20-23.) Salvation during that period will be provided through the benefits of the death of the Passover Lamb. That is why the Passover will be observed throughout the Millennial Age, as a memorial of the death of Christ (Ezekiel 45:21); and why blood sacrifices will be offered in the millennial temple as memorials of the death of Christ (Ezekiel 43:19-27). Jews living in the millennium will live in perfect obedience to the law of the king. This will be possible because the redeemed will enter into the fulfillment of the promise of Joel 2:3-8 and Ezekiel 36: 26-27, and the indwelling spirit will empower them to obedience. In addition, there will be a universal knowledge of the demands the king made to those who would walk in obedience to His law. (Jeremiah 31:34). What the king demands will not be written on external tablets as was the Law of Moses. Instead it will be inscribed on their hearts. (Jeremiah 31:33). The outbreak of sin will be punished by immediate death. (Isa 11:4). Rebellion against the authority of the king will be immediately judged. (Zechariah 14:16-19).

All those born during the millennial kingdom will have the opportunity to receive the salvation that the king has provided, and because of fear of judgment and respect for the power of the king they will outwardly live in conformity to His law.

Since Satan will be removed during Messiah's millennial reign, there will be no one to entice them to an organized rebellion. Thus at the conclusion of the Lord's earthly reign, it will be necessary to test those who have lived during this period. For that reason, Satan must be set free for a short time (Rev 20:3).

The subjects of the millennial rule of Christ at the beginning of the millennium will consist of those who survive the searching judgments of both Israel and Gentiles as the millennial reign of Christ begins. From many Scriptures it may be gathered that all the wicked will be put to death after the second coming of Christ, and only saints who have lived through the preceding time of trouble will be eligible for entrance into the millennial kingdom. This is demonstrated in the judgment of the Gentiles in Matt 25:31-46, where only the righteous are permitted to enter the millennium. According to Ezekiel 20:33-38, God will also deal with Israel and purge out all rebels, that is, unbelievers, permitting only the saints among Israel. The parables of the wheat and the tares (Matt 13:30-31) and of the good and bad fish (Matt 13:49-50) teach likewise that only the wheat and the good fish, representing the righteous will survive the judgment.

The millennial kingdom will display the fullness of the Holy Spirit. At the institution of the theocratic kingdom the prophecy of Joel will be fulfilled. Joel 2:28-29.

The prophecies picturing the millennium unite in their testimony that the work of the Holy Spirit in believers will be more abundant, and have greater manifestation in the millennium than in any previous dispensation. It is evident from the Scriptures that all believers will be indwelt by the Holy Spirit in the millennium even as they are in the present age (Ezekiel 36:27; 37:14, Jeremiah 31:33).

The fact of the indwelling presence of the Holy Spirit is revealed as part of the glorious restoration of Israel depicted in Ezekiel 36:24. In Ezekiel 37:14, it is stated, "And I will put my Spirit in you, and you shall live, and I will place you in your own land. The filling of the Holy Spirit will be common in the millennium, in contrast to the infrequency of it in other ages, and it will be manifested in worship and praise of the Lord and in willing obedience to Him as well as in spiritual power and inner transformation Isa 32:15; 44:3, Ezekiel 39:29, Joel 2:28-29.

In contrast to present day spiritual apathy, coldness, worldliness, there will be spiritual fervor, a love of God, holy joy, universal understanding of spiritual truth, and a wonderful fellowship of the saints. The emphasis will be on righteousness in life and on joy of the spirit.

The remarkable, astounding, outpouring of the Holy Spirit as presented in the millennial descriptions are so powerful in its transforming, glorifying and imparting miraculous gifts to the saints; so pervading in and over the Jewish nation that all shall be righteous from the least to the greatest; so wide-reaching over the Gentiles that they shall rejoice in the light bestowed; and so extended in its operation that the whole earth shall ultimately be covered with glory- this, with the magnificent portrayal of the millennial and succeeding ages, is so sublime with the indwelling, abiding, communicated divine, that no one can contemplate it, without being profoundly moved at the display of spirituality.

It must, thus, be observed that the outstanding characterization of the millennium is its spiritual nature. An earthly kingdom, to be sure, but spiritual as to its character.

Conditions Existing within the Millennium

Peace: The cessation of war through the unification of the kingdoms of the world under the reign of Christ, together with the resultant economic prosperity, since nations need not devote vast proportions of their expenditure on weapons, is a major theme of the prophets. Isaiah 2:4; 9:4-7; 11:6-9; 32:17-18; 33:5-6; 54:13; 55:12; 60:18; 65:25; 66:12. Ezekiel 28:26; 34:25, 28; Hosea 2:18; Micha 4:2-3, Zech 9:10.

The fullness of joy will be a distinctive mark of the age. Isa 9"3-4; 12:3-6; 14:7-8.

Holiness: The theocratic kingdom will be a holy kingdom, in which holiness is manifested through the king and the king's subjects. The land will be holy; the city holy, the temple holy, and the subjects holy unto the Lord. Isa 1:26-27; 4:3-4; 29:18-23, Joel 3:21, Zephaniah 3:11.

Full Knowledge: Because of the fact that Christ is in the world and ruling over all nations, the millennium is characterized as a time in which the truth of God is widespread. Isaiah writes, for instance "The earth shall be full of the knowledge of Jehovah as the waters cover the sea (Isa 11:9).

The removal of the curse placed upon creation (Gen 3:17-19) will be removed, so that there will be abundant productivity to the earth. Animal creation will be changed so as to lose its venom and ferocity. (Isa 11:6-9, 35:9; 65:25).

Sickness removed: The ministry of the king as a healer will be seen throughout the age, so that sickness and even death, except as a penal measure in dealing with overt sin, will be removed. (Isa 33:24; Jeremiah 30:17; Ezekiel 34:16).

Healing of the deformed: Accompanying this ministry will be healing of all deformity at the inception of the millennium. (Isa 29:17-19; 35:3-6; 61:1-2; Jeremiah 31:8; Micah 4:6-7; Zephaniah 3:19)

No immaturity: The suggestion seems to be that there will not be the tragedies of feeble- mindedness nor of dwarfed bodies in that day. (Isa 14:3-6; 42:6-7; 49:8-9; Zech 9:11-12).

Reproduction: The living saints who go into the millennium in their natural bodies will beget children throughout the age (Not the saints of the Church age. Church age saints will have a body like Jesus). The earth's population will soar. Those born in the age will not be born without a sin nature, so salvation will be required. Jeremiah 30:20; 31:29; Ezekiel 47:22; Zech 10:8.

Labor: The period will not be characterized by idleness, but there will be a perfect economic system, in which the needs of men are abundantly provided for by labor in that system, under the guidance of the king. There will be a fully developed industrialized society providing for the needs of the king's subjects. Isa 62:8-9; 65:21-23; Jeremiah 31:5; Ezekiel 48:18-19. Agriculture, as well as manufacturing, will provide employment. The perfect labor situation will produce economic abundance, so that there will be no want. Isa 4:1; 35:1-2; 30:23-25; 62:8-9; 65:21-23; Jeremiah 31:5, 12; Ezek 34:26; Micah 4:1, 4; Zech 8:11-12; 9: 16-17; Ezek 36:29-30; Joel 2:21-27; Amos 9:13-14.

Increase of Light: There will be an increase of solar and lunar light in this age. This increased light probably is a major cause in the increased productivity of the earth. Isa 4:5; 30:26; 60:19-20; Zech 2:5.

Unified Language: The language barriers will be removed so that there can be free social interaction (Zephaniah 3:9).

Unified Worship: All the world will unite in the worship of God and God's messiah. Isa 45:23; 52:1, 7-10; 66:17-23; Zech 13:2; 14:16; 8:23; 9:7; Zephaniah 3:9; Mal 1:11; Rev 5:9-11.

The fullness of the spirit's divine presence and enablement will be the experience of all who are in subjection to the authority of the king. Isa 32:13-15; 41:1; 44:3; 59:19, 21; 61:1; Ezekiel 36:26-27; 37:14; 39:29; Joel 2:28-29; Ezekiel 11:19-20.

The duration of the Millennium:

The duration of the millennium is 1000 years (Rev 20:1-6). It is generally held, even by those denying the literalness of the thousand-year period, that the angel, heaven, the pit, Satan, the nations and the resurrections mentioned in this chapter are all literal. It would be folly to accept the literalness of those and deny the literalness of the time element. Most of Christendom spiritualizes this chapter according to their whims. Six times in this passage it is stated that Christ's millennial kingdom will continue for a thousand years. An important section is 1 Corinthians 15:24-28. In these words, the apostle is stating the ultimate purpose of the theocratic kingdom, that God may be all in all". This envisions the absolute accomplishment of the original purpose in the establishment of the theocratic kingdom, "prepared before the foundation of the world". (Matt 25:34). The father has put all things under Christ's feet. And when all things are ultimately subjected unto Christ, then shall the Son also himself be subject unto the Father, who put all things under Christ that God may be all in all". God's original purpose was to manifest His absolute authority, and this purpose is realized when Christ unites the earthly theocracy with the eternal kingdom of God.

Concerning the question of the surrender of authority by the son to the Father, Chafer says, "The delivery to God of a now unmarred kingdom does not imply the release of the son. The truth asserted in 1 Corinthians 15:27-28 is that at last the kingdom is fully restored – the kingdom of God to God. The distinction to be noted lies between the presentation to the Father of a restored authority and the supposed abrogation of a throne on the part of the son." In the eternal state, Jesus Christ will go on ruling under that same authority of the Father's as subject as ever to the First Person. At the end of the millennium, Christ will hand over the mediatorial kingdom to God, to be merged into the eternal kingdom, so that the mediatorial kingdom is perpetuated forever, but no longer having a separate identity. (1 Corinthians 15:24-28). He shares the throne with the Father in the final Kingdom. (Revelation 22:3-5).

The Government in the Millennium

The government will be a theocracy. The Messiah is the King in the millennium. The New Testament records firmly establishes Christ's right to assume the Davidic throne.

David's role in the millennium. David is regent in the millennium. (Isaiah 55:3-4; Jeremiah 30:9; 33:15,17, 20-21; Ezekiel 34:23-24; 37:24-25; Hosea 3:5; Amos 9:11)

The Subjects in the Millennium. The earthly theocratic kingdom, instituted by the Lord Jesus Christ at His second advent, will include all the saved of Israel and the saved of the Gentiles, who are living at the time of His return.

Jerusalem and Palestine in the Millennium.

Because the covenants made with Israel guaranteed them the possession of the land, which is fully realized in the millennial age, Palestine and Jerusalem figure largely in the prophetic scriptures.

Jerusalem in the Millennium. Jerusalem will become the center of the Millennial earth. (Isaiah 2:2-4; Jer. 31:6; Micah 4:1; Zechariah 2:10-11). Because the world is under the dominion of Israel's king, the center of Palestine becomes the center of the entire earth.

Palestine in the Millennium

Palestine will become the particular inheritance of Israel. (Ezek. 36:8, 12; 47:22-23; Zech. 8:12). The land will be greatly enlarged in comparison to its former area. (Isa. 26:15; 33:17; Obadiah 17-21; Mich. 7:14). For the first time, Israel will possess all the land promised to Abraham: (Gen. 15:18-21). The topography of the land will be altered (Isa. 33:10-11; Ezek. 47:1-12; Joel 3:18; Zech. 4:7; 14:4, 8, 10). Instead of the mountainous terrain which characterizes Palestine today, a great fertile plain will come into existence at the second advent of the Messiah (Zech. 14:4), so that Palestine will truly be beautiful for the situation. (Ps. 48:2). This changed topography will permit the river to flow out from the city of Jerusalem and divide to the seas to water the land. (Ezek. 47:1-12). There will be renewed fertility and productivity in the land. (Isa. 29:17; 32:15; 35:1-7; 51:3; 55:13; 62:8-9; Jer. 31:27-28; Ezek. 34:27, 36:29-35; Joel 3:18; Amos 9:13). Then the plowman will overtake the reaper because of the productivity of the land. There will be an abundance of rainfall. (Isa. 30:23-24). Throughout the Old Testament the rain was a sign of God's blessing and approval and the absence of rain a sign of God's disapproval and judgment. The land will be reconstructed after being ravaged during the tribulation period. (Isa. 32:16-18; 49:19; 61:4-5; Ezek. 36:33-38; 39:9; Amos 9:14-15). The remnants of destruction will be removed that the earth may be clean again. Palestine will be redistributed among the twelve tribes of Israel. In Ezekiel 48:1-29 this redistribution is outlined. In that chapter the land is seen to be divided into three portions. In the northern portion land is apportioned to the tribe of Dan, Asher, Naphtali, Manasseh, Ephraim, Reuben and Judah.

(Ezek. 48:1-7). The land seems to be divided by a line running from east to west all across the enlarged dimensions of Palestine. In like manner in the southern portion land is allotted to Benjamin, Simeon, Issachar, Zebulon, and Gad. Ezek. 48:23-27. Between the northern and southern divisions is an area known as the "holy oblation" (Ezek. 48:8-20), that is, that portion of the land which is set apart for the Lord. This is to be an area twenty-five thousand reeds long and wide (Ezek. 48:8-20), to be divided into one area 25,000 by 10,000 reeds for the Levites (Ezek. 45:5; 48:13-14), the same area for the temple and the priests (Ezek. 45:6; 48:15-19). The reed would be 72 feet. The holy oblation would be a spacious square, 34 miles each way, containing about 1100 square miles.

The Temple in the Millennium

A large portion of the prophecy of Ezekiel 40 (v. 1-46; 24) is devoted to the temple, its structure, its priesthood, its ritual, and its ministry. Arno C. Gaebelein states, "The temple which the remnant built does in no way whatever corresponds with the magnificent structure which Ezekiel beheld in his vision. The fact is if this temple is a literal building (as it assuredly is); it has never yet been erected. Furthermore, it is distinctly stated that the glory of the Lord returned to the temple and made His dwelling place there, the same glory which Ezekiel beheld departing from the temple and from Jerusalem. But the glory did not return to the second temple. No glory cloud filled that house. And furthermore no high priest is mentioned in the worship of the temple Ezekiel describes, but the Jews after their return from Babylon had high priests again. Nor can the stream of healing waters flowing from the temple as seen by Ezekiel be in anyway applied to the restoration from the Babylonian captivity."

Some think this temple in Ezekiel symbolizes the spiritual blessings of the Church in the present age. But the true interpretation is the literal one which looks upon these chapters as a prophecy, yet unfulfilled, when Israel has been restored by the shepherd and when His glory is once more manifested in the midst of His people. The great building seen in his prophetic vision will then come into existence and all will be accomplished. Merrill F. Unger stated "Ezekiel's temple is a literal future sanctuary to be constructed in Palestine as outlined during the millennium." And he continues, "The temple itself would be located in the middle of this square (the holy oblation and not in the city of Jerusalem), upon a very high mountain, which will be miraculously made ready for that purpose when the temple is to be erected. This shall be 'the mountain of Jehovah's house,' established upon the 'top of the mountain and exalted above the hills,' into which all nations shall flow. (Isa. 2:4; Mich. 4:1-4; Ezek. 37:26). Ezekiel gives the picture in chapter 37, verse 27: 'my tabernacle also shall be with ("over or above") them.' The prophet sees the magnificent structure on a grand elevation commanding a superb view of all the surrounding country." In Ezekiel chapter 40 to 43 we can see the details of the temple. The extensive description of the throne is given in the prophecy (43:7-12), which is seen to be the very seat of authority.

Will there be Literal Sacrifices in the Millennium?

One of the problems accompanying the literal interpretation of the Old Testament presentation of the millennium is the problem surrounding the interpretation of such passages as Ezek. 43:18 – 46:24; Zech. 14:16; Isa. 56:6-8; 66:21; Jer. 33:15-18 and Ezek. 20:40-41, all of which teach the restoration of a priesthood and the reinstitution of a bloody sacrificial system during that age. An alleged inconsistency between this interpretation and the teaching of the New Testament concerning the finished work of Christ, which brought about the abolition of the Old Testament sacrificial system, has been used by the Amillennialists to reduce the premillennial system to an absurdity and to affirm the fallacy of the literal method of interpretation. The problem that confronts the premillennialists is the necessity of reconciling the teaching of the Old Testament that bloody sacrifices will be offered in the millennium with the New Testament doctrine of the abolition of the sacrifices of the Old Testament order because of the sacrifice of Christ. If a consistent literalism leads to the adoptions of literal sacrifices during the millennium, it becomes necessary to give reason why such a system should be re-instituted.

Is the Mosaic order re-established? A question which faces the advocate of animal sacrifice during the millennial age is that of the relationship existing between the former mosaic system and the system operative in the millennium. An opponent of premillennialism Oswald T. Allis says, "The crux of the whole question is undoubtedly the restoration of the Levitical ritual of sacrifice. This is referred to or implied a number of times. In Ezekiel, burnt offerings are mentioned. The bullocks, the he-goat, the ram are to be offered. The blood is to be sprinkled on the altar. The priests, who are Levites of the seed of Zadok, are to officiate. Literally interpreted, this means the restoration of the Aaronic priesthood and of the Mosaic ritual of sacrifices essentially unchanged." He states further: "Since the pictures of the millennium are found by Dispensationalists in the Old Testament Kingdom prophecies and are, consequently, marked by Jewish in character, it follows that the question of the re-establishment of the Mosaic economy, its institutions and ordinances, must be faced by them." J. Dwight Pentecost aptly replies: "There is one grave error in his observation and conclusion. The kingdom expectation is based on the Abrahamic covenant, but is in no way based on the Mosaic covenant. It is insisted that the covenants will be fulfilled in the kingdom age. This does not, however, link the Mosaic covenant with the kingdom necessarily. It is therefore fallacious to reason that because one believes in the fulfillment of the determinative covenants, he must also believe in the restoration of the Mosaic order, which was a conditional covenant, non-determinative and non-eschatological in intent, but given rather to govern the life of the people in their relation to God in the old economy. One great stumbling block that hinders the acceptance of literal sacrifices in the millennium is removed by observing that, while there are many similarities between the Aaronic and millennial systems, there are also many differences between them that make it impossible that they should be equated.

1) There are certain similarities between the Aaronic and millennial systems. In the millennial system we find the worship centers in an altar on which blood is sprinkled (Ezekiel 43:13-18) and on which are offered burnt offerings, sin offerings, and trespass offerings (40:39). There is the re-institution of a Levitical order in that the sons of Zadok are set aside for a priestly ministry (43:19). There are prescribed rituals of cleansing for the altar (43:20-27), for the Levites who minister (44:25-27), and for the sanctuary (45:18). There will be the observance of new moon and Sabbath days (46:1), morning sacrifices will be offered daily (46:13), perpetual inheritances will be recognized (46:10-18), the Passover feast will be observed again (45:21-25), and the feast of Tabernacles becomes an annual event (45:25). The year of Jubilee is observed (46:17). There is a similarity in the regulations given to govern the manner of life, the dress, and the sustenance of the priestly order (44:15-31). It can thus be seen that the form of worship in the millennium will bear a strong similarity to the old Aaronic order.

The very fact that God has instituted an order strangely like the old Aaronic order is one of the best arguments that the millennium is not being fulfilled in the Church, composed of Gentile and Jew, in the present age. That this worship was particularly planned for a redeemed Israel is well observed by William Kelly, who writes:

"Israel shall yet return to the land, and be converted indeed, and blessed, under Jehovah their God, but as Israel, not as Christians, which all believers do become meanwhile, whether Jews or Gentiles. They belong to Christ in heaven, where such differences are unknown, and therefore one of the great characteristics of Christianity is that such distinctions disappear while Christ is head on high, and His body is being formed on earth by the Holy Ghost sent down from heaven. When Ezekiel's visions shall be accomplished, it will be the reign of Jehovah Jesus of earth, and the distinction of Israel from the Gentiles will again be resumed, though for blessing under the new covenant, not as of old for curse under the law... The heavenly people rest upon one sacrifice, and draw near into the holiest of all, where Christ is at the right hand of God. But the earthly people will have a sanctuary as well as land suited to them, and such are all the ordinances of their worship."

it is the argument of the book of Hebrews that Israel sought access to God in the old economy through the order or arrangement of the Aaronic priesthood, but that we are brought to God through Christ as He ministered in a new order or arrangement, the Melchizedek priesthood. It is particularly emphasized in Hebrews 7:15 that Christ came to minister in a new order of the priesthood. The requirements or rituals of the two orders need not vary appreciably for them to be two different orders. Since both these orders point to Christ, it would be expected that similarities should exist.

2) There are many basic differences between the Aaronic and millennial systems. The significance is not in the similarities, but rather in the marked differences between the two systems. The millennial system is marked by omissions

from the Aaronic order that make the two systems so different.

a) First of all, there are changes in the millennial order. Nathaniel West states the differences: "There are changes in the dimensions of the Temple so that it is neither the temple of Solomon, nor that of Zerubbabel, nor that of Herod; changes in the measures of the outer court, the gates, the walls, the grounds, and the locality of the temple itself, raised on a high mountain, and even separate from the city. The Holy places have hardly anything like the furniture that stood in the Tabernacle of Moses or the Temple of Solomon."

This change in the physical temple and its environs is so marked that it is necessary for Ezekiel to give detailed descriptions of it. One of the major changes to be observed is in the relation of the Levites to this order. In a number of passages, the existence of a Levitical order is affirmed. (Ezekiel 40:46; 43:19; 44:15-31). Yet it is to be noted that the priests who serve are not taken from the whole Levitical line, for the line as a whole was set aside because of their apostasy, but are taken from the sons of Zadok. The Levites are restricted in their ministry to that of guarding and maintaining the temple and are excluded from the priestly ministry, with the exception of the sons of Zadok. Concerning the line of Zadok, F.W. Grant writes: "Zadok fills a prominent place in the history of Israel, being high priest in David's and Solomon's reigns. He remained faithful to David during Absalom's rebellion, and with Nathan the prophet espoused the cause of Solomon when Adonijah sought to secure the throne. David being of one mind with them instructed Zadok to anoint Bathsheba's son. (1 Kings 1:26, 32-45). Zadok thus stands as representative of the priesthood in association with the king of God's choice, and with the kingdom as established by him in David's seed-type of Christ."

It is thus to be observed that God has set aside the whole Levitical line because of their apostasy, has singled out the line of Zadok from within the Levitical line, and appointed to his seed the important priestly ministry of the millennial age. If it should be argued that tribal lines have vanished and no genealogy exists by which the line of Zadok should be established, let it be observed that the God who, in infinite wisdom, can call twelve thousand from each of the tribes of Israel (Rev. 7), can preserve and identify the line of Zadok.

b) The millennial system is marked by the deletion of much that had the highest place in the Aaronic system.

There is no Ark of the Covenant, no pot of manna, no Aaron's rod to bud, no tables of the Law, no Cherubim, no mercy-seat, no golden candlestick, no show-bread, no veil, no unapproachable Holy of Holies where the High Priest alone might enter, nor is there any High Priest to offer atonement to take away sin, or to make intercession for the people. None of this. The Levites have passed away as a sacred order. The Priesthood is confined to the sons of Zadok, and only for a special purpose. There is no evening sacrifice. The measurements of the Altar of Burnt Offering differ from those of the Mosaic altar, and the offerings themselves are barely named. The preparation for the singers is different from what it was. The social, moral, and civil prescriptions enforced by Moses with such emphasis, are all wanting.

While there is mention made of the five great offerings in force under the Aaronic order, in the millennial age, these offerings are given a different emphasis. The complete system is not restored. In like manner, while there is emphasis on the Passover in Ezekiel (Ezekiel 45:25), there is an omission of any reference to the feast of Pentecost. While portions of the Aaronic system are seen in the millennial system, yet it is marked by incompleteness and deletion of much that was observed formerly. The very center of the whole Levitical system revolved around the Day of Atonement, with its ritual of sprinkling of the blood of atonement by the High Priest on the mercy seat. It is significant that all necessary parts of this important ritual – the High Priest, the ark and mercy seat, and even the day itself – are all omitted from the record. The absence of that which was most vital to the Levitical system shows that the millennial age will not see the re-establishment of Judaism.

c) There are additions to the Levitical system to be observed in the millennial age.

Nathaniel West writes: "The entrance of the 'Glory' into Ezekiel's temple to dwell there, forever; the living waters that flow, enlarging from beneath the Altar; the suburbs, the wonderful trees of healing, the new distribution of the land according to the 12 tribes, their equal portion therein, the re-adjustment of the tribes themselves, the Prince's portion and the city's new name, "Jehovah-Shammah", all go to prove the New Israel restored is a converted people, worshiping God 'in spirit and truth.' As established by God, the Levitical order of the old economy was unaltered and fixed so that Israel might be confronted with a picture of the unchangeable holiness of God. The change in the order for the millennial age bespeaks an entirely new order."

One of the greatest changes to be observed in the coming millennial order is the person and ministry of "the prince", who not only has royal prerogatives but priestly ones as well. Ezekiel describes one who is a king-priest in the office of high priest. Concerning this one F.W. Grant writes: "We have 'the Prince' who has a unique and highly favored position. It is his privilege to occupy the eastern gate at which the glory of Jehovah entered. To him the offerings of the people are given, and by him administered in providing for the ritual sacrifice. It does not appear that the people bring sacrifices of themselves, but that it is the prince who gives all for the prescribed ritual including the daily burn offering (Ezekiel 45:17). The people are spoken of as simply worshiping at the times of offering by the prince, but the act of offering is his, the priests and Levites acting in their respective capacities. He thus fills a representative position on behalf of the people in the matter of specific offerings, while in all of these the people may be considered as having their part, since, in the first instance, they present their offerings to the prince (Ezekiel 45:13-17), and join in worship when he offers. It would seem also that he occupies a representative position for God toward the people, since he is privileged to commune with Jehovah at the East Gate." Concerning the person and the work of this prince, F.W. Grant writes in another place, "This important personage, the prince, is apparently one of the nations, not Christ Himself; his sons are spoken of (Ez. 46:16) and he offers a sin-offering for himself (Ez. 45:22). It seems clear that he occupies a representative position, yet neither the same as that of the high priest, of whom Ezekiel does not speak, nor that of the king as formerly known in Israel. He is not accorded the privileges nor the power of either. He seems to occupy an intermediary place between the people and the priesthood, since he is found among the former in their seasons of worship (46:10), not among the priests, nor privileged to enter the inner court, yet drawing nearer than the people themselves, since he may worship in the inner east gate which opens upon the inner court, while the people worship in the outer court as gathered at the door of this gate (46:2). But he is responsible to supply the various offerings at the feasts, the new moons, the Sabbaths, in the solemnities of the house of Israel, and he is therefore the recipient and holder of what the people offer for those occasions; and thus too the priesthood would look to him for the provision needed to carry on the national worship (45:13-22). Then he is given his own special portion in the land, and he is enjoined not to take any of the people's inheritance."

It must be obvious that such a person, with such an important ministry, is unique to the millennial age and has no counterpart in the Levitical order and thus represents a major change in that coming age. In all probability this personage will be an earthly representative of the king-priest ministry of Christ after the order of Melchizedek, perhaps resurrected David.

The system to be inaugurated in the millennial age will be a new order that will replace the Levitical order, for there are too many changes, deletions, and additions to the old order to sustain the contention that, literally interpreted, Ezekiel teaches the institution of the Levitical order again. The whole concept of the new covenant of Jeremiah 31 envisions an entirely new order after the passing of the old.

B) The Purpose of the Sacrifices

Several factors are observed concerning the millennial sacrifices which make them entirely legitimate.

1) It is to be observed, in the first place, that the millennial sacrifices will have no relation to the question of expiation. They will not be expiatory, for it is nowhere stated that they are offered with a view to salvation from sin.

2) In the second place, the sacrifices will be memorial in character. There is general agreement among premillennialists as to the purpose of the sacrificial system as

inaugurated in the millennial age. Interpreted in the light of the New Testament, with its teaching on the value of the death of Christ, they must be memorials of that death. F.W. Grant states: "This is the permanent memorial of sacrifice, maintained in the presence of the revealed glory. It is not sacrifice rendered with a view of obtaining salvation but sacrifices in view of accomplished salvation." Gaebelein takes the same view of the memorial character of the sacrifices. He writes: "While the sacrifices Israel brought once had a prospective meaning, the sacrifices brought in the millennial temple have a retrospective meaning. When during this age God's people worship in the appointed way at His table, with the bread and wine as the memorial of His love, it is in retrospect. We look back to the cross. We show forth His death. It is 'till He comes'. Then this memorial feast ends forever. Never again will the Lord's supper be kept after the saints of God have left the earth to be with the Lord in glory. The resumed sacrifices will be the memorial of the cross and the whole wonderful story of the redemption for Israel and the nations of the earth, during the kingdom reign of Christ. And what a memorial it will be! What a meaning those sacrifices will have! They will bring to a living remembrance everything of the past. The retrospect will produce the greatest scene of worship, of praise and adoration this earth has even seen. All the cross meant and has been accomplished will be recalled, and a mighty "Hallelujah Chorus" will fill the earth and the heavens. The sacrifices will constantly remind the people of the earth of Him who died for Israel, who paid the redemption price for all creation and whose glory now covers the earth as the waters cover the deep."

Adolph Sapphire describes the parallelism existing between the Lord's Supper in its relation to the death of

Christ and the memorial sacrifices in relation to that death: "May we not suppose that what was typical before the first coming of Christ, pointing to the great salvation which was to come, may in the kingdom be commemorative of the redemption accomplished?

In the Lord's Supper we commemorate Christ's death. We altogether repudiate the popish doctrine of a repetition of the offering of Christ; we do not believe in any such renewal of the sacrifice, but we gratefully obey the command of Christ to commemorate His death in such a way that both an external memorial is presented to the world, and an outward and visible sign and seal given to the believing partaker. May not a similar plan succeed the Lord's Supper, which we know shall cease at Christ's coming. It is also possible that both the glorified saints in heaven and the nations on the earth will contemplate during the millennium the full and minute harmony between type and reality. Even the church has as yet only a superficial knowledge of the treasures of wisdom in the Levitical institutions and its symbols."

Burlington B. Wale has stated the proposition clearly: "The bread and wine of the Lord's supper are, to the believer, physical and material symbols and memorials of a redemption already accomplished on his behalf. And this will be the case with the re-instituted sacrifices at Jerusalem; they will be commemorative, as the sacrifices of old were anticipative. And why should they not be? Was there any virtue in the legal sacrifices which prefigured the sacrifice of Christ? None whatever. Their only value and meaning was derived from the fact that they pointed to Him. And such will be the value and meaning of those future sacrifices which God has declared shall yet be offered in that future temple. Whatever the difficulty the reader may imagine in the way of the accomplishment of the prediction, it is sufficient for us that GOD HAS SAID IT."

It is concluded, then, that these sacrifices are not expiatory, for no sacrifice ever accomplished the complete removal of sin, but are memorials of the perfect sacrifice of the one typified by all sacrifice, the Lamb of God that takes away the sin of the world.

The Relation between Living and Resurrected Saints in the Millennium

There has been general confusion, even among premillennialists, concerning the relationship that would exist during the millennial age between the resurrected and translated saints of the Church age, the resurrected saints of the Old Testament, and the living saints from among both Jews and Gentiles, all of whom would bear some relationship to that period. There has been no specific delineation as to the positions these various groups would occupy, their spheres of activity, their relation to the role of the king, their relation to the earth, nor their relationship to each other. It has been recognized that the Church would reign as a bride with Christ. The Old Testament saints are to be resurrected and rewarded in that age. The saved Jews, who are found to be righteous at the judgment on Israel, together with the saved Gentiles, who are declared righteous at the judgment on the Gentiles at the time of the second advent, are to be the subjects of the King in the millennium. But there has been little said concerning their specific relationship to that period.

The Nature of the Old Testament Hope

The Old Testament scriptures abound with descriptions of the glory and blessing that wait the "heirs of promise". A glorious expectation was clearly presented as the hope of the saints. In order to present the relationship between the Old Testament and New Testament saints, between the resurrected and un resurrected individuals in the millennial age, it is necessary to distinguish certain aspects of the promises given in the Old Testament as to the hope of the saints.

A) National Promises

In the Old Testament, God made certain promises to the nation of Israel. The vast majority of the promises of future blessing and glory were given, not to individuals to buy their hope, but were given to the nation as the basis of their confidence and expectation. These promises rest on the eternal and unconditional covenants which God made with the nation and which find their fulfillment by the nation itself. The Abrahamic covenant, as originally stated in Genesis 12:1-3, and reiterated in Genesis 13:14-17; 15:1-21 and 17:1-18, while it included certain individual promises to Abraham, concerned itself with a posterity in the line of Abraham and their possession of the land given to Abraham by promise. All subsequent covenant promises were reiterations, enlargements, and clarifications of parts of this original covenant made through Abraham with the nation, and established certain national promises and hopes.

Thus we see that the Old Testament was occupied with national promises and programs and not primarily individual expectation.

B) Individual Promises

It is true; however, that certain individual hopes were indicated in the old economy. Israelites were given the hope of a resurrection. (Isaiah 26:19-20; Daniel 12:2-3, 13; Hosea 13:14 and Job 19:25-27 indicate this.) The Israelites were given the expectation of individual judgment and reward, as witnessed by such passages as Isaiah 40:10; Ezekiel 11:21; 20:33-34; 22:17-22; Daniel 12:3; Zechariah 3:7; 13:9, and Malachi 3:16-18; 4:1. The Israelites were promised blessings in the new heaven and new earth in Isaiah 65:17-18; and 66:22.

It is not until the New Testament that a more specific delineation of the individual Israelite's hope is given to us. See Hebrews 11:10.

THE BEGINNING OF ETERNITY
The Great White Throne Judgment

Rev.20:<u>11– 15</u> Satan has persuaded mankind for centuries that there is no future punishment; no final accounting before God. That lie is now fully exposed. Here in the beginning, John describes the background; we see a great white throne. Guilty men summoned to that throne, have no place to hide, nothing behind which to cower. All the foolish little delusions behind which men hide today will be gone, and men will be confronted by a fact too terrible to contemplate – the great white throne judgement. John sees Him at once and knows Him as the Lord. The nail prints are in His hands; the scars are upon His back and brow, the spear wound is in His side. The marks of what wicked men did to Him. There He is! Men have ignored Him, denied Him, cursed Him, disbelieved in Him, sold Him. Now He is their judge. There is a terrible fear gripping each heart. To look upon the face of Jesus is bliss beyond words for the child of God, but for the ungodly, it will be the first agonizing stab of hell. From the face of Christ, the earth and heavens fled away. Heaven and earth have been defiled by sin, and need to be made anew. What a face it is! The ungodly spat in it once and wrenched the beard from its cheeks, leaving it more marred that any man's. Now they gaze on it in fear and torment.

The dead, small and great, stand before God. Dead souls are united to dead bodies in a fellowship of horror and despair. Little men and paltry women whose lives were filled with pettiness, selfishness, and nasty little sins will be there. The great will be there, men who sinned with a high hand. Men like Alexander and Napoleon, Hitler and Stalin will be present, men who went in for wickedness on a grand scale with the world for their stage, and who died unrepentant at the last.

The Books

Psychologists assure us that nothing we have experienced is really forgotten. The subconscious mind stores it all up in neat compartments, awaiting the appropriate trigger to recall it to the conscious mind. God keeps records of everything. It is all written down. God keeps books. There are two in particular that are mentioned by John.

There is the book of life of the Lamb. John says, "And the books were opened: and another book was opened, which is the book of life." This book is the Lamb's book of life, in which are written the names of all those who, from the beginning of time to the end, have been saved through faith in Christ. The book is vast, for the names are many. Every kindred and nation, people and tongue, every strata of society and every culture, are represented in that book. It contains the names of hopeless sinners who trusted in God's Son and were saved from wrath through Him. It contains the names of those long deluded by false religion who finally turned to Christ to be saved by Him alone. It contains the names of those saved in childhood's tender years, as well as those saved with life's final breath. It contains the names of those who have gone from strength to strength and of those who have stumbled again and again. No matter! Is your name written in there? That is the important thing.

Then there is the book of the lives of the lost. John says, "And the dead were judged out of those things which were written in the books, according to their works." Nothing can save the man who is determined to stand on his record: who insists, "I am doing the best I can." Salvation as proclaimed in the Bible is always according to faith. (Ephesians 2:8-9). Judgment is always according to works. The sinner can either ask God for a free pardon or demand a fair trial. If he chooses the fair trial, it will land him in the lake of fire, for he will be judged according to his works. To receive the free pardon, he must plead guilty, cast himself upon the mercy of God, and accept the salvation He offers through Christ. This he must do before it is too late.

When the books are opened, God is going to judge "the secrets of men" (Romans 2:16), as well as the open, flagrant sins. He is going to judge the things we have left undone as well as the things we have done. Read the indictment of the nations in Matthew 25:41-46. Every count is a sin of omission. We will be judged not only for what we do, but for what we are, for we are sinners. We are not sinners because we sin; we sin because we are sinners; we do what we do because we are what we are. The lost will be weighed and measured by the holy character of Jesus and will be shown that they "have sinned and come short of the glory of God." (Romans 3:23).

All of the deeds that men do in this world are written down in God's Books. To those who trust in Jesus, whose sins are washed away in the blood of the lamb, who have looked in repentance to Him, to those who are saved, the things that are written in the Book are things that are blessed.

It is most evident why these judgments are at the end of time. A man does not die when he dies. His life continues. His influence continues. The deeds of this life continue. God only is able to unravel out of all of the skeins of human history the influence of a life. For those whose sins are covered and who are saved, God unravels the good of their lives and the record becomes our crowning reward at the final Bema of Christ when we stand before our Lord. However, at the end of millennium, at the white throne judgment, the Lord unravels the skein of the lives of the lost and these iniquitous records become the basis of their eternal of damnation. It cannot be done until the end of time. When the lost, the damned, the doomed, the unbelieving, the Christ-rejecting get to the end to that white throne judgment, oh, what an appalling thing when God sums up the wickedness of a man's life! What a somber, what a fearful summation.

The Summons

Rev.20:13. The Holy Spirit now goes back to describe how men will be brought before the great white throne. John says, "And the sea gave up the dead which were in it; and death and hell delivered up the dead which were in them: and they were judged every man according to their works." There will be no hiding place. The first question put to man by God was, "where are you?" As that word rang out across Eden, Adam and Eve came out of hiding to stand naked and ashamed before their judge.

That cry will go forth again, and out of their tombs they will come, up from the depths of the sea, from the arctic wastes, up from the burning sands, and out of the tropical bush. From this age and from that they will come, those newly dead and those whose bones are but dust. He knows where every speck of human dust is hidden, and at His word it will come scurrying back to make again the forms of the departed. The bodies will rise from the dust, and the souls will come up from Hades. Back they will come, with faces wrecked and ruined by sin and with souls knotted and gnarled, shriveled and shorn by lust, and hate, envy and scorn, passion and pride, iniquity and crime. Back they will come to be judged according to their works.

The Fire of Hell

And whosoever was not found written in the book of life was cast into the lake of fire. Rev 20:15

Rev. 20:14-15. The dragon, the Beast, the False Prophet, and now all the unbelieving, from the days of Cain, find themselves in one horror of horrors, in one place where memory will give point and sting to the agony of eternal separation from God, from light and happiness. The fearful sentence is proclaimed. The terrible words are spoken: "Depart from me, ye cursed, into everlasting fire, prepared for the devil and his angels." (Matthew 25:41) It was to save men from this judgment, that Christ came and suffered, bled, and died. It was to warn men of this, that God wrote the Bible and for centuries has striven by His Spirit with men.

The verse in the Book of Hebrews becomes real at this time, "It is a fearful thing to fall into the hands of the living God. For our God is a consuming fire." Jesus and all the prophets and writers of the Bible gave this solemn warning.

The Awesome Judgment of God upon Sin

It was the curse upon the sin of lost humanity that brought down our Lord from heaven. Paul says that Christ was made a curse for us, that we might be redeemed from the damnation pronounced by the law. Our Lord became a man, was given a body, that He might be sacrificed for our sins, that He might pour out His holy blood for our salvation. Never let anyone persuade you that our Lord came down from heaven in order to teach us as a better example. We had all the fine examples we needed. What drew our Lord down from heaven was the tragic plight of our souls, facing eternal damnation in the presence of a holy God. He came to deliver us from evil, to offer us remission of sins in His blood. Against this background of damnation, a true minister preaches. With the hope of a soul's salvation he delivers his message from God. Always and always over every gathering there is that shadow of what it means to be damned. Always before the faithful worker is the tragedy involved in the rejection of a man who says "No" to God and "No" to Christ and "No" to the wooing appeal of the Holy Spirit of grace and intercession. It is a fearful thing to fall into the hands of the living God. "And whosoever was not found written in the book of life was cast into the lake of fire."

The Separation between the Saved and the Lost

Time and time again, over and over again, page after page, God says in the Bible that there will someday be a separation between the lost and the saved, between those whose sins are forgiven and those who die in unforgiven sin. There is an example of this in the parable of the tares.

(Matthew 13:24-30) In Matthew 13 is the parable of the fish caught in the net, the good fish are kept and the bad fish are thrown away. "So shall it be," said our Lord at the time of the great separation between the good and the bad, between those whose sins are forgiven and those who die in unforgiven sin." "As it was in the days of Noah when Noah was taken out and the judgment of God fell upon this earth, so shall it be at the time of the coming of Christ." Two shall be sleeping in a bed, one shall be taken and the other left. Two shall be grinding at a mill, one shall be taken and the other left. Two shall be working in a field, one shall be taken and the other left. (Matthew 24:37-41). This is the great separation. As we turn the pages of the Bible, this great separation is evident everywhere.

Finally, we come to the Great White Throne Judgment where the records are searched, "and whosoever was not found written in the Book of Life was cast into the lake of fire." This tragic sentence is made all the more awesome with the words of Revelation 21:7-8...over and over God reveals that tragic, final separation between the saved and the lost.

Another great thing God reveals in His Book: As there is an eternal abode for the saved, so there is an everlasting habitat for the lost. The scripture says that angels came and carried Lazarus to Abraham's boson, to Paradise, to the presence of God, where the people of the Lord dwell with their savior. The same scripture also says that when the rich man died he lifted up his eyes in torment, in the flame and the fire of his sins, unforgiven. He died without God. And those two states in which Lazarus and the rich man found themselves are eternal and fixed.

Matthew 25:40

According to William Kelly, "The meaning clearly is that one is taken away judicially, and the other left to enjoy the blessings of His reign, who shall judge God's people with righteousness and His poor with judgment. It is the converse of our change, (rapture) when" the dead in Christ shall rise first, and we, the living who remain, shall be caught up together to meet the Lord in the air; for those who are left in our case are left to be punished with everlasting destruction from His presence."

There is a great gulf fixed in- between. The residents cannot pass from one side to the other. There is an eternal abode for those who are saved and there is an eternal abode for those who are lost. The abode of the saved is in heaven, when God has washed away the sins of His children; they stand in His presence, perfect without spot and without blemish, their names written in the Lamb's book of life. These are the children of God. But there is also an eternal abode for those who reject the – mercies, the overtures and the intercession of the Spirit of grace.

In the Greek language Jesus called the place of torment "Gehenna" or hell. Gehenna means "the valley of Hinnom." It was located outside of Jerusalem and was the place where the heathen had burned their children to the fiery god Moloch. God cursed the place and it became the dumping ground for the filth of Jerusalem through the centuries. In that refuse of Gehenna the worm never died as it ate into the putrid mass; the fire was never quenched as it burned the endless waste: and the gnashing of teeth never ceased as the jackals fought with one another over the dead carcasses that were cast into that horrible place. This is the Gehenna of hell. It is our Lord who speaks of it, even Jesus.

No lost man is ever saved beyond death. No lost man is ever saved in that eternity when the great separation is made and he falls into hell. That is the end forever and forever. There is no other chance.

The Choice that Confronts Every Human Soul

Now let us speak of the choice God gives us concerning our eternal destiny. No man can ever say that God sent him to perdition. No man can ever say that God damned his soul. No man can ever say that he is tormented in the flame because of the injustice and cruelty of Almighty God.

Matthew 24:41 says "Then he will say to those on his left, 'Depart from me, you who are cursed into the eternal fire prepared for the devil and his angels." The fire is not made for us; it is not made for any man; it is not made for you. It is prepared, that flame of fire that torment in hell, for the devil and his angels. The only people who are there are those who choose to cast their lot, life and destiny with the devil and his angels. For a man to fall into hell with the devil and his angels is for a man to choose to go there.

How certain and obvious is this judgment! God says this world shall pass away; the very fashion of it shall perish. And if your life is in this world, when the world is lost, you are lost, too. The judgment is the obvious result of an investment of your life. God says there is a judgment upon sin. When you give your life to iniquity and to unbelief, when the judgment of God comes upon righteous rejection, then the judgment falls upon you. In that day you may say something like this in hell, "Oh, I felt the tug of the Holy Spirit of God, I felt the call of my conscious turning me to Jesus, I felt the call of the preacher when he made an appeal for Christ; but I gave up Christ for the bottle; I gave up Christ for a lewd and a lecherous life; I gave up Christ for my profession and my job; I gave up Christ for the cheap rewards of the world." When the judgment of God falls upon this world if you are in it, it is because of your choice. No man ever goes to damnation, except when he chooses to be lost and damned. There is a choice for every man in this world.

If Anyone or "Whosoever" Revelation 20:15

In Revelation 20:7, we see that Satan is loosed at the end of the millennium. Every man who ever lived will have a choice as to whether he worships God or Satan, whether he chooses heaven or hell, whether he will give his life to Christ or invest it down here in the cheap rewards of the world. In the period of that thousand-year millennium many think that there are those born who will never have been tempted and who will never have been tried by evil. But at the end of that period of time called the millennium, Satan is loosed to go out to tempt the nations of the earth who number as the "sands of the sea." People of these nations must decide for or against the Lord.

This "whosoever" or anyone in Revelation 20:15 is the same kind of a "whoever" as is found in Revelation 22:17. It is the same "whoever" found in John 3:16. "It is appointed unto men once to die and after this the judgment." (Hebrews 9:27). "And whoever was not found written in the Book of Life was cast into the Lake of fire."

The Holy Spirit pleads with lost men to look in saving faith to Jesus. Bow down in the presence of the Lord; ask Him to forgive your sins. Christ says that if we confess Him before men, He will confess us before God in heaven.

REVELATION CHAPTER 21

Now we come to the last and the climactic vision, recorded in chapters 21 and 22. These passages in the Bible are so rich in meaning. The wisdom and truth of God are unfathomable.

Three New Things Made by the Hand of God

This passage presents three new things made by the hand of God. "I saw a new heaven and I saw a new earth...And I John saw the holy city, New Jerusalem." The first new thing is a new heaven. The Bible speaks of three heavens. The first heaven is the atmosphere world around us, the heaven through which the birds fly and the clouds float. The second heaven described in the Bible is the heaven of the starry sky, the Milky Way, the sidereal universes, all that you see when you stand at night under the blue firmament of the sky. The third heaven is the heaven of heavens. It is the throne and the dwelling place of God.

When the Bible says there is to be a new heaven, it refers to the heaven immediately above us, the heaven of the atmosphere, the heaven that brings storms and fury, the heaven of lightning and thunder, the heaven of the lowering, swarming clouds. There is to be a new atmosphere heaven above us. The new heaven also includes the heaven of the starry skies, for in that universe beyond us there are stars that have turned to cinders and solar systems that have become ashes. In the recreation of God, the whole universe above us will be remade in primeval, primordial and pristine glory.

The apostle continues the description: "And I saw a new earth." The miseries of this present earth in its deep and dark apostasy from God are seen and felt everywhere. This earth is blighted and cursed. The desert places that are burned and seared, the floods that wash our villages and cities away, the earthquakes that tear down the handiwork of man, the diseases and death that waste the very life of millions, these are but evidences of the wages of sin. But this earth is to experience redemption. No longer will it be torn by hooks and irons in order that it yield its increase and its fruit. No longer will it be infested with thistles and thorns and briers. No longer will it be cut into graves and plotted into cemeteries. No longer will it be stained with the crimson of human blood. No longer will its highways bear the processions of those who are brokenhearted and bereaved. There is to be a new, redeemed world. It is to be a paradise regained, an Eden restored, the whole beautiful creation of God remade and rebuilt. "And I saw a new earth." "And I John saw the holy city, New Jerusalem." John saw a capital city made by the glorious workmanship of our infinite Lord. In the new creation, God will build a new heavenly city as a center for God's government and God's people and God's dwelling place. In Revelation18:1-24, there was described for us the city of Babylon, the ultimate work of the hands of men, built in defiance and in blasphemy against God. But this city will reflect the glory of the Lamb, a new, heavenly capital city of God.

Renovation of the Earth

When John says, "I saw a new heaven and a new earth: for the old heaven and the old earth were passed away," does John mean that the old, first heaven and the old first earth were annihilated, that they entered into extinction and nothingness, that they were swept into non-existence? Is that what he means? Does John mean that it is the same heaven renovated and redeemed and that it is the same earth purified and regenerated? William Kelly states, "Here in revelation not merely the present dispensation but the present heaven and earth have passed away, and give place to 'all things made new'. Doubtless the new heaven and earth will be made out of the old. Just as the resurrection — body will be formed out of the present body of humiliation, by the present earth and heavens destined to a kindred transformation. After the dissolution they will reappear in the form of the new heavens and earth. "No more sea" would be impossible without a miracle, as long as life in its present condition has to be maintained. The sea is absolutely necessary to animate nature as it is, man could not exist without it; and so with regard to every animal and even vegetable upon the face of the earth, not to speak of the vast world of waters."

There's really very little said about the nature of the new heaven and the new earth. The earth will definitely be populated, and it will be restored as it was in the Garden of Eden. There will be no deserts or ice poles or snow. God, Himself, will supply all the natural resources that are needed to keep an earth running smoothly. He will be the source of light and heat and water.

The new earth as a whole will not be the principal residence of the believers, though they will have free access to it. The New Jerusalem is where Jesus has been preparing mansions for His own and is the capital from which He will rule. It will be the center of the new universe, with a beauty and a holiness that can hardly be fathomed. Revelation 21 and 22 describe the glories of this city.

The Location of the New Jerusalem

In Revelation 21:2 John said he saw the Holy City coming down out of heaven from God. Some Bible interpreters believe that this city has existed from the time

Jesus left the earth to go to prepare a place for His bride, the Church. If that's true, this city is in in existence during our present age, although it is invisible, and it will exist during both the tribulation and the millennium. It may be that the Holy City will be suspended above the earth during the thousand-year kingdom, and that the immortal believers will principally live there. This would help to explain the question of how mortal and immortal beings can live together in the millennium, since the mortals (those believers who live through the Tribulation) will continue to marry, have children, and live ordinary lives. This, of course, won't be true of the immortal believers, since these saints will already have received their resurrection bodies.

If this view is correct, then the city would have to be temporarily withdrawn when the earth is destroyed at the end of the millennium. After the re-creation or renovation of the earth, the city will apparently descend to the new earth and actually rest on it, since the New Jerusalem is said to have foundations, which implies a firm means of support. Also, the New Jerusalem has twelve gates through which the peoples of the nations will go in and out of the city. The New Jerusalem will be the center of the universe. All light will emanate from it, and all life in the universe will revolve around it.

The Inhabitants of the New Jerusalem

John pictures this magnificent city as a new bride adorned for her husband. Because of the term "bride", some interpreters feel that only the bride of Christ, the Church, will live in this city. However, we know that Abraham was promised a city, for the writer of the Book of Hebrews tells us, "For he looked for a city which has foundations, whose builder and maker is God...But now they desire a better country, that is, a heavenly one; wherefore, God is not ashamed to be called their God: for He has prepared for them a city." (Hebrews 11:10, 16).

There can be no question that this promised city is the New Jerusalem. While it may be the bride's city, it also has other permanent inhabitants – the saved of the house of Israel. You will notice that the foundation stones of the city have the twelve apostle's names on them, while the twelve gates are named for the twelve tribes of Israel. These 24 spiritual leaders represent the two main groups who will inhabit this city: they symbolize the foundation and access to the New Jerusalem.

A third group of people will also have access to the city, though their principal place of residence will be the new earth. This group is called the "nations", which means "peoples". They will be comprised of believers who didn't happen to be among Israel in the Old Testament or the church in the New Testament. Noah and Job also would be in this group, as well as many of the Old Testament people who knew God and believed in Him and found salvation, but were never part of Israel. All the Gentiles who are saved during the Tribulation will also be in this company of believers.

God Will Wipe Away Our Tears

Rev. 21:6 – 7. Just to read the text is a benediction to our souls. It is a comfort to God's saints in our pilgrimage through this weary world. Out of all of the subjects in the Bible, the most difficult to speak on is the subject of heaven.

The vast difficulty in describing heaven is illustrated in the utterances of the men of God who have written the Bible.

For example, the Apostle Paul says, as he describes his celestial experience in 2 Corinthians 12:1-4 that he was taken up into Paradise, into the third heaven, the heaven of heavens where God dwells. Can Paul describe his experience? Does he say what he heard and what he saw? No. All the Apostle says is this: 2 Corinthians 12:1, "It is doubtless not profitable for me to boast. I will come to visions and revelations of the Lord: I know a man in Christ who fourteen years ago – whether in the body I do not know, God knows – such a one was caught up to the third heaven. And I know such a man – whether in the body or out of the body I do not know, God knows – how he was caught up into Paradise and heard inexpressible words, which it is not lawful for a man to utter." Our spirits, our very minds and souls, cannot imagine it; this creation of God which we will call our heavenly and eternal home.

John here writes "And I heard a great voice out of heaven saying, Behold, the tabernacle [Greek, *skene*, 'dwelling place'] of God is with men, and he will dwell [Greek, *skenoo*, 'tabernacle'] with them. The dwelling place, the pavilion, the house of the Lord will be visibly with us. In the days past the Lord tabernacled with us. The Lord dwelt with our parents in the Garden of Eden. He walked with them and visited them. God tabernacled with the patriarchs. He spoke to Abraham as a man would talk to his friend, face to face. The Lord cast His tabernacle among the children of Israel and His presence was seen among them, a pillar of fire by night and a cloud by day. In the days of the temple, the Lord dwelt in the darkness of the Holy of Holies.

In the Gospel of John, 1:14 he says, "And the word was made flesh and dwelt among us" *(skenoo)*, 'tabernacled', the same and identical word used in our text here in Revelation 21:3. The Lord tabernacles today in His Church, and lives in our hearts by the Holy Spirit. But how shall it be and with what words could we describe it, when God Himself shall live in our midst and our eyes shall see Him, our ears shall hear Him and we shall behold the glory and beauty of the Lord God Jehovah.

"And there was no more sea." What does that mean in this new creation of God? And there was no more sea is to be a symbol of the fact that there will be no more separation.

John was on a lonely island in exile, sent there to die of starvation and exposure. Across the sea were those he loved, the church at Ephesus, all the friends and the saints of the household of faith. The dark sea rolled in- between. In glory, there will be no more exile and no more separation. There is certainly a dark sea that rolls between time and eternity. There is a dark river of death, a flood that rolls between us and our loved ones gone before. But in heaven "there will be no more sea."

In John's day the sea was a frightful, a fearsome and an awesome monster. They had no compass, for example, and when the cloudy day came, their ships were absolutely lost on the vast bosom of the deep. Their frail barks were subject to destruction before the face of those fearful storms that suddenly arose. The loss of life in the sea was beyond measure, innumerable. To the ancient the sea was a horrible monster, a fearsome enemy. Now no more sea.

John now writes a beautiful thing. "And God shall wipe away all tears from their eyes; and there shall be no more death, neither sorrow, nor crying, neither shall there be any more pain; for the former things are passed away." As long as we are in this life, tears will be in our eyes. Until we come to the gate of heaven itself, God's people will know how to cry. We may forget how to laugh, but we will never forget how to cry. Not until we enter the New Jerusalem will God wipe away the tears from our eyes. Our pilgrimage in this world is like the pilgrimage of the children of Israel to the Promised Land. We are delivered in the grace of God from so much of the hurt and trial of the journey, but we are not delivered from the heartaches, diseases and afflictions of this life. Suffering is a common denominator and the experience of all of God's people. Even Jesus wept. He bowed His head in sorrow, in strong crying and tears. It is only there, beyond the pearly gates and the Jasper walls, that the Lord will wipe away our tears.

There is another encouraging thing to be said about this passage. We are not to forget, in our earthly pilgrimage with its burden and trials, its losses and its crosses, that our crying and bereavement yield for God's people a marvelous and heavenly reward on the other side of the river. For example, Paul says in 2 Corinthians 4:17: "For our light affliction, which is but for a moment, is working for us a far more exceeding and eternal weight of glory." Paul says the things we suffer down here, the agony, the tears, the burden, the heartache and the disappointment of our lives, work for us a far more and exceeding weight of glory. If we are to be like our Lord, we must suffer. Our Lord suffered. He was called a man of sorrows and acquainted with grief. Paul said in 2 Corinthians 1:5 "For as the sufferings of Christ abound in us, so our consolation also abounds by Christ." Having suffered here, wept here, cried in agony and died here, we shall find heaven as God's release from our bondage of tears and death. Let us follow the text word by word. "And God shall wipe away all tears from their eyes." The story of this world is a story of bereavement. Jesus wept with Mary and Martha at the tomb of their brother. Here in this earth is misfortune and poverty, as Lazarus was laid at the door of dives (Rich Man). Here in this world of woe is lamentation like the cry of Jeremiah, "Oh that my head were waters, and mine eyes a fountain of tears, that I might weep day and night for the slain of the daughter of my people." (Jeremiah 9:1). Here are despair, agony, and disappointment. But God purposes some better things for His people. All our tears will be wiped away.

"And there shall be no more death." Can you conceive of a world without the scythe and the stroke, without the dreadful visit of the pale horseman? A world in which "there shall be no more death"? There is no home without its shadow in the circle of every family, a mother; or a wife or a husband or a daughter or a son or a friend is gone.

There is no flock however watched and tended,

But one dead lamb is there!

There is no fireside,

howsoe'er defended,

But has one vacant chair.

- Henry W. Longfellow

"Death is swallowed up in victory. Death, an enemy, the last and the final one, is cast with the false prophet and Satan into the lake of fire."

When a baby dies, what will the baby be like in heaven? Does the baby grow? Is the baby still a child? There is so much that is not revealed to us, so much of which we are not told. But God has revealed this much, that there are no stonecutters chiseling epitaphs in glory. There are no wreaths on the mansion doors in the sky. There are no graves on the hillsides of heaven. There are no obituary columns in the newspapers. There are no funeral processions over the streets of gold. The whole creation echoes with the glad and triumphant refrain of God's holy redeemed when they sing, "Death is swallowed up in victory". "And there shall be no more death." Death, an enemy, the last and final one, is cast with the false prophet and Satan into the lake of fire. "And there shall be no more sorrow, nor crying, neither there does any more pain." Sorrow follows us like a shadow. Every heart knows its bitterness. How many pillows at night are wet with the teardrops that this world never sees and will never know, but is known and seen only by our Lord. Sorrow, Sorrow!

W.A. Criswell narrates a story about a preacher who conducted revival meetings in Dallas:

"We had a great preacher in this pulpit. He held a revival meeting here. From the days of my teen-age boyhood I loved that marvelous, wonderful man. While here in the revival, he began telling me about the days of his childhood. He was a mountain boy. His father was killed when he was a little boy. His stepfather was vile and vicious. One day at the breakfast table, the stepfather in anger picked up the plate of biscuits that displeased him and threw the plate into the face of the boy's mother. He cursed her. He doubled up his fist and beat her. He then strode away from their mountain cabin. The little boy went over to the side of his mother and said, 'Mother, let's leave, let's leave. I don't know how, but I will make a living for you. Mother, let's leave.' The mother replied: 'Son, not so. There has never been a separation in our family, never. And son, I shall not live long. Soon I will be with the Lord Jesus. God will take care of you, my boy.' And according to this intuitive knowing that God revealed to her, she died soon after. The little boy went to live in the city, and according to the prayers of his mother, he was saved there and became the preacher that I loved and admired so much."

The Heavenly City of God

Rev.21:9-22:5. There should be no chapter division between Revelation 21:27 and 22:1. Revelation 22:1-5 are the concluding verses in chapter 21. Beginning at verse 6 in chapter 22, John writes an epilogue to the book. The visions, however, close at Revelation 22:5. In this last vision, John sees the holy city, New Jerusalem. He describes it first from the outside as he saw it descend out of heaven; then he describes it from the inside as though he entered within the gate of the city.

The dazzling glory of the new city of Jerusalem that is to come down from God out of heaven is beyond man's ability to comprehend. It is pictured in Revelation as the ultimate preparation of God for man's habitation. The same difficulty of comprehension may be observed in the ministry of many missionaries. As they live amid a primitive tribe for a period of time and try to communicate to them scenes of the outside world, the natives look at them in bewilderment. How can one describe an electric stove, television, or telephone to a native who has never seen anything but an open wood fire? Only by comparing the unknown with the known is the missionary able to convey facts of the outside world, or more importantly, the eternal truths of God. Thus it is with us as we try to comprehend the glories God has prepared in the Holy City for them that love Him. He has used terms and descriptions with which we are familiar, to describe the things that are beyond our finite frame of reference.

The New Jerusalem – The Bride of Christ

Inviting John to a high mountain, the angel showed him the Bride, the Lamb's wife. But the Bride is described in the tenth verse as that great city, the holy Jerusalem. This does not suggest that the Bride of Christ is a city. Since Chapter 19 described the marriage of the Lamb to the Bride, we find that the Bride is not a physical city, but the Church. The Holy Spirit here is telling us about that city which the Lord promised His disciples in John 14 when He said, "I go to prepare a place for you". Now that prepared city is coming to the earth, and the inhabitants of it are the members of the Bride. When this city comes to the earth, it will be a people-filled city – people in their resurrected bodies to dwell with Christ for eternity. That is why this city, which surpasses the splendor of anything comprehended by man, is called the Bride, the Lamb's wife. A city is more than buildings and streets, for these are merely the means of providing for the inhabitants which compose the real city. The Old Testament saints also will be the inhabitants of the city.

The city has 12 gates, and at the gate 12 angels, and names written on the gates, which are the names of the twelve tribes of the children of Israel. Obviously the number twelve takes on great significance in this city. Since the Bible is inspired by God, we can expect, in spite of the various authors and the length of time engaged in its writing, that there would be an unusual, even supernatural continuity in the use of numbers. F.W. Grant, one of the greatest Christians who ever lived after St. Paul, discovered the numerical structure of the scripture.

The Bible numerology points out this thrilling thread of consistency that attests to divine authorship. For example, it is suggested that the number one stands for unity, two for union, three for the trinity; four is the number of the earth (four directions: East, West, North, South, four seasons, etc.), five is the divisional number (five wise and five foolish virgins), six is the number of man. Everything in the Bible that has to do with man seems to be in the realm of six. For instance, "six days shalt thou labor". The height of an average man is about six feet. The Antichrist uses for his number three sixes, called the number of man. Seven seems to be the perfect number, or God's number. Twelve seems to be the governmental or administrative number. Thus, we find multiples of twelve in the administration of God's universe. Note the many references of twelve in this picture of the Holy City that will come down from heaven. Twelve gates: twelve entrances will always be open for God's people to have access to the City. Verse 13 indicates there will be three gates on each of the four sides of this gigantic city. Twelve Angels: Again we see the relationship of angels in the eternal order and their work with man. Twelve foundations: The foundation walls will be magnificent beyond comprehension. In verse 19 to 21 they are described as "garnished with all manner of precious stones".

The various foundations are represented as layers built upon each other, each layer extending around all four sides of the city.

Jasper – gold in appearance but like clear glass in substance, namely glass with a gold cast to it.

Sapphire – a stone similar to a diamond in hardness and blue in color.

Chalcedony – an agate stone from Chalcedon (in Turkey), thought to be sky blue with other colors running through it.

Emerald – introduces a bright green color.

Sardonyx – a red and white stone.

Sardius – refers to a common jewel of reddish color, also found in honey color which is considered less valuable. The sardius is used with Jasper in Revelation 4:3 in describing the glory of God on the throne.

Chrysolite – a transparent stone, golden in color, according to the ancient writer Pliny, and therefore somewhat different from the modern pale green Chrysolite stone.

Beryl – is sea green.

Topaz – is yellow-green and transparent.

Chrysopraus – introduces another shade of green.

Jacinth – is a violet color.

Amethyst – is commonly purple.

Though the precise colors of these stones in some cases are not certain, the general picture here described by John is one of unmistakable beauty, designed to reflect the glory of God in a spectrum of brilliant color. The light of the city within shining through these various colors in the foundation of the wall topped by the wall itself composed of the crystal-clear Jasper forms a scene of dazzling beauty in keeping with the glory of God and the beauty of His holiness. The city is undoubtedly far more beautiful to the eye than anything man has ever been able to create, and it reflects not only the infinite wisdom and power of God, but also His grace, as extended to the objects of His salvation.

The foundation stones contain the names of the apostles, indicating that the Holy City will contain the redeemed by the blood of Christ, who heard the word through the faithful witnessing of the servants of God in the first century, the apostles. The gates of the city contain the names of the twelve tribes, clearly indicating that they were the vehicles through which the oracles of God were revealed in the Old Testament days, and to whom the Messiah came.

The Size of the City

Rev.21:15-16. The New Jerusalem is shaped four-square like a cube. The city is 1,380 miles (2220 km) on each face, including height, with a wall 72 yards (66m) thick. It has been calculated that even if only 25 percent of this space were used for dwellings, 20 billion people could be accommodated spaciously. Bible scholars do not agree as to whether this will be a square-shaped or a pyramid shaped city. "And the twelve gates were twelve pearls." Every gate will be one pearl, large enough to cover the gateway of this huge city. In addition, the streets of the city will be pure gold, as it were, transparent glass, clearly indicating that we will walk on gold. In our mind's eye, gazing at this city with its fantastically beautiful and expensive foundational stones, for foundations, its gigantic pearl gates, and its gold streets, we are impressed with the superiority of this city over anything known to man. Today we use concrete and stone for foundations, scarcely the most beautiful material on earth, but selected because of its durability, supply and low cost. Our streets are made of concrete or blacktop for the same reasons. By comparison, the Holy City of God will be so magnificent that we will literally walk on precious metals that today are used for costly bracelets, necklaces, and rings. The city's foundation will consist of precious stones that today are used for ornaments only, and due to their expense, are very small. This presentation, when taken literally, emphasizes the phenomenal omnipotent power of our God.

Twelve gates were twelve pearls; every single gate was of one pearl. How appropriate! All other precious gems are metals or stones, but a pearl is a gem formed within the oyster – the only one formed by living flesh. The humble oyster receives an irritation or a wound, and around the offending article that has penetrated and hurt it, the oyster builds a pearl. The pearl, we might say, is the answer of the oyster to that which injured it. The glory-land is God's answer, in Christ, to wicked men who crucified heaven's beloved and put Him to open shame. How like God, it is to make the gates of the New Jerusalem of pearl. The saints as they come and go will be forever reminded, as they pass the gates of glory, that access to God's home is only because of Calvary. Think of the size of those gates! Think of the supernatural pearl from which they are made! What gigantic suffering is symbolized by those gates of pearl! Throughout the endless ages we shall be reminded by those pearly gates and the immensity of the sufferings of Christ. Those pearls, hung eternally at the access routes to glory, will remind us forever of one who hung upon a tree and whose answer to those who injured Him was to invite them to share His home.

John then tells us more about the street. He says, "And the street of the city was pure gold, as it were transparent glass." All the walks and ways of that city will reflect the glory of God. Every step taken, every move made will be a step or a move along a path that brings glory to God.

The Missing Temple

Rev. 21:22 There is no need for a temple in heaven. The city itself is a sanctuary. God's presence is there. No need of veils, curtains, ceremonies, rites or altars. No need for explanation, atonement, covenants, arks and intermediaries. We shall live in the presence of God and shall worship Him immediately and directly. The place could be called Jehovah Shammah, "God is here". God is present as He was in the Garden of Eden. This is paradise restored and regained. The Lord God is there and we do not need a temple. We shall see Him face to face.

John continues in Revelation 21:23, "The city had no need of the sun or of the moon to shine in it, for the glory of God illuminated it. The Lamb is its light." The garments of God reflect the glory, the iridescence, the incomparable effusion of beauty, color, splendor and light that stream from His person. His resplendent, radiant and effulgent glory will illuminate the city. When Moses talked with the Lord and came down from the mountainside, his face shone. He had been with God. On the mount of Transfiguration, the face of our Lord became bright above the glory of the sun. When Paul on the road to Damascus met the Lord, above the splendor of that Syrian orb that shone in the sky, he saw the light of the glory of God in the face of Jesus Christ. There is an inherent light and glory in the city because Jesus is there, and the Lamb is its light. All light, hope, and blessings stream from His blessed face. From the first promised blessing in Genesis, to the last benediction in the Revelation, it is Jesus; as He was then, is now, and ever shall be, world without end. Amen.

John now presents a remarkable parallel between what he saw in the Paradise of God, in the beautiful city, and what was described in the first and the second chapters of the Book of Genesis.

REVELATION CHAPTER 22

Rev.22:1-5 In concluding the most wonderful record of our eternal home, John gives four final impressions. He mentions the life of that city. He says, "And he showed me a pure river of water of life, clear as crystal, proceeding from the throne of God and of the Lamb." Most of earth's cities are built along the banks of important rivers that soon become polluted by the cities to which they give rise. Here, however, is a river whose streams make glad the city of God. (Psalm 46:4).

There is a remarkable parallel between what he sees in the paradise of God, in the beautiful city, and what is described in the first and the second chapters of the Book of Genesis. John sees a pure river of the water of life, clear as crystal. In Eden there was a beautiful river with four branches that watered the garden. The heavenly paradise also is glorified with a beautiful river.

In numerous ways the earthly Jerusalem is a counterpart of the heavenly Jerusalem during the millennium. Both cities are seats of government, both have a river flowing from them, and both have trees of fruit. In the earthly Jerusalem the river will flow from the Temple (Ezekiel 47:1-12); in the heavenly Jerusalem the river flows from the throne.

But there is more.

Rev.22:2 We are going out to eat in heaven. Who could object to that? The angels ate when they were entertained by Abraham. Our Lord Jesus ate when He was raised from the dead.

This tree is reminiscent of the Garden of Eden where the test of loyalty had to do with a tree, the fruit of which was forbidden to men. The tree of life was not forbidden while man was sinless. But once sin entered, the race could no longer be trusted with the tree of life. Possibly Adam and his posterity, had they remained sinless, would have been enabled to live forever by means of the tree of life. God removed that tree and thus put temptation beyond Adam's reach, for had he eaten it in his fallen condition; he would have been doomed to live forever in his sins.

The tree of life now flourishes in glory. It graces the celestial city, lines the banks of the river, and runs in splendor down the central boulevard. The saints in glory can enjoy the fruit of that tree, and the nations on earth benefit from the healing of its leaves. We are not told what the fruit of that tree tastes like; the full delights of glory are not revealed and possibly cannot be.

John tells also of the Lord of that city. "And they shall see his face; and his name shall be in their foreheads."

Here is the climax of everything! John has learned from his master; he keeps the best wine until the last. "They shall see his face". The ancient mariners, sailing westward along the coastlines of the Mediterranean, came at last to the Pillars of Hercules, the Straits of Gibraltar. When they came to this point in their travels, they drew back. It was one thing to sail from isle to isle, but it was something else to venture forth into the great unknown whence came the fearful billows of the mighty deep: "Ne plus ultra", they said, "There is nothing beyond." Says John, "They shall see His face" Ne plus ultra! There is nothing beyond. It is heaven's crowning joy, for what we have in the next verse is merely a repetition of what has been said before. There is nothing beyond in terms of bliss when once we have seen the face of Jesus.

Conclusion to Revelation

Revelation 22:6-21

John has come to the end of his book and to the end of the Bible. Most people's last words are of special interest, and God's last words before the centuries of silence descend must be of great significance indeed. Our attention is drawn to the faithful word of God, to the finished work of Christ, and to the final witness of the spirit. It would be hard to think of a more appropriate way of ending the Book of God.

The Faithful Word of God

Rev.22:6-10 Sin entered this world when Satan questioned the word of God and when Eve, entertaining the question, was led to doubt the accuracy and the authority of

God's word. God concludes the scriptures with a fresh emphasis on both.

The accuracy of the word of God (22:6). John's attention is again attracted by the angel. The immediate reference is to the great truths of the Apocalypse that sooner or later all will come to pass. But the statement is wider than that, and embraces the whole Bible. God's word is accurate, and the truths it contains have been transmitted, recorded, arranged, and preserved exactly as God had in mind. In the original, autographed manuscripts, every jot and tittle, every word, ever letter was God-breathed. Men may scoff at that fact, deride it, and deny it, but God declares that His sayings are faithful and true.

The Authority of the Word of God

Rev.22:7-9 John has three things to say about the book's authority. He points out how positively this truth is declared. The Lord says to him, "Behold I come quickly: Blessed is he that keep the sayings of this book." The words of the angel give way before the direct word of Christ. The Lord breaks in, as it were, as though what he had to say was too good to be passed along merely by an angel. "I am coming quickly" He says. Then He adds, "keep the sayings of this book." The spur to holy living is the imminent appearing of the Lord Jesus; the steps to holy living are given in His word.

John reveals how patently this truth was denied. He says, "And I John saw these things, and heard them. And when I had heard and seen, I fell down to worship before the feet of the angel which showed me these things." Once already John has been told not to worship an angel, but he is so overwhelmed with the glory of the revelations entrusted to him that he does it again. Such is the heart of man! What a patent denial John's act really was of the entire message of the Word of God, and especially of the message of the closing book of revelation, is concerned with the unveiling and exaltation of the Lord Jesus. John, in his frail mortality, attempts to worship an angel. The Lord himself has just burst in with the news of His imminent return, and John worships an angel! He at least has the grace to confess it for our warning and instruction. We would count John's act incredible if we did not carry around in our own hearts the seeds of every imaginable form of disobedience and a whole pantheon of secret idols. Johns then tells us how plainly this truth is detailed.

John says (v. 9), "Then he said to me, see that you do not do that. For I am your fellow servant, and of your brethren the prophets, and of those who keep the words of this book. Worship God." The angel took his place with all those who govern their lives by the revealed word of God. He says in effect, all authority is in this book; it speaks of God; it brings you to His Feet If we abandon the word of God, we abandon the gold standard and bankrupt ourselves of everything worthwhile.

The accessibility of the Word of God (22:10). The angel says to John, "Seal not the sayings of the prophecy of this book: for the time is at hand." Daniel was told to seal up one of his visions (Dan.12:4-9) because another dispensation was to intervene before the vision would be fulfilled. But that is not the case with the great truths revealed in Revelation. They are written in an open book for all to read. In the light of the completed revelation of God, we can understand most, if not all, of what God has revealed in both Testaments. The word is accessible to us. Paul says, "The word is near you, in your mouth and in your heart" (Romans 10:8).

So then, God draws our attention to His faithful word. Visions and voices may have their place, and John has been receiving communications in both ways. But it is the word of God, which is accurate, authoritative, and accessible that matters. The word of God is our court of appeal and final arbiter in matters of faith and morals.

Rev.22:12 Once again, does the divine speaker proclaim the certainty and nearness of His return, not simply as a cheer to His waiting and expectant saints (v.7), but with rewards, many and varied to be bestowed according to the quality and character of service recorded. The least service shall be fittingly rewarded by the Lord when He comes, not into the air for us (1 Thess. 4:17), but into the kingdom with us. Not the Father's house into which we are first removed (John 14:2-3), but the kingdom is the sphere and scene where rewards are bestowed according to our service and faithfulness.

"I am Alpha and Omega, the beginning and the end, the first and the last."

Four times in the revelation do we read the words: "I am the Alpha and Omega." The first time is in Revelation 1:8: "I am Alpha and Omega, the beginning and the ending"; this is an avowal of the omnipotence of the Lord Christ. The Alpha is the beginning letter of the Greek alphabet as the Omega is the concluding letter. Our Lord Christ is the beginning and the ending, the first and the last, the all-inclusive revelation of the reality, the being, the existence of God Himself.

The second time that expression is used in this same first chapter, Revelation 1:10: "I am Alpha and Omega, the beginning and the ending". Here Christ avows that He is the Lord of time and of history. All of the unfolding ages are in His hands. Revelation 21:5-6, is the third time that expression is used: "I am Alpha and Omega, the beginning and the ending". Here it is affirmed that He is the Lord God of the new order and the new creation. The last, the fourth time the expression is used is in this epilogue, Revelation 22:12-13: "I am Alpha and Omega, the beginning and the ending". Here it is affirmed of our Lord Christ that He is the judge of all men. He is the great judge of the earth, sitting in jurisdiction upon time, history and creation. All four of these passages are affirmations of the deity of our Lord Christ. The Prophet Isaiah wrote about the marvelous and glorious preexistence of Christ. In Isaiah 9:6, He is called the everlasting father. Many readers are confused about this verse. The everlasting father means, Jesus Christ is the Father of eternity. The beginning of all time and of all creation is found in Him.

Revelation 22:14 "Blessed are those who do His commandments, that they may have the right to the tree of life, and may enter through the gates into the city" (NKJV). The following is the Darby translation: "Blessed are they that wash their robes, that they may have the right to the tree of life, and that they should go in by the gates into the city."

Revelation 22:14 is the last beatitude in the Bible. It is written in the King James Version, the Authorized Version, and the New King James Version in the words: "Blessed are they that do his commandments that they may have right to the tree of life, and may enter in through the gates into the city." That is the way the verse reads in the Textus Receptus, the Greek text that was used as the basis for the translation of the King James Version. But that is not the way John wrote it. When John wrote the verse, he said "Blessed are they that wash their robes that they may have right to the tree of life, and may enter in through the gates into the city." Hundreds of years before printing was invented, a scribe copying the Bible saw that passage in the Revelation, "Blessed are they who wash their robes (plunontes tas stolas) ..." But he said to himself, "No man can be saved just by trusting Jesus. One cannot go to heaven and enter through those beautiful gates just by washing his robes in the blood of the Lamb. A man has to earn heaven." Said that scribe to himself, "A man has to obey the laws of God in order to be saved." So the scribe took upon himself the authority to change that "plunontes tas stolas auton" (washing their robes) into "poiountes tas entolas autou" (doing his commandments).

The Textus Receptus is the Greek text that Erasmus, the famous Renaissance scholar, published in A.D. 1516. It was the first New Testament Greek text ever published. The basis for the Textus Receptus was three minuscule, three cursive manuscripts that Erasmus had before him. One was copied in the tenth century, the second was copied in the twelfth century, and the third, the one he mainly relied upon, was copied in the fifteenth century. The Textus Receptus became the standard Greek text for over three hundred years. It contained this changed reading in Revelation 22:14, "Blessed are they that do his commandments".

Since 1516 the world of scholarship and archeology has discovered thousands of earlier Greek texts. The great uncials that were copied from the very beginning when the books of the New Testament were first gathered into one have been discovered since Erasmus. An uncial is a Greek text written in large, square capital letters. We have thousands of Greek manuscripts written cursively. They are called minuscules. The writing of uncials with big, square letters was slow and difficult. In the seventh century, a way was invented to write cursively, as you write longhand in English, writing in a running hand. After the seventh century all of the manuscripts were written in that cursive style. There are thousands of Greek minuscules.

Enumeration of Greek New Testament manuscripts. This list was compiled in 1967 by Kurt Aland:

Papyri	81
Majuscules	267
Minuscules	2,764
Lectionaries	2,143
Total	5,255

There are presently 5,687 Greek manuscripts in existence today for the New Testament.

There are thousands of New Testament Greek manuscripts, than any other ancient writing. The internal consistency of the New Testament documents is about 99.5% textually pure. That is an amazing accuracy. In addition, there are over 19,000 copies in the Syrian, Latin, Coptic, and Aramaic languages. The total supporting New Testament manuscript base is over 24,000. This is an astonishing and an amazing total when you remember there is only one manuscript of the annals of Tacitus, the great Roman historian. There is only one manuscript of the Greek anthology. So much of the literature of the ancient world of Plato, Sophocles, and Euripides would depend upon one or two manuscripts. But there are thousands and thousands of manuscripts of the Greek New Testament and its versions into Latin, Syrian, Coptic, and other languages. By comparing those thousands of manuscripts, you can see where a scribe emended the text here, where he wrote a little explanation of the text there, where he changed a word here. Essentially, practically, doctrinally, for all worship purposes, for our own reading and edification, the King James Version, the Authorized Version, the Textus Receptus, is superlative. But once in a while you will see where a scribe has made a change, has interpolated, has emended, has (what he thought) corrected. These emendations are most apparent, and are not a part of the word of God.

John Nelson Darby's Translation

Darby did not feel such a need for a new translation in English because he considered the King James Version to be adequate for most purposes, and he encouraged his followers to continue to use it. However, he decided to produce a highly literal English version of the New Testament for study purposes. The version is exceedingly literal, based upon modern critical editions of the Greek text, and abundantly supplied with text-critical and philological annotations. The annotation is by far the most comprehensive and detailed to be found in an English version. It was consulted by the translators of the English Revised version of 1881. (See F.F. Bruce, History of the Bible in English, 3rd ed; 1978 page 132). When Mr. Darby first issued his new translation into English, he wrote in the preface to the Revelation. "If the reader finds my translation exceedingly similar to Mr. William Kelly's, I can only rejoice in it, as mine was made a year or two before his came out, and he has never seen mine up to the time of my writing this."

Kelly Translation

William Kelly was a highly capable scholar, textual critic of the Greek New Testament, and expositor of Scripture. Except for Matthew, Mark and Luke, his translation of the NT is found in his books; and his critical comments on the English Revised Version are available in The Bible Treasury, which he edited. Responding to a critic of Darby, William Kelly wrote "It is to be hoped that but few professors of the Lord's name on earth could descend so low in the blindness of ill-feeling. No man is infallible; but the translator (J.N. Darby) thus recklessly assailed, contributed to present the Scriptures in English, French, and German beyond any man that ever lived; and no wonder, as he had adequate power, commanding knowledge of all helps, and spiritual acumen unequaled." William Kelly also stated another occasion about Darby's linguistic skill ancient and modern. "He knew English, German, French, Italian, and Dutch, as well as Greek and Hebrew, and perhaps Sanskrit and no doubt, Latin. Darby visited for a short time in New Zealand (September 15, 1875-April 1876) and learned Maori. During his stay at J.G. Deck's home in Sand ridge, Moteuka, it is said that Darby also preached to the Maoris of the district, and when he left he had learnt enough of the language to preach to them without a translator."

F.F. Bruce remarked about the key of accurate translation.

"Translation is not simply a matter of looking up a word in a dictionary and selecting the equivalent which one would like to find in a particular passage. It is this manifest mastery of Greek usage which makes William Kelly's New Testament commentaries, especially those on Paul's epistles, so valuable. "And you know what is restraining him now," says the RSV of 2 Thessalonians 2:6, following some earlier interpreters. This construing of 'now' with what is restraining' Kelly describes as a solecism, pointing out that the 'now' is simply resumptive.' Kelly is right. But how did he discover that the construction of the adverb with 'what is restraining' is solecism? No grammar-book or dictionary would tell him that; it was his wide and accurate acquaintance with Greek usage that made it plain to him, an acquaintance which is the fruit of long and patient study. (In Retrospect, P.293).

Let us come back to Revelation 22:14. An emendation of a copyist is found in our text in Revelation 22:14. Why did that scribe change that gospel message from one of faith and trust to one of obedience and works? For the plain and simple reason that there is the everlasting tendency in a man to try to merit, to try to achieve, to try be self-advancement to find his way into heaven. That is a weakness of human nature, and it is seen everywhere in religion.

This system of merit represents the great religions of the world. it represents much of Christianity. Many churches in Christendom believe that we are saved by works, that a man toils his way into the kingdom of heaven, that he deserves heaven as a reward after he has done certain things that he thinks are acceptable unto God. Certainly the great religions; like the Hindu, the Confucian, the Buddhist, are religions of works. So much of Christianity is built around the doctrine of trying to deserve the favor of heaven. A man is saved, says one preacher, by trusting in Jesus and by being baptized. Another preacher says a man is saved by trusting Jesus and doing all kinds of good works. Another says a man is saved by believing in Jesus and taking the Lord's Supper. Another says a man is saved by trusting in the Lord Jesus and becoming a member of the Church, and by being obedient to all of the commandments of the Church.

The doctrine of merit is a reflection of human pride. The falsely proud, conceited man says, "I can do this assignment myself. I can merit heaven myself. I can work out this problem of sin by myself. And when I am saved it is because I have done it. Look at me. Here I am walking golden streets, going through the gates of pearl, mingling with the saints of God because I did good, I obeyed commandments, I kept laws and I did great things. Therefore, I am here in the presence of God." That is the religion of the flesh; that is the religion of human pride; and that was the religion of the scribe who, when he found this passage in Revelation, changed the text from one of washing robes to one of doing commandments.

Revelation 22:17

This message is one of the most meaningful and beautiful of all the texts in the word of God. Beginning at Revelation 22:6 John, by the Holy Spirit, writes and epilogue, a final, concluding passage, not only to the book of Revelation but to the entire canon of Holy Scripture.

It is fitting indeed that the sacred canon of scripture should close with a reference to the Holy Spirit. For He is the Author of the Book, the one who has inspired every chapter, every verse, and every line.

These verses of this epilogue are like the final moment of a great concerto in which the instruments of the orchestra all join in one vast flood of triumph. The different voices in this epilogue are all heard alternately. Sometimes it will be the voice of the seer who is speaking, the Apostle John. Sometimes it will be the voice of the angel. Sometimes it will be a deeper voice from the throne, the Lord Christ Himself speaking.

The first three "comes" are an answering cry to the tremendously significant and triumphant messages of our Lord, who announced in verse 12 above: "Behold I come quickly". The spirit says "come!" The saints (bride) say "come!" and the very sinners who hear the message and respond say "come!" - come, Lord, come!

"And the spirit says 'come'". When the Lord announced 'Behold I come quickly', the Spirit of Jesus in the earth answered with deep seated longing. "Come, Lord, Come."

Our Savior said it was expedient that He go away; for if He went away He would send as His vice-regent on earth the spirit of truth, the Paraclete, who would teach us the way of truth and who would be our comforter, our guide, and our keeper. But for the years of this dispensation, how the rejection and wickedness of the world has grieved and quenched the Holy Spirit of God. The forty years of wandering in the wilderness when Israel provoked the spirit of God, are nothing compared to the centuries and generations of these last 2000 years that have known no other thing than the rejection of Christ and the grieving and provoking of the Holy Spirit. When the Lord announced: "Behold I come quickly," a grieving, agonizing spirit replied "come, Lord, come, blessed Jesus." It is the desire, the longing, the assignment of the Holy Spirit to glorify the Lord Jesus. The last time this unbelieving world ever saw our master was at Calvary, when He was raised between the earth and the sky on a cross. The world saw Him die in shame, between two felons. The longing and the desire of the Holy Spirit of God is to exalt the Lord Jesus; to reveal Him in beauty and in glory, in splendor and in triumph. When the Lord announced, "Behold, I come quickly", the spirit replied, "come, Lord, do come," for the day of Christ's glory is at hand.

"And the bride says, 'come'. The spirit and the bride say, 'come'". The bride of Christ, His Church, through all of these ages and centuries and now these two millenniums, has been in prayer, waiting for her coming Lord. However, the different groups may interpret the manner of His coming, the true Church of Christ is ever moved by that prayer of appeal: "Thy kingdom come, yea, come, Lord Jesus". Do you notice with reference to the spirit and the bride that there is just one "come"? The spirit and bride say, "Come." Not two. Not the spirit says, "Come" and the bride says, "come". They are identified in that longing. If the church is filled with the Holy Spirit and if the Holy Spirit speaks through His Church, they have a common prayer, "come blessed Lord Jesus." The Church cries in the spirit and the spirit prays and cries in the church, "come Lord, come blessed Jesus." The true Church is espoused to the Lord, but the marriage is not yet. It is not until the return of our Lord that the wedding supper of the Lamb is celebrated. The Church now looks up to her espoused husband, waiting for that final consummating day when she shall belong to her Lord and the Lord shall possess His own. "And let him who hears say, 'come'". At the sublime announcement of our Lord, "Behold I come quickly", let every individual member of the congregation, let every member of the household of faith, when he hears the word that is read and the revelation that is delivered, let him say in his heart, "yes Lord, come blessed Jesus." That is the token and the sign of a born-again Christian, a true child of the Lord. No unsaved man, no world ling longs for the return of the Savior. To him the day of the return of the Lord is a day of foreboding, it is a day of judgment, it is a day of perdition and damnation. It is a day of loss and terror. That is why the unsaved man says, "Where is the promise of his coming? For since the fathers fell asleep, all things continue as they were from the beginning of creation" (2 Peter 3:4). To the unbeliever the coming of the Lord is a dreadful thing, but not so with the true child of God. The Lord announces, "behold, I come quickly", and when the true child of God reads of that blessed promise in the Bible, he says: "In Revelation I am taught that Jesus shall surely come. Amen. It is a blessedness and a happiness to my soul. Even so, come Lord Jesus." That is the sign of a true, devout, God-fearing Christian. "Let him who hears each individual saved member of the household of faith, let him answer 'come Lord, yea, come'".

In the midst of the answering cry of the spirit and of the bride and of the individual church member, the Lord speaks. Do you see the difference between those two 'comes'? Now the text turns in its grammatical construction. "And let him who thirsts come...whoever desires; let him take the water of life freely." There are two different 'comes' in the invitation. One is voiced by the spirit and the individual hearer. The other is the message of our Lord to the sinner, to the unbeliever who is not prepared for the triumphant day. It is as though the Lord remembered those who are lost, especially you. It is as though He took up the pen and before the last, final benediction was written, before the canon was closed, before the last prophet and the last apostle had concluded, He says: "Let me make one last appeal to the lost that they might be saved, that they might come." The Lord appeals: "Come, let him who thirsts take the water of life freely, whoever desires, come."

The word 'come' is a favorite of the Lord God in His Holy Book. In the face of the terrible judgment of the flood, the Lord commanded Noah to build an ark, and when it was built He said to Noah: "come, Noah, come, you and your family, into the ark of safety, come." The great lawgiver, Moses, standing in the midst of the camp among his people in idolatry and an orgy of sin, said "Let him who is on the Lord's side, let him come and stand by me." It is the message of the Gospel of the Old Testament in Isaiah 1:18, "come now and let us reason together, says the Lord 'Though your sins be as scarlet, they shall be as white as snow; though they be red like crimson, they shall be as wool. Come now, says the Lord.'" Or in Isaiah 55:1, "Ho! Everyone who thirsts, come to the waters; come buy and eat, yes come buy wine and milk."

The word 'come' was the constant word of invitation on the lips of our blessed Lord. Passing by the sea, He saw the first disciples fishing and He said, "Come follow me and I will make you fishers of men." The Lord said "suffer little children to come unto me." Throughout gospel we see this word 'come'. Here in Revelation the spirit, bride, and who hears, say come. They all invite the lost to be saved. "Whoever desires let him take the water of life freely."

We have now arrived at the last, the most inclusive, summation of all the invitations of God in all of the word: whoever will – the invitation is broad. God does not use force. All who enter in do so of their own choice. Oh, what a simple Gospel and what a simple message. Let the lost sinner take the gift of salvation freely. It is theirs without price.

Revelation 22:18-19

This message is the summation of the whole Book of the Revelation. Some people have raised a theological problem by the text in its dire warning and somber threat. Is it possible for God's people to be blotted out of the Book of Life? Having been saved and regenerated, can they fall away from the grace and keeping of our Lord? The answer is simple and plain. This passage is not discussing the possibility of the saved being ultimately lost. The text is but a warning from God, solemn and serious, that His word is immutable, eternal. "Forever, O God, thy word is fixed in Heaven." God's word is like Himself, the same yesterday, and today and forever. This is God's serious solemn mandate that His word is not to be changed or mutilated or impaired; it is not to be added to and it is not to be taken away from. But what, then, is the meaning of this dire warning that if any man takes away from the Book, God will take away his name out of the Book of life and his part out of the Holy City?

Does the warning imply that a man, who is regenerated, saved, born again, could fall away and finally be lost? Impossible! It is as impossible; as is the suggestion that a regenerated man would mutilated God's Holy Word. He would not do it. It does not belong to the elect of God to change God's word; nor would it enter the heart of a man who was regenerated to do ought else but to reverence God's Holy Book. A preacher may be an intellectually trained minister of Christ, and he may stand in a great pulpit, and he may have a vast following, but if he does not honor God's word, he exhibits a sign that he does not know the Lord as his personal Savior. He is not born again. Those who love Jesus, who are elect, who belong to His kingdom, would never mutilate or change God's Holy revelation.

The vision was given to a man named John. Three times He calls his name, "John". He says in Revelation 1:4, "John to the seven churches which are in Asia". Then in Revelation1:9, "I, John, who am also your brother, and companion in tribulation, and in the kingdom and patience of

Jesus Christ, was in the isle that is called Patmos, for the word of God, and for the testimony of Jesus Christ." In Revelation 22:8, in the epilogue he says, "I John saw these things, and heard them."

Who is this John? He is a man of such authority in the churches that his word is immediately accepted as the word of God Himself. Who is this John, who has such an unusual place and prominence among those early Christians? The answer is simple and plain. He is the Apostle John. When the Judean war broke out against Rome in the latter part of the A.D. 60's, John left the city of Jerusalem and finally came to the Roman Province of Asia in A.D. 69. He became an elder of the Assembly at Ephesus and the spiritual leader of all God's people in that part of the Eastern Roman Empire. Irenaeus, a disciple of Polycarp, who was an elder of the Assembly at Smyrna and a disciple of the Apostle John, Polycarp, said that in the latter part of the reign of Domitian, John saw the Revelation. Domitian reigned as emperor of the Roman Empire from A.D. 81 until A.D. 96. Cement of Alexandria, another father of the early church, said that after the death of the Roman emperor Domitian, John left his exile in Patmos and returned to Ephesus. So the vision was seen and written down about A.D. 96, toward the latter part of the reign of the Emperor Domitian.

We are in the Laodicean period of the church now. The Philadelphian era of the open door has closed. Now the vast population of this earth is shut out for the Gospel. Nation after nation is closed to the Gospel. Nation after nation is closed to the preaching of the gospel. The door to the gospel to India closed 3 decades ago.

There is apostasy everywhere: in the chairs of theology, in the pulpits, in the unconcern and indifference of the people. The Lord's Day has become like any other day. The great commandments and teachings of our Savior are beginning to be looked upon as those of any other philosopher, his mind being the produce of his own times. To most of the world today religion is altogether optional. If a man wants to go to church, it is his business. If a man wants to join the country club, that is his business. The conception of the church being the very fountain of life and the difference between hell and heaven is impossible to the average man of today. The very ideas of damnation are offensive to the modern, intellectual mind. There is no God of wrath, there is no God of judgment, there is no damnation, there is no fire of hell. The traditions of the Christian church are looked upon as being part of the cultured life of a people and therefore are still evolving. This is the Laodicean era of the church. This is the day in which we live. The Apocalypse is a book of prophecy, outlining these great eras in the history of the church. As described in Revelation 3:20, in the Laodicean era the Lord is standing on the outside. Our Lord says, "I stand at the door and knock; if any man hears my voice..." But God has His own in every age. There are people devout and holy, and there are churches who preach the truth in any age, in every age, in this age. May God bless the congregations that seek to be faithful to the true message of the Revelation of our Lord.

The Last Promise

Revelation 22:20-21

We have now come to the end of the Revelation and to the end of the Bible. Our text, the last and closing verses, chooses the canon of the Holy Scriptures. There are no more prophets to proclaim the mind of God. There are no more apostles to write with infallible authority. There are no more instructions and mandates from heaven. The visions recorded here reach to the end of time and into the eternity of eternities. They encompass all history, all ages and all dispensations. There is one great remaining event and that is the Parousia; the presence, the descent, the coming, the return of our Lord God from heaven.

In this text is the last time Christ's voice is heard on earth. The next time we hear the voice of the Son of man it will be when He descends in glory with a shout, with a voice of the arch angel and with the trump of God. This last and concluding sentence, these last verses that close the canon of the Holy Spirit sum up in these few words the whole revelation and testimony of the Lord throughout the ages. First, we have the certainty of His coming. Second, the last words of a man, the affirmation, the last prayer that fell from the lips of a human being. And third, the last benedictory remembrance of the love and grace of the Lord Jesus upon His people.

The Bible opens with a promise of our coming Lord. The Holy Spirit closes the scriptures with a promise of the coming again of our Lord. In the book of Genesis, in 3:15 God said to the serpent, the devil, the dragon that has brought heartache and tears, that sowed the earth with death and sorrow, the Lord said to that serpent, "And I will put enmity between thee and the woman, and between they seed and her seed; you shall bruise his heel." In this mighty prophecy, according to Romans 16:20, there are two comings promised by the Lord God. The first coming of our Lord saw Satan bruise our Savior, "Thou shall bruise his heel".

The Lord was crucified in ignominy, in shame, in sorrow, in tears and agony. His life and blood were poured out because of our sins. But there is another part to that first promise. There is a day of coming, the lord avows, when the Christ of heaven shall crush Satan's head; when God shall reign over His people in triumph, when righteousness shall fill the earth as the waters cover the sea. The Lord in His personal glory shall reign over His own redeemed people. There are two comings in that first Genesis promise. The Bible opens with that prophecy, and the Bible closes with that same promise.

First, the Savior is to come so that He might be crushed, bruised, crucified and made an offering for sin. He is to come to die as the redeemer for the souls of men. After God made that promise in Eden, hundreds of years passed, millenniums passed, and the Lord did not come. When finally, He did arrive He "came unto His own and His own received Him not". He was in the world and the world was made by Him and the world knew Him not. The thousands of humanity had forgotten the promise, or else they scoffed at the fulfillment. When finally, the announcement came that He had arrived, the learned scribes pointed out the place where He was to be born, but never took the time to journey the five miles from Jerusalem to Bethlehem to welcome this promised Savior of the world. But however long he delayed and however men forgot and scoffed and however few of a faithful band waited for the consolation of Israel, as old Simeon, yet He came. In keeping with the holy, faithful promise of God, the Lord Jesus came. It is thus in the text that God speaks in closing His Bible, "surely I come quickly". Here a second time, infidels may scoff and others may reject Him and the centuries may grow into the millenniums, this is the immutable word and promise of the Lord God, "surely, I come."

It is interesting to see the first time God used that word "surely". In chapter 2 of the Book of Genesis, the Lord said to Adam and Eve, verse 17 "but of the tree of the knowledge of good and evil you shall not eat, for in the day that you eat of it you shall surely die." This is the first time God uses the word "surely". It is also interesting to see the second time that word 'surely' is used. Genesis 3:4: "Then the serpent said to the woman "you will not surely die'." The denial of the word of God is always the beginning of a fall. "Surely, surely, you shall die says the Lord God." But Satan says, "Yea, did God say such a thing? You shall not surely die answered Satan." Whatever that 'surely' meant, when God first said it, is what that 'surely' means when God last uses it. When Adam partook of that forbidden fruit, that day his soul died. And in a day of the Lord's calendar (2 Peter 3:8), which is a thousand years, Adam's body died. Did you ever notice that in these long records of the longevity of men, there has never been a man yet that outlived that thousand-year day of the Lord? Adam died when he was 930 years of age. Genesis 2:17: "For in the day that you eat of it you shall surely die." Every grave cut into this earth, every tear unbidden that falls on the ground, ever heartache, every pain, every sorrow, every despair is an exclamation point after God's "surely" surely you shall die. But there is a second "surely". There is another part to that promise. There is another side to that awful curse of death and despair. The Savior is coming. He will bruise Satan's head and crush out his life of evil forever. There is a redeemer coming, there is a Savior coming. One of the most interesting of all the passages in the Hebrew text of the Old Testament is this one "And Adam knew Eve his wife; and she conceived, and bare Cain, and said I have gotten a man from the Lord". That is the way it is translated in the King James Version. But in the Hebrew text there is revealed a startling and an amazing thing on the part of Eve as she remembered God's promise of a coming redeemer. When she bare Cain, she said "I have gotten a man even the Lord Jehovah." Genesis 4:1. Let us see the Darby Translation: "I have acquired a man with Jehovah." When that child was placed in the bosom of Eve she thought he was the answer to the promise from the Lord; she thought the Deliverer had come. She thought Christ had come, the final, the ultimate, the glorious redeemer. She thought Him to be Cain. She was mistaken, but the promise, the hope and the expectancy of that coming Lord has never died in the earth, or in the hearts of men.

The answering prayer and benediction of the holy apostle who listened to this last promise spoken by our Savior, was, "Amen, even so, come Lord Jesus." These are the last words of a man recorded in the Bible

And now the final benediction, "The grace of our Lord Jesus Christ be with you all. Amen."

Appendix I

THE SYRIAN CIVIL WAR

Today the world faces an International crisis unparalleled in all of man's history.

The world is aflame with violence and demonic power. Since 2010, the Syrian Government is fighting different groups of rebels. Looking at today's geo-political landscape, it is not difficult to envision the scenario outlined in Isaiah 17, Jeremiah 49: 23-27 and Psalm 83: 1-8.

Isaiah 17 (NKJV)

Proclamation Against Syria and Israel

17 The burden against Damascus.

"Behold, Damascus will cease from *being* a city,
And it will be a ruinous heap.
² The cities of Aroer *are* forsaken;]
They will be for flocks
Which lie down, and no one will make *them* afraid.
³ The fortress also will cease from Ephraim,
The kingdom from Damascus,
And the remnant of Syria;
They will be as the glory of the children of Israel,"
Says the LORD of hosts.

Jeremiah 49:23-27 (NKJV)

Judgment on Damascus

²³ Against Damascus.

"Hamath and Arpad are shamed,
For they have heard bad news.
They are fainthearted;
There is trouble on the sea;
It cannot be quiet.
²⁴ Damascus has grown feeble;
She turns to flee,
And fear has seized *her.*
Anguish and sorrows have taken her like a woman in labor.
²⁵ Why is the city of praise not deserted, the city of My joy?
²⁶ Therefore her young men shall fall in her streets,
And all the men of war shall be cut off in that day," says the LORD of hosts.
²⁷ "I will kindle a fire in the wall of Damascus,
And it shall consume the palaces of Ben-Hadad."

Psalm 83:1-8 (NKJV)

Prayer to Frustrate Conspiracy Against Israel

A Song. A Psalm of Asaph.

83 Do not keep silent, O God!
Do not hold Your peace,
And do not be still, O God!
² For behold, your enemies make a tumult;
And those who hate You have lifted up their head.
³ They have taken crafty counsel against Your people,
And consulted together against Your sheltered ones.
⁴ They have said, "Come, and let us cut them off from *being* a nation,
That the name of Israel may be remembered no more."

⁵ For they have consulted together with one consent;
They form a confederacy against You:
⁶ The tents of Edom and the Ishmaelites;
Moab and the Hagrites;
⁷ Gebal, Ammon, and Amalek;
Philistia with the inhabitants of Tyre;
⁸ Assyria also has joined with them;
They have helped the children of Lot.

In the last days, the Bible tells us of a horrible series of events that will take place in the land of Israel and Syria. One of these events is the disappearance of Damascus as one of the premier cities in the world. Since Damascus exists today, this prophecy remains unfulfilled. Isaiah 17: 1 – 3.

According to Jeremiah 49:1– 2: The destruction of Damascus apparently spills over into northern Jordan.

Jeremiah 49:1-2 (NKJV)

Judgment on Ammon

49 Against the Ammonites.

Thus says the LORD:

"Has Israel no sons?
Has he no heir?
Why *then* does Milcom inherit Gad,
And his people dwell in its cities?
² Therefore behold, the days are coming," says the LORD,
"That I will cause to be heard an alarm of war
In Rabbah of the Ammonites;
It shall be a desolate mound,

And her villages shall be burned with fire.
Then Israel shall take possession of his inheritance," says the LORD

The sequence of events should be as follows: Damascus and Rabbah are destroyed. In the aftermath of a war, Israel possesses her inheritance.

The destruction of Israel's Damascus and Jeremiah's Rabbah are closely related to the Psalm 83 events. Assyria, which comprised part of modern day northern Syria when Psalm 83 was written, is also part of the Arab confederacy.

Psalm 83 describes, the concluding Arab - Israeli war that was prophesied by Asaph the Seer, about three thousand years ago. Psalm 83 is a prayer in which Israel asked the Lord for deliverance from a group of nations that verses 3 – 5 show are united in a confederacy or League for one purpose- the destruction of the nation of Israel. In the 1950s, the Arab League of Nations was formed. It united the Arab Nations together for the very purpose of the destruction of Israel. Psalm 83 describes the blatant Arab attempt to confiscate the Promised Land. But Israel is going to wipe them out completely. (Read Jer. 31: 35 – 37)

Jeremiah 31:35-37 (NKJV)

[35] Thus says the LORD,
Who gives the sun for a light by day,
The ordinances of the moon and the stars for a light by night,
Who disturbs the sea,
And its waves roar
(The LORD of hosts *is* His name):

[36] "If those ordinances depart
From before Me, says the LORD,

Then the seed of Israel shall also cease
From being a nation before Me forever."

[37] Thus says the LORD:

"If heaven above can be measured,
And the foundations of the earth searched out beneath,
I will also cast off all the seed of Israel
For all that they have done, says the LORD.

According to connecting prophecies in Obadiah 1:18, Ezekiel 25: 14, 37: 10; Jer: 49: 1 – 6, the Israeli Defense forces prevail in the Psalm 83 war. Now Arabs are cursing Jews. As such, they must be cursed, according to the divine policy issued in (Gen.12: 2 – 3)

Obadiah 1:18 (NKJV)

[18] The house of Jacob shall be a fire,
And the house of Joseph a flame;
But the house of Esau *shall be* stubble;
They shall kindle them and devour them,
And no survivor shall *remain* of the house of Esau,"
For the LORD has spoken

Ezekiel 25:14 (NKJV)

[14] I will lay My vengeance on Edom by the hand of My people Israel, that they may do in Edom according to My anger and according to My fury; and they shall know My vengeance," says the Lord GOD.

Ezekiel 37:10 (NKJV)

¹⁰ So I prophesied as He commanded me, and breath came into them, and they lived, and stood upon their feet, an exceedingly great army.

With his priests and his princes together.
⁴ Why do you boast in the valleys,
Your flowing valley, O backsliding daughter?
Who trusted in her treasures, *saying,*
'Who will come against me?'
⁵ Behold, I will bring fear upon you,"
Says the Lord GOD of hosts,
"From all those who are around you;
You shall be driven out, everyone headlong,
And no one will gather those who wander off.
⁶ But afterward I will bring back
The captives of the people of Ammon," says the LORD.

Genesis 12:2-3 (NKJV)

² I will make you a great nation;
I will bless you
And make your name great;
And you shall be a blessing.
³ I will bless those who bless you,
And I will curse him who curses you;
And in you all the families of the earth shall be blessed."

In Psalm 83, the Arabs, by their own choice, ignore the foundational understandings contained in Jer: 31: 35 – 37, and fundamental precepts in Genesis 12: 3.

They seek to destroy the Jews, which means they will extract literal judgment upon themselves.

In retrospect, the Arab spring of 2011 appears to have primed the pump for the prophetic fulfillment of Psalm 83. Verse 6 mentions some of these nations.

Psalm 83 or Ezekiel 38- what is the next Middle East Headlines.

Current Middle East events seem to be setting the stage for the final fulfilment of the Israeli war prophecies of (Psalm 83 and Ezekiel 38-39)

Ezekiel 38 (NKJV)

Gog and Allies Attack Israel

38 Now the word of the LORD came to me, saying, [2] "Son of man, set your face against Gog, of the land of Magog, the prince of Rosh,[1] Meshech, and Tubal, and prophesy against him, [3] and say, 'Thus says the Lord GOD: Behold, I *am* against you, O Gog, the prince of Rosh, Meshech, and Tubal. [4] I will turn you around, put hooks into your jaws, and lead you out, with all your army, horses, and horsemen, all splendidly clothed, a great company *with* bucklers and shields, all of them handling swords. Persia, Ethiopia, and Libya are with them, all of them *with* shield and helmet; [6] Gomer and all its troops; the house of Togarmah *from* the far north and all its troops—many people *are* with you.

[7] "Prepare yourself and be ready, you and all your companies that are gathered about you; and be a guard for them. [8] After many days you will be visited. In the latter years you will come into the land of those brought back from the sword *and* gathered from many people on the mountains of Israel, which had long been desolate; they were brought out of the

nations, and now all of them dwell safely. ⁹ You will ascend, coming like a storm, covering the land like a cloud, you and all your troops and many people's with you."

¹⁰ 'Thus says the Lord GOD: "On that day it shall come to pass *that* thoughts will arise in your mind, and you will make an evil plan: ¹¹ You will say, 'I will go up against a land of unwalled villages; I will go to a peaceful people, who dwell safely, all of them dwelling without walls, and having neither bars nor gates'— ¹² to take plunder and to take booty, to stretch out your hand against the waste places *that are again* inhabited, and against a people gathered from the nations, who have acquired livestock and goods, who dwell in the midst of the land. ¹³ Sheba, Dedan, the merchants of Tarshish, and all their young lions will say to you, 'Have you come to take plunder? Have you gathered your army to take booty, to carry away silver and gold, to take away livestock and goods, to take great plunder?'"'

¹⁴ "Therefore, son of man, prophesy and say to Gog, 'Thus says the Lord GOD: "On that day when My people Israel dwell safely, will you not know *it?* ¹⁵ Then you will come from your place out of the far north, you and many peoples with you, all of them riding on horses, a great company and a mighty army. ¹⁶ You will come up against My people Israel like a cloud, to cover the land. It will be in the latter days that I will bring you against My land, so that the nations may know Me, when I am hallowed in you, O Gog, before their eyes." ¹⁷ Thus says the Lord GOD: "Are *you* he of whom I have spoken in former days by My servants the prophets of Israel, who prophesied for years in those days that I would bring you against them?

Judgment on Gog

[18] "And it will come to pass at the same time, when Gog comes against the land of Israel," says the Lord GOD, *"that My fury will show in My face.* [19] For in My jealousy *and* in the fire of My wrath I have spoken: 'Surely in that day there shall be a great earthquake in the land of Israel, [20] so that the fish of the sea, the birds of the heavens, the beasts of the field, all creeping things that creep on the earth, and all men who *are* on the face of the earth shall shake at My presence. The mountains shall be thrown down, the steep places shall fall, and every wall shall fall to the ground.' [21] I will call for a sword against Gog throughout all My Mountains," says the Lord GOD. "Every man's sword will be against his brother. [22] And I will bring him to judgment with pestilence and bloodshed; I will rain down on him, on his troops, and on the many peoples who *are* with him, flooding rain, great hailstones, fire, and brimstone. [23] Thus I will magnify Myself and sanctify Myself, and I will be known in the eyes of many nations. Then they shall know that I *am* the LORD."'

I will bless those who bless you, and I will curse him, who curses you and in you all the families of the earth shall be blessed.

Throughout much of 2010, Turkey distanced itself from Israel. This moved many to the edge of their seats, thinking that Ezekiel 38 was an imminent event, because it meant that Turkey and Iran both members of the Ezekiel 38 coalition shared a common enmity toward Israel.

Ezekiel 38 describes nine distinct populations by their ancient names including Russia, Iran, Turkey, Libya, and several others, but omits these Arab countries and terrorist organizations.

The Psalm 83 lists ten entirely separate members not included among the Ezekiel 38: 1 – 6 invaders.

Israel will defeat Psalm 83 coalition, and then the Ezekiel 38 coalition will come to attack Israel.

The Psalm 83 confederates lists 10 nations.

1. Tents of Edom – Palestinians and Southern Jordanians
2. Ishmaelite - Saudis (Ishmael - Father of Arabs)
3. Moab – Palestinians and Central Jordanians.
4. Hagarenes –Egyptians (Hagar Egypt – Matriarch)
5. Gebal – Hezbollah and Northern Lebanese
6. Ammon – Palestinians and Northern Jordanians
7. Amalek – Arabs of the Sinai area.
8. Philistia – Hamas of the Gaza Strip
9. Tyre – Hezbollah and Southern Lebanese
10. Assyria – Syrians and Northern Iraqis

The above Psalm 83 nations present the first confederate attempt to destroy modern day Israel.

The second such confederacy is prophesied in Ezekiel chapter 38 and 39.

Ezekiel 39 (NKJV)

Gog's Armies Destroyed

39 "And you, son of man, prophesy against Gog, and say, 'Thus says the Lord GOD: "Behold, I *am* against you, O Gog, the prince of Rosh, Meshech, and Tubal; [2] and I will turn you around and lead you on, bringing you up from the far north, and bring you against the mountains of Israel. [3] Then I will knock the bow out of your left hand, and cause the arrows to

fall out of your right hand. ⁴ You shall fall upon the mountains of Israel, you and all your troops and the peoples who *are* with you; I will give you to birds of prey of every sort and *to* the beasts of the field to be devoured. ⁵ You shall fall on the open field; for I have spoken," says the Lord God. ⁶ "And I will send fire on Magog and on those who live in security in the coastlands. Then they shall know that I *am* the Lord. ⁷ So I will make My holy name known in the midst of My people Israel, and I will not *let them* profane My holy name anymore. Then the nations shall know that *I am* the Lord, the Holy One in Israel. ⁸ surely it is coming, and it shall be done," says the Lord God. "This *is* the day of which I have spoken.

⁹ "Then those who dwell in the cities of Israel will go out and set on fire and burn the weapons, both the shields and bucklers, the bows and arrows, the javelins and spears; and they will make fires with them for seven years. ¹⁰ They will not take wood from the field nor cut down *any* from the forests, because they will make fires with the weapons; and they will plunder those who plundered them, and pillage those who pillaged them," says the Lord God.

The Burial of Gog

¹¹ "It will come to pass in that day *that* I will give Gog a burial place there in Israel, the valley of those who pass by east of the sea; and it will obstruct travelers, because there they will bury Gog and all his multitude. Therefore, they will call *it* the Valley of Hamon Gog. For seven months the house of Israel will be burying them, in order to cleanse the land. ¹³ Indeed all the people of the land will be burying, and they will gain renown for it on the day that I am glorified," says the Lord God. ¹⁴ "They will set apart men regularly employed, with the

help of a search party, [c] to pass through the land and bury those bodies remaining on the ground, in order to cleanse it. At the end of seven months they will make a search. [15] The search party will pass through the land; and *when anyone sees a man's bone, he shall set up a marker by it, till the buriers have buried it in the Valley of Hamon Gog.* [16] *The name of the city will also be Hamonah. Thus they shall cleanse the land.*'"

A Triumphant Festival

[17] "And as for you, son of man thus says the Lord GOD, 'Speak to every sort of bird and to every beast of the field:

"Assemble yourselves and come;
Gather together from all sides to My sacrificial meal
Which I am sacrificing for you,
A great sacrificial meal on the mountains of Israel,
That you may eat flesh and drink blood.
[18] You shall eat the flesh of the mighty,
Drink the blood of the princes of the earth,
Of rams and lambs,
Of goats and bulls,
All of them fatlings of Bashan.
[19] You shall eat fat till you are full,
And drink blood till you are drunk,
At My sacrificial meal
Which I am sacrificing for you.
[20] You shall be filled at My table
With horses and riders,
With mighty men
And with all the men of war," says the Lord GOD.

Israel Restored to the Land

"I will set My glory among the nations; all the nations shall see My judgment which I have executed, and My hand which I have laid on them. So the house of Israel shall know that I *am* the LORD their God from that day forward. The Gentiles shall know that the house of Israel went into captivity for their iniquity; because they were unfaithful to Me, therefore I hid My face from them. I gave them into the hand of their enemies, and they all fell by the sword. According to their uncleanness and according to their transgressions I have dealt with them, and hidden My face from them.'"

"Therefore thus says the Lord GOD: 'Now I will bring back the captives of Jacob, and have mercy on the whole house of Israel; and I will be jealous for My holy name— after they have borne their shame, and all their unfaithfulness in which they were unfaithful to Me, when they dwelt safely in their *own* land and no one made *them* afraid. When I have brought them back from the peoples and gathered them out of their enemies' lands, and I am hallowed in them in the sight of many nations, then they shall know that I *am* the LORD their God, who sent them into captivity among the nations, but also brought them back to their land, and left none of them captive any longer. And I will not hide My face from them anymore; for I shall have poured out My Spirit on the house of Israel,' says the Lord GOD."

The Magog map displays the nine confederate members. The post Psalm 83 period Israel will become a great power with enlarged borders.

A Sign from God

In July 2006, during the height of the Israeli - Hezbollah conflict, a miracle was reported on the news outlets across the world. An Irish construction worker operating a backhoe (a backhoe, also called a rear actor or back actor, is a piece of excavating equipment or digger consisting of a digging bucket on the end of a two – part arm) saw something very unusual in the swampy pit that he was about to dig up. His find turned out to be an ancient 20-page portion of the Psalms dated to the years 800 – 1000 AD. Experts say that the manuscript had been lying in the mud for the past 1000 to 1200 years. The National Museum of Ireland issued a statement saying "In discovery terms, this Irish equivalent to the Dead Sea scrolls are being hailed by the Museum's experts as the greatest find ever from a European bog. The Museum's director, Pat Wallace referred to the find as a "miracle find" telling the Associated Press, "It is unlikely that something this fragile could survive burial in a bog at all and then for it to be unearthed and spotted before it was destroyed is incalculably more amazing".

But what is even more miraculous than the nature and the manner in which the book was found is the timing of the find and the nature. For, not only did the find occur at the height of the Israeli Hezbollah conflict, but the Psalter itself was found opened to Psalm 83 - a very fitting Psalm indeed to be found in the midst of a historical conflict between Israel and Hezbollah, which was backed by Syria and Iran.

Israel already discovered huge natural gas and oil fields. Houston based Noble Energy is the Prime Operator of those fields. Israel will dwell securely for a time. Ezekiel 38 lists nine nations. Israel's great booty includes Arab Spoils of war. Jordan surrenders sovereignty to Israel. (Jer.49: 2; Isaiah 11: 14; Zeph. 2: 9.)

Then Israel shall take possession of his inheritance," says the LORD.

Zephaniah 2:9 (NKJV)

⁹ Therefore, as I live,"
Says the LORD of hosts, the God of Israel,
"Surely Moab shall be like Sodom,
And the people of Ammon like Gomorrah—
Overrun with weeds and salt pits,
And a perpetual desolation.
The residue of My people shall plunder them,
And the remnant of My people shall possess them."

Today Jordan, represented in these passages as, Ammon, Moab, and Edom, rests within the promised land that was allotted to Abraham in (Gen.15: 18)

Ezekiel 37: 10 inform us that Israel, rising from a seemingly helpless fate, will establish for itself an "exceedingly great army". The Jews will change from victims to victors, from destroyed to destroyers, and from hunted to hunters.

Ezekiel 37:10 (NKJV)

¹⁰ So I prophesied as He commanded me, and breath came into them, and they lived, and stood upon their feet, an exceedingly great army.

God gathers the Jews into the land of Israel. (Ezekiel 36: 24; 37: 12; Isaiah 11: 11-12)

Ezekiel 36:24 (NKJV)

²⁴ For I will take you from among the nations, gather you out of all countries, and bring you into your own land.

Ezekiel 37:12 (NKJV)

¹² Therefore prophesy and say to them, 'Thus says the Lord God: "Behold, O My people, I will open your graves and cause you to come up from your graves, and bring you into the land of Israel.

Isaiah 11:11-12 (NKJV)

¹¹ It shall come to pass in that day
That the Lord shall set His hand again the second time
To recover the remnant of His people who are left,
From Assyria and Egypt,
From Pathros and Cush,
From Elam and Shinar,
From Hamath and the islands of the sea.

¹² He will set up a banner for the nations,
And will assemble the outcasts of Israel,
And gather together the dispersed of Judah
From the four corners of the earth.

Appendix II

The Bozrah Deliverance

In the Prophecies of Isaiah and Micah there are a number of apocalyptic passages relating to the second coming of Christ that are rarely mentioned or given reference to by Bible teachers. These refer to the return of the Messiah at a place the Bible calls "Bozrah". Exegesis of the Bozrah scriptures in Isaiah 63 and in Micah 2 is an intriguing exercise. Something of epic and cataclysmic significance will happen at the end of this age at a place the Bible calls "Bozrah. Quite clearly we are dealing with a mystery. It is a hidden truth yet to be revealed.

Bozrah was a city south – southeast of the Dead Sea in the land of the Edomites.

This was the land of the children of Esau. Ancient Bozrah is not a significant place today. The sons of Esau have spread out into the world. They left their ancient homeland a long time ago. Esau's descendants are now far away from those harsh places of the Middle East. Esau's old stomping grounds were in the region of mount Seir. His descendants lived in that area south of Judah and this included Petra and certain other geographical places of South East of the Dead Sea.

When we look at the Bozrah passages in:

Isaiah 63:1-4 (NKJV)

The LORD in Judgment and Salvation

1 Who *is* this, who comes from Edom,
With dyed garments from Bozrah,
This *One who is* glorious in His apparel,
Traveling in the greatness of His strength? —
"I who speak in righteousness, mighty to save."

² Why *is* Your apparel red,
And Your garments like one who treads in the winepress?

³ "I have trodden the winepress alone,
And from the peoples no one *was* with Me.
For I have trodden them in My anger,
And trampled them in My fury;
Their blood is sprinkled upon My garments,
And I have stained all My robes.
⁴ For the day of vengeance *is* in My heart,
And the year of My redeemed has come.

Revelation 19:11-16 (NKJV)

¹¹ Now I saw heaven opened, and behold, a white horse. And He who sat on him *was* called Faithful and True, and in righteousness He judges and makes war. ¹² His eyes *were* like a flame of fire, and on His head *were* many crowns. He had a name written that no one knew except Himself. ¹³ **He *was* clothed with a robe dipped in blood**, and His name is called The Word of God. ¹⁴ And the armies in heaven, clothed in fine linen, white and clean, followed Him on white horses. ¹⁵ Now out of His mouth goes a sharp sword, that with it He should strike the nations. And He Himself will rule them with a rod

of iron. He Himself treads the winepress of the fierceness and wrath of Almighty God. ¹⁶ And He has on *His* robe and on His thigh a name written: KING OF KINGS AND LORD OF LORDS.

Micah 2:12-13 (NKJV)

Israel Restored

¹² "I will surely assemble all of you, O Jacob,
I will surely gather the remnant of Israel;
I will put them together like sheep of the fold,
Like a flock in the midst of their pasture;
They shall make a loud noise because of *so many* people.
¹³ The one who breaks open will come up before them;
They will break out,
Pass through the gate,
And go out by it;
Their king will pass before them,
With the LORD at their head."

This end time place the Holy Scriptures refers to as "Bozrah" will be the scene of an awesome end-time drama. It will see the unveiling of the Messiah during the apocalypse. So Bozrah is apparently a very important destination for the returning Messiah. The Prophet Micah is quite specific in the prophecy. The sheepfold gathering of Jacob, which is spoken by the prophet Micah, is at Bozrah. Bozrah in the latter days of this age must be a special territory under the authority of a principality which the Bible identifies as belonging to Edom.

Cross Reference

Revelation 12 describes the flight of the woman.

This is another perspective on this re-gathering of Jacob. This epic re-gathering or exile will be taking place during the final 3.5 years or 1260 days of this age. Revelation 12.

Revelation 12 (NKJV)

The Woman, the Child, and the Dragon

12 Now a great sign appeared in heaven: a woman clothed with the sun, with the moon under her feet, and on her head a garland of twelve stars. ²Then being with child, she cried out in labor and in pain to give birth.

³ And another sign appeared in heaven: behold, a great, fiery red dragon having seven heads and ten horns, and seven diadems on his heads. ⁴His tail drew a third of the stars of heaven and threw them to the earth. And the dragon stood before the woman who was ready to give birth, to devour her Child as soon as it was born. ⁵ She bore a male Child who was to rule all nations with a rod of iron. And her Child was caught up to God and His throne. ⁶ Then the woman fled into the wilderness, where she has a place prepared by God that they should feed her there one thousand two hundred and sixty days.

Satan Thrown Out of Heaven

⁷ And war broke out in heaven: Michael and his angels fought with the dragon; and the dragon and his angels fought, ⁸ but they did not prevail, nor was a place found for them in heaven any longer. ⁹ So the great dragon was cast out, that serpent of old, called the Devil and Satan, who deceives the

whole world; he was cast to the earth, and his angels were cast out with him.

[10] Then I heard a loud voice saying in heaven, "Now salvation, and strength, and the kingdom of our God, and the power of His Christ have come, for the accuser of our brethren, who accused them before our God day and night, has been cast down. [11] And they overcame him by the blood of the Lamb and by the word of their testimony, and they did not love their lives to the death. [12] Therefore rejoice, O heavens, and you who dwell in them! Woe to the inhabitants of the earth and the sea! For the devil has come down to you, having great wrath, because he knows that he has a short time."

The Woman Persecuted

[13] Now when the dragon saw that he had been cast to the earth, he persecuted the woman who gave birth to the male *Child*. [14] But the woman was given two wings of a great eagle, that she might fly into the wilderness to her place, where she is nourished for a time and times and half a time, from the presence of the serpent. [15] So the serpent spewed water out of his mouth like a flood after the woman, that he might cause her to be carried away by the flood. [16] But the earth helped the woman, and the earth opened its mouth and swallowed up the flood which the dragon had spewed out of his mouth. [17] And the dragon was enraged with the woman, and he went to make war with the rest of her offspring, who keep the commandments of God and have the testimony of Jesus Christ

The Bozrah prophecies are obviously matters of enormous importance and yet these Bozrah passage in Micah is rarely spoken about today by our popular preachers.

In Rev.12 we see the woman, her seed and the dragon once again. The drama between the woman and the serpent we saw back in the Garden of Eden. It has now come full circle. The 'woman' of destiny is now in the end time. She is in travail and in great tribulation.

Revelation is a symbolic overview of all of Israel's history. The woman is symbolic of Israel.

1260 days is exactly 3.5 years – the standard lunar years of the Bible with 360 days each. Also it connects to (Matt.24: 15 – 22) Jerusalem surrounded by Armies.

Matthew 24:15-22 (NKJV)

The Great Tribulation

[15] "Therefore when you see the 'abomination of desolation,' 'spoken of by Daniel the prophet, standing in the holy place" (whoever reads, let him understand), [16] "then let those who are in Judea flee to the mountains. [17] Let him who is on the housetop not go down to take anything out of his house. [18] And let him who is in the field not go back to get his clothes. [19] But woe to those who are pregnant and to those who are nursing babies in those days! [20] And pray that your flight may not be in winter or on the Sabbath. [21] For then there will be great tribulation, such as has not been since the beginning of the world until this time, no, nor ever shall be. [22] And unless those days were shortened, no flesh would be saved; but for the elect's sake those days will be shortened.

The parallel passage in Luke 21 adds what Mathew does not tell us that Jerusalem will be surrounded by hostile armies at the time of the end.

Luke 21:22-24 (NKJV)

[22] For these are the days of vengeance, that all things which are written may be fulfilled. [23] But woe to those who are pregnant and to those who are nursing babies in those days! For there will be great distress in the land and wrath upon this people. [24] And they will fall by the edge of the sword, and be led away captive into all nations. And Jerusalem will be trampled by Gentiles until the times of the Gentiles are fulfilled.

This same scene as depicted by the Old Testament Prophet Zachariah (Zach.14: 1 – 3)

Zechariah 14:1-3 (NKJV)

The Day of the LORD

14 Behold, the day of the LORD is coming,
And your spoil will be divided in your midst.
[2] For I will gather all the nations to battle against Jerusalem;
The city shall be taken,
The houses rifled,
And the women ravished.
Half of the city shall go into captivity,
But the remnant of the people shall not be cut off from the city.

[3] Then the LORD will go forth
And fight against those nations,
As He fights in the day of battle

Flight of Jews from Judea.

The prophet Joel foresaw this calamity (Joel 2: 1 – 10).

Joel 2:1-10 (NKJV)

The Day of the LORD

2 Blow the trumpet in Zion,
And sound an alarm in My holy mountain!
Let all the inhabitants of the land tremble;
For the day of the LORD is coming,
For it is at hand:
² A day of darkness and gloominess,
A day of clouds and thick darkness,
Like the morning *clouds* spread over the mountains.
A people *come,* great and strong,
The like of whom has never been;
Nor will there ever be any *such* after them,
Even for many successive generations.

³ A fire devours before them,
And behind them a flame burns;
The land *is* like the Garden of Eden before them,
And behind them a desolate wilderness;
Surely nothing shall escape them.
⁴ Their appearance is like the appearance of horses;
And like swift steeds, so they run.
⁵ With a noise like chariots
Over mountaintops they leap,
Like the noise of a flaming fire that devours the stubble,
Like a strong people set in battle array.

⁶ Before them the people writhe in pain;
All faces are drained of color.
⁷ They run like mighty men,
They climb the wall like men of war;
Every one marches in formation,
And they do not break ranks.
⁸ They do not push one another;
Every one marches in his own column.
Though they lunge between the weapons,
They are not cut down.
⁹ They run to and fro in the city,
They run on the wall;
They climb into the houses,
They enter at the windows like a thief.

¹⁰ The earth quakes before them,
The heavens tremble;
The sun and moon grow dark,
And the stars diminish their brightness.

Many scholars believe this Godly remnant will find refuge in the ancient rock –hewn Cliff city of Petra, and in the surrounding region in the land of Edom (southern Jordan).

These fleeing refugees from Jerusalem will become a part of a believer's underground in those days. These believers will be converted by the preaching of the 144,000 evangelists. These converts will not be allowed the privileges of citizenship and commerce in the Antichrist's world government. They will refuse to participate in worship of the beast, and consequently will not be allowed to buy or sell anything. Therefore, they will be forced to hide in secret places, or die as the early Christians did when the Church was young.

Christians went underground during the persecutions in Rome. They literally lived in the vast network of catacombs beneath the city of Rome. Visitors to Rome today can see the places where they lived, including large cavernous rooms where they met for worship and prayer, and hundreds of tombs carved into the sides of the tunnels for those who died during this time.

Groups of underground believers during the Tribulation period will no doubt form their own alliances for survival, including sharing of resources, bartering and standing guard for one another.

According to Revelation 12, which records the cosmic drama of Israel and the Dragon the, Antichrist will be thwarted in his attempt to capture the fleeing remnant of Israel and will be enraged at the rest of her offspring who are described as true believers in Jesus. (Rev.12: 14-17)

Revelation 12:14-17 New King James Version (NKJV)

[14] But the woman was given two wings of a great eagle, that she might fly into the wilderness to her place, where she is nourished for a time and times and half a time, from the presence of the serpent. [15] So the serpent spewed water out of his mouth like a flood after the woman, that he might cause her to be carried away by the flood. [16] But the earth helped the woman, and the earth opened its mouth and swallowed up the flood which the dragon had spewed out of his mouth. [17] And the dragon was enraged with the woman, and he went to make war with the rest of her offspring, who keep the commandments of God and have the testimony of Jesus Christ.

Evidently this latter group will be converts from all the Gentile nations.

It is possible that the underground followers will receive special divine guidance and help from this place to which Israel will flee, because it will be protected by God.

The fifth seal Martyrdom

The Greek word "Martyr" actually means "witness" or one who gives a testimony. The early Christians were very bold witnesses for Christ in fulfillment of His command to be His witnesses in all the earth (Acts 1: 8)

Acts 1:8 (NKJV)

[8] But you shall receive power when the Holy Spirit has come upon you; and you shall be witnesses to Me in Jerusalem, and in all Judea and Samaria, and to the end of the earth."

In those days every Roman subject was expected to acknowledge Caesar as god. They were required to say "Caesar is Lord". Christians, of course could not say this. Instead they acknowledged "Jesus is Lord" (1 Cor.12: 3)

1 Corinthians 12:3 (NKJV)

[3] Therefore I make known to you that no one speaking by the Spirit of God calls Jesus accursed, and no one can say that Jesus is Lord except by the Holy Spirit.

For this reason, many early Christians were put to death by a variety of cruel methods, such as crucifixion, burning at the stake, beheading and being fed to lions. Historical accounts of these people refer to them as martyrs.

There have been a great many Christian martyrs down through the centuries. The 20th century has seen more persecution and death of Christians than any other age.

During the Tribulation there will be many martyrs. The fifth seal (Rev. 6:9– 11)

Revelation 6:9-11 (NKJV)

Fifth Seal: The Cry of the Martyrs

[9] When He opened the fifth seal, I saw under the altar the souls of those who had been slain for the word of God and for the testimony which they held. [10] And they cried with a loud voice, saying, "How long, O Lord, holy and true, until You judge and avenge our blood on those who dwell on the earth?" [11] Then a white robe was given to each of them; and it was said to them that they should rest a little while longer, until both *the number of* their fellow servants and their brethren, who would be killed as they *were,* was completed.

It is also clear that those who trust in Christ and refuse to receive the mark of the beast will be put to death for treason against (Anti Christ's one-world government (Rev.13: 10; 20: 4)

Revelation 13:10 (NKJV)

[10] He who leads into captivity shall go into captivity; he who kills with the sword must be killed with the sword. Here is the patience and the faith of the saints.

Revelation 20:4 (NKJV)

The Saints Reign with Christ 1,000 Years

⁴ And I saw thrones, and they sat on them, and judgment was committed to them. Then *I saw* the souls of those who had been beheaded for their witness to Jesus and for the word of God, who had not worshiped the beast or his image, and had not received *his* mark on their foreheads or on their hands. And they lived and reigned with Christ for a thousand years.

Surely the Lord will give them the strength to stand for Christ even if it means suffering in this extreme way. Believers are not promised deliverance from persecution. 2 Tim 3: 12 says "In fact everyone who wants to live a godly life in Christ Jesus will be persecuted."

The historical background of Petra.

The ancient capital of Edom was the city of Bozrah – the Hebrew Bozrah means sheepfold. It lies 30 miles southeast of the Dead Sea in present day Jordan. The present Jordanian city of Buseirah is not on any modern road but is a remote mountain village of difficult access. Ancient Bozrah at the same location, however, was on the main North West trade route known as the King's Highway (Num 20: 17). The city was noted for its weaving industry and export of dyed garments.

Numbers 20:17 (NKJV)

[17] Please let us pass through your country. We will not pass through fields or vineyards, nor will we drink water from wells; we will go along the King's Highway; we will not turn aside to the right hand or to the left until we have passed through your territory.'"

Edom is the territory allotted to Jacob's brother Esau, documented in Genesis 36. A man named Bozrah was a descendant of Seir the Horite, who inhabited the land before there were any kings in Israel. Also read (Deut. 20: 10 -12)

Edom's long standing enmity against Israel ultimately brought God's judgment on Edom. Obadiah the prophet devotes his short but potent, message to the judgment of Edom telling us of her pride and arrogance and the reasons for God's final judgment on these people. Amos the shepherd of Tekoa wrote of impending judgment on Edom. (Amos 1: 11-12).

Amos 1:11-12 (NKJV)

[11] Thus says the LORD:

"For three transgressions of Edom, and for four,
I will not turn away its *punishment,*
Because he pursued his brother with the sword,
And cast off all pity;
His anger tore perpetually,
And he kept his wrath forever.
[12] But I will send a fire upon Teman,
Which shall devour the palaces of Bozrah."

Several wonders have written descriptions of Petra and the history of that region of ancient Edom.

The Nabateans displaced the descendants of Esau around in the 6th Century BC. They controlled the entire region as far North as Damascus until the first century. The Greeks and Romans built extensively in Jordan and the area around Bozrah and Petra was well populated as late as Roman times. Today the area is desolate and sparsely populated because of the very low rainfall and scarcity of natural resources there.

South of Bozrah, about 20 miles on the King's Highway, is Petra, the capital city of the Nabateans. Towns and houses carved into the bedrock over a vast area at Petra, would be suitable for temporarily housing of many thousands of people.

Mount Hor is nearby where Aaron died after Moses passed the high priestly garments of Aaron on to Eliezer in the sight of the congregation. (Num. 20: 23-29).

Numbers 20:23-29 (NKJV)

[23] And the LORD spoke to Moses and Aaron in Mount Hor by the border of the land of Edom, saying: [24] "Aaron shall be gathered to his people, for he shall not enter the land which I have given to the children of Israel, because you rebelled against My word at the water of Meribah. [25] Take Aaron and Eleazar his son, and bring them up to Mount Hor; [26] and strip Aaron of his garments and put them on Eleazar his son; for Aaron shall be gathered *to his people* and die there." [27] So Moses did just as the LORD commanded, and they went up to Mount Hor in the sight of all the congregation. [28] Moses stripped Aaron of his garments and put them on Eleazar his son; and Aaron died there on the top of the mountain. Then Moses and Eleazar came down from the mountain. [29] Now when all the congregation saw that Aaron was dead, all the house of Israel mourned for Aaron thirty days."

The route of escape for the Jewish believing remnant from the Antichrist's military pursuit as he seeks to annihilate them has been made ready by the Lord (Dan. 11:41)

Daniel 11:41 New King James Version (NKJV)

[41] He shall also enter the Glorious Land, and many *countries* shall be overthrown; but these shall escape from his hand: Edom, Moab, and the prominent people of Ammon.

Evidently Jordan is given special protection during the last great invasion of Israel which will in fact devastate the land. Isaiah, the prophet instructs the believing remnant of Israel to find a safe hiding place during the time of Judah's trouble. (Isa. 26:20-21)

Isaiah 26:20-21 (NKJV)

Take Refuge from the Coming Judgment

[20] Come, my people, enter your chambers,
And shut your doors behind you;
Hide yourself, as it were, for a little moment,
Until the indignation is past.
[21] For behold, the LORD comes out of His place
To punish the inhabitants of the earth for their iniquity;
The earth will also disclose her blood,
And will no more cover her slain.

During the second half of the tribulation period there will be no safe place to hide anywhere on the earth, except in the refuge God has provided. The condition of the unbelievers is described when opening of the 6th seal of judgment. (Rev.6:12-17)

Revelation 6:12-17 (NKJV)

Sixth Seal: Cosmic Disturbances

[12] I looked when He opened the sixth seal, and behold, there was a great earthquake; and the sun became black as sackcloth of hair, and the moon became like blood. [13] And the stars of heaven fell to the earth, as a fig tree drops its late figs when it is shaken by a mighty wind. [14] Then the sky receded as a scroll when it is rolled up, and every mountain and island was moved out of its place. [15] And the kings of the earth, the great men, the rich men, the commanders, the mighty men, every slave and every free man, hid themselves in the caves and in the rocks of the mountains, [16] and said to the mountains and rocks, "Fall on us and hide us from the face of Him who sits on the throne and from the wrath of the Lamb! [17] For the great day of His wrath has come, and who is able to stand?"

There are disputes among scholars about the actual location of Bozrah. Here I am providing a different version about the location of Bozrah by Gavin Finley MD.

Here are the facts that hopefully will put this sham, this cover story to rest. Petra has **never** been able to house and accommodate more than 1,000 people. There is no water there and no sewage, - just empty caves and tombs of hard rock. Clearly Petra is not big enough to house and shelter nor supply food and other supplies for the huge numbers of people God will be sheltering in the latter days. And certainly not for three and a half years in a war zone with no good roads, no railway, and no airfields. Getting supplies into Petra under these circumstances would be difficult.

Petra is an unlikely, even impossible place, for an exile of the nation of Israel or even the small 5 million populations from

Judah and Jerusalem. The place is too small. And Petra certainly wouldn't accommodate a wider company of Christian and Messianic believers in an exile that numbers in the hundreds of millions. And if we are considering a refuge for Israel during the Armageddon siege then we need to be brought up to date. Yes, in ancient times Petra was a retreat for the Idumeans. The narrow passes were easily defended with swords and bows and arrows. But in these days of modern warfare the Israeli military would never allow their women and children to be led to an unsafe place like Petra in Jordan. In this day and age there is no shelter there. They would be far better off staying at home back in Israel in their underground bomb shelters. Petra would **never** qualify as a retreat in this day and age, except in the fevered imaginations of Bible prophecy storytellers and their unthinking audiences. Even getting a population of people out to Petra would expose them to great dangers on the way. Then to put a population of civilians in Petra at a dangerous location right inside a war zone would be sheer madness. It would seal their doom. Petra would be a deathtrap.

And why? Because one bomb down in that deep gorge would be the end of all the people in there. And with a chemical bomb the gas would just sit in the gorge and go nowhere. A gas attack would kill the whole population in that valley very quickly. And in the modern era of napalm bombs and fuel bombs a retreat to Petra would be utterly suicidal. The gorge would soon become a fiery furnace. The supposed "place of refuge" would soon become an oven full of charred corpses. No one would survive.

The scripture passage they focus in on to support this is in Zechariah 14.
But as we shall see, they have the wrong city.

Zechariah 14:1-5 New King James Version (NKJV)

The Day of the Lord

¹ Then I turned and raised my eyes, and saw there a flying scroll.

² And he said to me, "What do you see?"

So I answered, "I see a flying scroll. Its length *is* twenty cubits and its width ten cubits."

³ Then he said to me, "This *is* the curse that goes out over the face of the whole earth: 'Every thief shall be expelled,' according *to* this side of *the scroll;* and, 'Every perjurer shall be expelled,' according *to* that side of it."

⁴ And in that day His feet will stand on the Mount of Olives,
Which faces Jerusalem on the east.
And the Mount of Olives shall be split in two,
From east to west,
Making a very large valley;
Half of the mountain shall move toward the north
And half of it toward the south.

5 Then you shall flee *through* My mountain valley,
For the mountain valley shall reach to **Azal.**
Yes, you shall flee

As you fled from the earthquake
In the days of Uzziah king of Judah.

Thus the Lord my God will come,
And all the saints with You.

Vision of the Woman in a Basket

⁵ Then the angel who talked with me came out and said to me, "Lift your eyes now, and see what this *is* that goes forth."

THE ESCAPE FROM THE EARTHQUAKE BY THE INHABITANTS OF JERUSALEM.
WHEN THE MOUNT OF OLIVES IS SPLIT THEY EVACUATE TO NEARBY AZAL.

As we can see, there is no mention of Bozrah or Petra at all in this passage.
This is a flight of the inhabitants of Jerusalem out of the city during an earthquake.
That earthquake is the "big one" and it splits the Mount of Olives.
One element of the Second Coming is Jesus' return at the Mount of Olives.
He is the One who at His Second Coming causes the earthquake!

In all the prophecies involving Edom, there is no mention at all of the city of Petra. And there is no mention of Petra in any other part of the Bible for that matter.
But here **is** a clear message of a flight out of Jerusalem that will end up in a nearby city.

That city is not way down in Jordan. It is in fact quite close to Jerusalem.
It is the **city of Azal**.

This "flight to Azal" happens at the very end of the age at the second coming of Christ.
The "flight to Azal" we see in the passage above involves a short time short distance evacuation of a city. Zechariah gives no mention of a prolonged Tribulation refuge way down in Petra which is in Jordan. This "flight to Azal" will not satisfy the prophecy of the 'flight of the woman' in Rev. 12:6 & 12:14. Nor will it satisfy the scripture of the Bozrah exile and the Bozrah deliverance we see in Micah 2:12-13.

The so called "flight to Petra" is a doctrine without any scriptural foundation whatsoever.
The 'Azal evacuation' scripture in Zechariah 14 is the real story.
And yet it and the Bozrah scriptures have both been used to build up this Petra fable.
This "flight to Petra" and "refuge in Petra" fable is religious folklore.
They are used in a fast and loose way to "cover up" the rue stories at Azal and at Bozrah.
The Petra retreat fable becomes a "cover story" for these real prophecies.
Because we know that there will be a citywide evacuation of Jerusalem to nearby Azal.
And we know that Messiah will be paying a visit to Bozrah at His Second Coming. (Isa. 63 and Micah 2:12-13)

Made in the USA
Lexington, KY
10 July 2018